JACKED UP

Bill Lane

The Inside
Story of How
Jack Welch
Talked GE into
Becoming the
World's Greatest
Company

New York   Chicago   San Francisco   Lisbon   London
Madrid   Mexico City   Milan   New Delhi   San Juan   Seoul
Singapore   Sydney   Toronto

The *McGraw·Hill* Companies

1 2 3 4 5 6 7 8 9 0 DOC/DOC 0 9 8 7

ISBN: 978-0-07-154410-8
MHID: 0-07-154410-0

McGraw-Hill books are available at special quantity discounts to use as premiums and sales promotions, or for use in corporate training programs. For more information, please write to the Director of Special Sales, Professional Publishing, McGraw-Hill, Two Penn Plaza, New York, NY 10121-2298. Or contact your local bookstore.

Library of Congress Cataloging-in-Publication Data
Lane, Bill, 1944–
  Jacked up / by Bill Lane.
      p. cm.
  Includes bibliographical references and index.
  ISBN-13: 978-0-07-154410-8 (alk. paper)
  ISBN-10: 0-07-154410-0 (alk. paper)
  1. Business presentations. I. Title.
HF5718.22.L36 2008
658.4'52—dc22
                                        2007044726

This book is printed on acid-free paper.

For My Beloved Beth …

CONTENTS

INTRODUCTION   **xi**

PART I

Torched by an A-Hole   **1**

Retiring But Not Shy   **5**

Reflections of a Pimp   **11**

Bore Wars: Chet Lang and the Big Bang   **13**

Death of a Pitchman   **17**

PART II

I Can't Deal with this Anymore   **23**

Mike's Big Day   **27**

Crotonville High   **35**

Prior Planning Prevents Piss-Poor Performance   **37**

Fred's Bad Day   **39**

Triumphs, Train Wrecks, Coronations,
and Jack's Biggest Miss   **43**

You're Going Nowhere at GE Unless…   **45**

How to Succeed in Business by Really Trying   **49**

Love—or Hate—at First Sight   **51**

The View from the Bowling Alley   **55**

The Bogus Boca Presentation   **61**

Died and Went to Headquarters   65

Selling Hats to Each Other   69

PART III

The Russians Are Coming   73

Hectoring the Hobbit   77

Movin' On, Sideways   79

Death to Strategic Planning   83

Blubbering on the Stand   85

From Grunt to Flunky   87

The Marionette Meister   95

Jacking Up the Commo   101

Don't Dive. Swim!   103

PART IV

Restuffing Guts   107

Gentle Meddling   111

Called on the Carpet   113

More Change via Negative Reviews   117

Takes One to Know One   119

Dead Man Talking   121

"Stop Construction Today"   123

Every Biopsy Doesn't Have to Come Back Positive   127

I'm Okay; You're an A-Hole   **129**

Bulletproofing the Love-In   **131**

PART V

Death by Presentation at NBC   **137**

Peeing on the Kidder Body   **141**

A Shout from the Bathroom   **143**

The Wright Stuff (Righted)   **147**

Diversity Is Our ... er ... Strength   **149**

PART VI

Fly Ball at The Pierre   **155**

Black Clouds Lift the Stock   **163**

The Chairman and the Strawman   **165**

Don't Screw This Up   **169**

Don't Care About It? Don't Do It!   **173**

The 110 Percent Solution and Jack's Perks   **175**

Wanna Drink Lunch with Us?   **181**

The Firing Squad   **185**

PART VII

Why Gary Wendt   **191**

Lack of Care Packages   **199**

Seinfeld in Fairfield: The Yogurt Incident   **203**

Order and Logic Out of Chaos 205

Doin' Time 209

Better Than the Best 211

Herb Smokes Jack; Warren Lurks in His Nightmare 213

The Welch Work Ethic 217

The Fist Through the Drapes 221

Crotonville Turkey Shoot 225

A Pad in Front of You 229

PART VIII

If Your Wife Thinks It's Boring, It's *Boring* 233

Danger: Flying Carrot Fragments 237

Ringo's Rule 239

The Perfect Annual Report 243

"Not a Pennyworth of Difference" 249

PART IX

Bore Wars Continue … 251

Lloyd's Law: A Learning Company 257

The Bore Test. Are You Relevant? 261

Larry Leaves. Lane Grieves. (On the Way to the Bank) 263

The Inevitable (But Very Short) Golf Section 269

Tough Jack to Follow 271

Know Your Potential Enemy   275

Out of the Gate and Serious   277

PART X

Tell Me a Story   281

The Dogs Are Your Friends   285

What You Face If You're Black, Asian, or a Woman   289

Ten Minutes! No More!   293

PowerPoint Is the Enemy. Never Surrender.   297

On Being a Leader Rather Than a Projector Operator   301

Do It All in Five Charts   303

At the End of the Day   307

Love Story   311

FINAL THOUGHTS   315

INDEX   317

BORING ACKNOWLEDGMENTS SECTION   323

Is there a crying—or even whimpering—need for this book? I'm not sure. My book fills three gaps, that you, the reader, can decide were better filled or not.

Gap one is my life, which to be candid, has not been interesting enough to justify a book—maybe not even an essay. But there are vignettes from my years with Jack Welch at GE, from my earlier years at the Pentagon, and from an earlier year in Vietnam that taught me things about communications that I offer you as having applicability in your life.

Gap two is about how Jack Welch transformed GE—specifically the way we spoke to each other and to the outside world.

There have many books written about Welch. There have been two books written by Welch himself—one with John Byrne of *BusinessWeek*, and one with Jack's wife, Suzy. There have also been several fawning hagiographies and a couple of crappy and dishonest hatchet jobs.

My book is none of these, although, on balance, it is decidedly positive. In truth, Welch is a flawed, but good man, and possibly the best CEO ever.

In the 20 years I worked for him, most of those years as his Manager of Executive Communications and his speechwriter, I observed a hilarious, terrifying, inspiring, and crazy side of Jack. I often urged him to put this side of himself into his memoirs, which he never did. I think he thought the portrayal of this side would make him look less than serious.

My focus here is largely on how he changed the way, as a company, we talked to each other, and how we came to teach each other.

I've skimmed dozens of books on the subject of corporate communications and on leadership. I agree with most of them, so there probably is no desperate need for another; but I wrote it anyway. I wrote this because we changed things at GE with a wildly different approach, backed by a wildly different leader.

Gap three is the need to help you become a better communicator. You will find me coming out of the narrative periodically, with brief sermons on what you *must* do and *must not* do, in mass communications, whether you are an entry-level intern, or a leader of anything from an Army platoon, or a small division of a company, or the chairman of a major multinational.

Jack transformed communications at GE; and I helped him.

If you do as I suggest in this book, you can transform your company, your organization, and yourself.

Part I

Torched by an A-Hole

It was a dark and stormy afternoon (Welch-moodwise) at the turn of the century.

I had just returned from five days in a dismal plant outside Boston, overseeing the printing of the GE Annual Report, and was dueling, loudly and obscenely, over the phone with Jack Welch, in front of wide-eyed junior GE finance people. "Don't you listen? We took *that* out two weeks ago. Why is it back in there?" Jack snapped. He was referring to an obscure sentence in one of the business write-ups that few, besides analysts, read.

"No, Jack, we didn't take it out. Don't you remember? We said we'd do it *this way*," I replied.

"Bullshit. Get it out! I don't want it in there!"

I forget exactly what it was, probably a word like "risk," which was *not allowed* to appear in the annual report.

He read the boring financial section—about half the annual report—maybe four or five times. He also scoured the CEO Letter he and I spent *50* to *100 hours* on—minimum—and he combed the business write-ups (submitted by the dozen-or-so GE businesses), over and over, as if looking for lice.

"Lice," in Jack's view (but my word), included phrases such as the aforementioned *risk*, and *off balance-sheet transactions*, which prompted Flair-pen comments to me like "scary!!!!" A typical phone conversation between Jack and a submitting business leader ran roughly like this:

"I know it's *legal*. I just don't want anything that sounds like that shit in the annual report. Don't you read the papers?

"Okay? Good. How are you doing? Did you get rid of that asshole? I thought we agreed to send him home? March? That's okay. But I want him out of here. How's your family? Laura okay? Great.

"We're gonna do Augusta right after the annual meeting, and I want you to play with Sam and Si. Okay? Great! See ya."

So I got back to the office from Boston, with a fistful of first-edition GE Annual Reports, hot off the press—it's literally the most widely read corporate book in the world—and dropped the first copies off with Rosanne, Welch's secretary. Jack was out of town but returning via Air-GE later in the day.

I was chillin' in my office, deleting a week's worth of stupid e-mails, and planning on blowing out early to go home and see my family when Rosanne called. "Bill, I just looked at the Annual Report. Mr. Welch is *not* going to be happy with his picture in the Board section."

"Why not? It's the one I sent up there two weeks ago for him to look at."

A bit later, I'm still at my desk and the phone rings. It's Jack, friendly, animated, warm, on some other project we were working on.

"Jack, what do you think of the Annual Report? Doesn't it look great?"

"What? Where is it? You dropped it off? *Ro!*" (calling Rosanne) I hear her yell, "I put it on your desk!"

"Oh, okay. Here it is. Bill, let me look at it and call you back."

Approximately 25 seconds later, the phone rings again.

"You asshole! You put the wrong picture in the back. I hate that fucking picture."

"Jack, I sent it up to you two weeks ago and told you that if I didn't hear from you I was gonna print it. You didn't look at it."

"Bullshit! No you didn't! You fucked up."

"No, *you* did. *You're* the asshole. You didn't look at it." The screaming escalates. People are actually gathering outside my office and looking in the open door with alarmed faces. They all know who's on the other end of the line.

"Get up here, now!"

I venture up to his office, reassuring my concerned colleagues as I walk the 75-foot, one-floor journey up to the lion's den.

I decide to employ an offensive strategy as I blow into his outer office, where he awaits, standing, annual report in hand.

"You looked at that thing for 20 seconds. You went right to the picture in the back. I busted my ass for three months to make this the best annual report in the world—which it is—and all you give a shit about is your picture?"

"You put the wrong picture in! Don't give me that shit. It makes me look *bald.*"

"Yeah?" I wore a snotty sarcastic smile on my face even though I was as stressed and crazed as if I were in a fist fight.

"You didn't look at the picture I sent you up. It's your fault," I say.

"No, No, *No!!!,*" Jack retorts as he reaches over and punches me in the upper left arm—not hard, but with a grimace that says, "I wish this were in your face."

My right fist jerks up involuntarily and stops. The two secretaries—five and ten feet away are ashen, eyes averted. One or two senior people in the usually quiet hall are looking in, concerned.

"Awww! You fucked up. Now get out of here...."

Silence followed for three days. No calls. And then I happened to encounter him in an elevator full of strangers at 30 Rockefeller Center in New York.

I love the bastard, so I said, mournfully, "You still hate me, Jack?"

He softened and replied, "Bill, you have to understand vanity."

The book you are holding is about vanity.

It is a shot at clarifying the character and personality of perhaps the most significant business leader in history. But, much more important and focused than that, the book is a 20-year foray into how Welch's "vanity" drove him to change the way the world's greatest company spoke to the world, and how you can better communicate with and present yourself to *your* world.

The vanity of communications is about never—*ever*—allowing anything but your best face, and that of your organization, to ever, *ever,* appear in front of your constituencies or your employees or your mates.

Come with me...

Retiring But Not Shy

Retirement ceremonies are often pathetic—even depressing—and, as Steinbeck might have put it, "predictable as peristalsis and as interesting as its result." Too many speeches, "gag gifts," a set of golf clubs, over-praise, exaggeration of achievements, fake laughter, and fake applause.

Inevitably the retiree will get up and say, "After 28 years, Marge and I thought it was time to 'stop and smell the roses.'" More often than not, everyone in the room knows that the retiree decided to smell the roses after the *company* decided to "package" his ass up and get him out of there. The retiree will then recount, in hideous detail—sometimes punctuated by embarrassing and often crapulous choke-ups, accompanied by discomforting silences—his view of the contributions he made to the company.

I've attended between 50 to 100 of these affairs and have left most of them swearing to myself that I would eat my .357 magnum before I would ever have a "retirement" party.

One or two of them were fun. Bruce Bunch, probably one of the best media relations pros in the business and a friend of mine, left GE after experiencing a miserable and frustrating year of "irreconcilable differences" with senior management. After 30 years, he just quit—no package, and no "deal."

Welch came down to Bruce's office, closed the door behind him and I heard him say, "You're doing the right thing." Jack regarded Bruce highly and hated to lose him, but he always said that an employee should never stay in a bad situation and die a little bit every day, just to keep a "good job."

So Bruce quit, and we had a party over at the opulent GE guest house to celebrate his courage, with skits, songs, and hilarious commentary. The word "retire" was not uttered once. Bruce has lived happily ever after.

In the early '80s, one particular early retirement didn't go over so well. The future "retiree" planned to bring his wife into the impressive GE headquarters lobby, where the recently commissioned million-dollar painting, *Arabesque*, by Robert Motherwell, hung next to the reception desk.

Once in the lobby, he allegedly planned to shoot his wife, and then blow out his own brains. When one of the vice chairmen asked, for laughs, how *I* would handle this situation, I replied that the *first* thing they needed to do was move the Motherwell out of the lobby to avoid bullet damage or "splatter." I don't recall being consulted on any HR issues again.

"So, Bill, are *you* gonna have a party?"

"No way in hell. I hate them."

But as the months rolled on (I was still an employee, but with a cleaned-out desk), they started to wear me down. There were, it turns out, a fair number of people who actually liked me—no accounting for taste—and who wanted to say goodbye at a good party.

I was told that Mr. Welch would like to come to a party for me, and that I should "get on his calendar." I should get on *his* calendar to plan *my* retirement party? Why couldn't he get on *my* calendar? A brief reality check cured me of that delusional excursion, and I got on Jack's calendar.

I agreed to a party on a late summer evening, after my old friend and ex-boss, Joyce Hergenhan, graciously offered her beautiful home and its back deck and pool in Southport, Connecticut, down the street from one of Jack's houses, and across the street from Bob Wright, former NBC President and GE Vice Chairman.

Before I agreed to this party, I had a few conditions:

1. that I be permitted to pick every single name on the guest list;
2. no hokey gifts—gag or otherwise. I screwed myself on this count and wound up getting nothing, not even golf clubs or a laptop; and
3. there would be only *one* speech, which *I* would deliver.

The rest of the evening would be devoted to old friendships, laughter, and fun; and seeing if anyone would get drunk enough to fall in the pool.

I spent three or four days working on my five-minute speech. I sat at the dining room table, as I always did—and continue to do—with yellow pad and Flair pen, writing, crossing out, rewriting. At one point my wife strolled by. With a curiosity about these things that is not usually her wont, she said, "So what are you going to say in your speech?"

I replied, "I'm going to talk about business communications, and how we changed them at GE."

She smiled. "My, that should be interesting."

Bitch.

The party was a pleasant one. Jack and a number of senior people from the company, with whom I had worked over the decades, showed up, along with a bunch of people at my level, and all my favorite secretaries. Everyone had smiles on—*real* smiles, which I pointed out to a friend, who suggested that they were probably getting the first rush of the weekend Cialis buzz.

After an hour or so of GE-catered hors d'oeuvres and moderate booze consumption, the crowd seemed ready to "get the bullshit over," so I meandered toward the lectern that Joyce had set up, holding the manila folder containing my notes.

Frank Doyle, a former Executive VP of GE and a former boss, sprang toward me, grabbed my notes, ran to poolside, and cocked his arm to throw them in. The crowd went wild with approval.

I promised Frank I'd be brief if he gave me back my notes, and he did. I walked to the lectern, waved my manila folder at the crowd and told them, "Do not be intimidated by this. Five minutes and that's it. So listen to me."

I began by professing my affection for everyone who was there that night, which was genuine, since I liked them all, and even loved one of them (my wife, not Welch). In 23 years at GE I cannot name five people whom I disliked to any great degree, and I hated no one, despite being one of the most opinionated and judgmental people on earth—even "a prick," as Welch has described me. "He's worse than I am," he would tell people, in front of me.

I began my retirement pitch with a 45-second dissertation on the role that chance plays in life; and recounted how I was seated at my junky metal desk one day in my low-rent D-ring Pentagon office (where a 767 would plow through 22 years later), and politely examined a want-ad my friend and boss, army colonel "Van" Van Fleet, had clipped for me. The ad sought a "speechwriter and public relations professional for a major global company."

I told Van that frankly, I wasn't interested. I loved Washington. I worked in a building with *ten thousand* women. I had a nice bachelor condo, a motorcycle, and I liked what I was doing, which was helping the Army get stuff from Congress to kill Russians with. Why would I leave?

"Because," said the colonel, "you don't want to be a pathetic old fool walking around this dump 20 years from now trying to pick up girls. What do you have to lose? Why not answer the ad?"

And so I did, mostly to please him.

A few weeks later I got a call from a man named Lou Marsh, who would later become one of the great people in my life. Although sick with cancer, he was at my retirement party in Southport that night.

Lou told me that he was from General Electric in Fairfield, Connecticut; he liked my résumé and samples, and wanted to come to Washington and speak with me.

At that point I nearly said, "I don't want to waste your time, but I'm not leaving Washington to go to Connecticut," which I considered a wealthy, boring wilderness. I grew up across the Sound on Long Island, and would occasionally alight on a nondescript AM Connecticut radio station with a faraway voice as I twisted the dial in search of "Murray the K" or "Cousin Brucie" for 50s rock and roll.

But then my healthy *what the hell* instinct kicked in. I agreed to the meeting, and one year later, found myself sitting in a much nicer office, complete with a genuine veneer wood-like desk, in Fairfield, Connecticut.

Three years after joining GE, I was home alone one snowy night, looking forward to curling up for an evening in front of the television with a big martini, when the phone rang. A friend of mine, another speechwriter from GE, had the much-younger woman he was dating over to his condo to watch a football game, and she had invited her friend. I could tell from his voice that this was no *ordinary* friend.

"Why don't you come over?" he asked.

I had been burning the social candle at both ends—Westport, Connecticut during most weeks, and Washington on the weekends. "I'm just not up to it. And it's snowing," I told him.

"You *need* to get your *ass* over here," he said, with some urgency.

Twenty minutes later I trudged up to his condo, carrying a couple of six-packs. Shortly thereafter, the door swung open; and I faced a six-foot tall, 21-year-old, UConn nursing senior with a face like a young Cheryl Tiegs and a body that my mother would describe as "a cute figure." I would describe it as an ACUTE figure.

I've always been known for my witty persiflage and endearing banter with women, so once I closed my jaw—which had gone into free fall—I smiled engagingly and said, *"My, you're a big one."* She went home that night and told her mother, "I just met the man I'm going to marry… and he's an asshole."

Eighteen months later I was distracted from the potential depression of my 40th birthday by our honeymoon in Las Vegas and San Francisco.

The vagaries of chance have always intrigued me, so I expended almost a minute of my retirement speech on the subject. Welch had often spoken of careers in terms of the "parachutes" we all jump with—some land in the steel or rubber industries, while some occasionally find a lucky landing zone like GE.

But the subject of my little poolside pitch that night, and the subject of this book, was not chance—but rather the *act of seizing chances by companies, by people like us.*

I pointed out that I was proud of my contribution to the change of culture in communications—specifically business presentations—at GE.

Welch came up to me that night, and said, "You're gonna make a gazillion dollars, with your credentials." I asked, "What are my credentials? You?" He said, "Exactly."

We had totally changed communications at the corporate level, though we had limited success in transforming the communications cultures of "the field"—the dozen or so huge GE businesses scattered around the globe.

But we proved it could be done. And you can do it at your organization if you care enough about doing it.

When I joined GE the corporate presentations at the major company meetings were among the most polished (and expensive) in corporate America. But they were—if not outright dishonest—mostly useless and, often, just plain dull. After Chet Lang's shotgun blast, which I'll tell you about later, they had sunk back into a soporific, suffocating sea of boredom and corporate bullshit.

Jack told me once of a sector meeting he went to in 1977 or 1978 where, "in three days, not a single true thing was said." *Not a single true thing!*

Back then, GE meetings were "shows"; and that's what we called them. Marshall McLuhan might have aptly described them as "a wasteland."

Within a few years, Jack's impatience with crap and sham grew, and I was able to guide presenters (with Welch's backing) toward changing GE meetings into what I would call "helpful conversations"—which resembled family gatherings, where men and women shared what they had learned, sometimes painfully. They discussed things like customer insights, exciting pieces of technology, market opportunities, and common threats. Meetings that were once typified by demonstrations of corporate pomposity, laughed at in hushed tones at late-night bar conversations, became opportunities to develop *useful, competitive* tools. Speakers had no hidden agenda and no other objective than to share with one another, and to look good in the process.

As the '80s rolled along, it became increasingly apparent that the stock price, more than any other factor, was the key to achieving significant wealth in this short time on earth we were allotted. Salary was not a significant factor—at least not in my case. I remember being asked what my salary was, because I got badgered into filling out a Sears credit card application or rather, was forced to by a pretty woman at the mall. I couldn't get my salary right within $25,000.

The bonus, or "incentive compensation," was a significant but predictable number—another "dental plan" as Jack called it. But *options* were in a class by themselves, and five stock splits during Jack's watch caused more than a few mid-level grunts like me to furtively pull out the calculator and option sheet after a particularly good day in the market for GE. I remember sitting alone in my office and quietly, but audibly, saying, "Holy shit!" after I added up the numbers; "I don't deserve this." And I didn't, but my parachute had found the right landing zone.

Leaving the Pentagon and the Department of the Army for GE, after seven years of impassioned pleas for new tanks and helicopters, I had some twinges of regret and considerable guilt. Even as a civilian, I still loved my army, which defended my country in the still-hot Cold War during the '70s.

And now I was leaving this noble calling, as I told my friends, "to go up to Connecticut and be a pimp for light bulbs."

Reflections of a Pimp

I searched out the familiar faces of my friends around the pool as I proceeded with my little retirement speech, speaking of what I'd first observed after reporting to Fairfield to "begin pimping."

I soon realized, after my arrival, that I was dealing with the smartest people I had ever encountered in my life. At the Pentagon, there was a noticeable gap in intelligence between the generally smarter "field grade" and general office-level military personnel, with whom I worked, and the career civilian workers—some of whom were dull drones, comfortable in their career sinecures. Other civilians were classic bureaucrats, cunning in their manipulation of the system, but essentially dull. Occasionally a diamond intellect who was content with the mediocre pay and quiet life would shine.

The classic bureaucrats were not uncommon at GE; but, after the ascendancy of Welch, they quickly became an endangered species. By the mid-'80s, most were long gone.

Some of those smartest people in the company were at my retirement party that evening: Doyle, Welch, Phil Ameen, Joyce Hergenhan, Bob Nelson, who was Jack's financial analyst, and Vice Chairman John Opie. I drop all these names only because they all taught me some good and bad things about communicating that I'd like to pass along to you, if you'll stick with me.

I finished up, within the promised five minutes, by reviewing how we had raised the bar of communications at the company from the sterile, boring, and wasteful days of yesteryear. We had become a group of men and women who spoke only to teach, to warn, and to inspire others in "the family." No longer did we brag and strut and posture and fool each other the way some did in the old days.

Before I left the lectern, I tried to make one final point: Regardless of the personalities in any management or ruling group, they *will* cooperate, share, and teach each other willingly *if the leader demands it*—and if the leader rewards or punishes the group based on their adherence to his philosophy. The leader can change the way an organization communicates *at will.* If members of the group resist change, and refuse to bring candor, sharing, and passion to their presentations, they must, in Jack's apocalyptic words, be "ridiculed and removed."

A forceful leader can turn a culture on a dime.

My final plea was for our new CEO, Jeff Immelt, his Vice Chairmen, and the leaders of the dozen or so big GE businesses, to change the way the *entire company* conversed with their people, their customers, and each other. It was my parting wish that GE, *at every level*, could somehow eliminate the endless, ritualistic "shows," talk to one another with care and passion, and *reason* with one another.

I ended my little speech by quoting Nancy Reagan, who, as the President moved further toward his sunset, told a friend of mine that "GE is still Ronnie's favorite company." I added that GE would always be *my* favorite company as well. I took my smatter of warm applause and signaled for the bar to reopen and the stuffed mushrooms to resume their circulation.

John Opie, who ran lighting for years, chided me for "picking on lighting" with my "pimping for lightbulbs" comment.

A few people that night told me, "You need to write a book about what you and Jack did to make communications better at GE."

I didn't do that much. It was all Welch. But what I did, and still do, is observe. I can see what works and doesn't work, and I can spot the elements that make a presentation a triumphant success, and those that spell disaster or even career death.

What follows in this book, is what I—this fly on countless walls— learned about effective communications during the massive changes that took place over the course of the Welch years at GE.

I truly believe that if you agree with what I say, and take my advice, you will never make a bad presentation for the rest of your career; and if you are already near or at the top, you'll never tolerate another bad presentation made to you.

I know you can do it at your company, in your organization. You can dramatically transform your institution, exponentially increase its speed, and give it a powerful competitive advantage—at no cost (you'll save, in fact), without having to resort to consultants, and without having to subscribe to any "program." All that is needed is your will as a leader.

Bore Wars: Chet Lang and the Big Bang

One warm morning in the '50s, a GE officer named Chet Lang had determined to end the dreary drivel that was the standard fare at GE corporate meetings. A couple hundred senior GE executives were gathered at the annual general managers meeting on a little GE-owned island in Lake Ontario called Association Island. The meeting was an annual ritual and continues to this day.

Two hundred and fifty white males would board small boats for the island, where they would stay in neat rows of huts. They would dine on the lawns, smoke cigars, Chesterfields, Camels, and Luckies at the cocktail hour, which would often last long into the night. The cocktail hour would open the event (for many, it would also *close* the event) and took place at the bar on the island, which GE people called—until the '80s—the "Black Catte."

Most of the 18 or 20 presentations delivered over the two days were the same boring spewings that characterized business communications in America then—and characterize them today. Back then, however, the sharing, the warmth, the direct eye contact, and the impassioned arguments all ended when the last of the general managers left the Black Catte in the wee hours.

Their *formal* meetings were a sterile wasteland that consisted of highly scripted acts rather than real human interaction.

For his morning presentation, Chet Lang was not about to deliver yet another head-throbbing snoozer to which everyone had grown accustomed—he was planning to deliver a *real* challenge. After elaborate preparations that involved hiding a shotgun (loaded with a "blank" shell) behind the lectern and positioning a trainee in the loft over the stage, who was poised to drop a stuffed duck on the stage at the appropriate moment, Chet drove passionately through his harangue—appealing to his bored and hungover cohorts to "Aim High!" At the climactic moment, he suddenly withdrew the shotgun from behind the lectern, *aimed it high*, and fired a deafening blast. The trainee—squatting on a crossbeam overhead, stuffed duck in hand—took the full force of the blast and the wadding in the "blank" on his hind parts, screamed an obscenity, and fell onto the stage, landing, injured, next to the stuffed duck.

Pandemonium erupted, the boredom vanished, and the most famous business presentation in the history of GE was now complete.

Unsurprisingly, Chet's presentation was not regarded by the company as a "best practice," so the dark waters of insipid business presentations rolled back over the GE communications landscape, until a wonderful maniac named Jack Welch blew up communications and banished boredom for good.

I worked for Jack Welch for the better part of two decades, first as the head of the speechwriters shop at GE corporate, and then as his speechwriter and Manager of Executive Communications. I was responsible for everything inside the meeting hall of the major company meetings, such as "The Program," and the 20 or 25 presentations that comprised it. I was also responsible for co-writing and polishing the CEO letter in the annual report—Jack's yearly masterpiece, and one of the most sought-after communications in the business world. I had a great run as a speechwriter for a CEO who was so good he didn't really need one. I never told him that, of course, it might have set him to thinking.

By late 2001, Jack's run had pretty much ended—as had my own. Before Jack handed over the keys to the greatest company that has ever existed, a wonderfully opulent party was thrown to celebrate Jack's tenure at GE; Crotonville—GE's Management school—located upriver from New York City, was chosen at the location for the bash.

It was early September 2001, days before the unthinkable struck, as we watched the daylight fireworks and drank Château Lafite Rothschild, that I marveled how a *nobody* like me would wind up hanging out with the tycoons, celebrities, GE superstars, the *Today Show* cast, and the CNBC "Squawk Box" commentators. By late morning the next day, the bleary-eyed partygoers, almost all of whom had stayed over, had gone home. The Board of Directors remained for a meeting. After 20 years under Welch, GE had a new boss: Jeff Immelt.

I had known Jeff for more than a decade; I knew all the big players who were called on to present at the major company meetings. He always seemed to like me, as many of them did—probably because they knew, through all my editing of their pitches, rehearsing, and nagging, that my objective was always and only to make them look good and ensure that their presentations would be the proverbial GE "home runs." If they didn't look good; or if Jack or one of the vice chairmen hated their presentations, I would get hammered for it. I didn't allow that to happen. They trusted my judgment—many still do—as to what makes a business presentation a triumph or a disastrous ordeal.

You should trust my judgment, too.

Jeff Immelt had announced, after his designation as CEO, but before he took the reins, that he did not plan on having a speechwriter. This was relayed to me in ominous tones during a few "sit downs" I'd had with the new vice president to whom I reported. I understood what this meant, and even agreed what it *should* mean: a package.

I was simply making too much money not to be the CEO's speechwriter; running the Company meetings and Annual Report could not justify the numbers I was pulling down.

In three of the last six years of my career at GE I took home seven figures—*well into seven figures* at the end. I was ready to go.

I should never have told them that I was ready and you shouldn't either. Let them sell the package to you. Never offer to take one. Feign reluctance. Speechwriters are especially vulnerable, since they are creatures so intimately connected with established cultures that they need to be ushered (gently) into the night, when the new regime enters. Change is good, and no matter how adaptable and skilled the writer is, the dead hand—or mouse—of the past will reach into the words of the new leader.

Death of a Pitchman

Twenty years before, I had watched the sad career demise of the speech-writer to Jack's predecessor, Reg Jones, whose title was Manager, Chief Executive Officer Communications. His office was near the Chairman's on the third floor of the East Building in Fairfield—the "holiest of holies" at GE. He was an older man with intellectual substance, and he was a great writer, who certainly played a major role in the honors and adulation heaped upon Reg Jones. In many cases Reg simply marked-up and read what he was given. The prose was good enough to do so, although I don't believe any CEO should ever simply read what is written for him. Welch *never* would, at least on anything substantive.

Reg used to speak in Washington regularly, defending business and American capitalism, and this writer's cerebral approach and polished phrasing were perfectly suited to Jones's style. When Reg retired in 1981, his speechwriter was understandably reluctant to give up the immense prestige and third-floor perch, and hoped he could continue on with the new chairman.

However, a few years earlier, in an incident I'm not even sure he remembered, this Manager of CEO Communications had made the elevator speech from hell, and committed career suicide as surely as if he had withdrawn a .357 magnum from his suit jacket and blown his own head off.

Jack described the scene to me two or three years later. He and a few other senior vice presidents—all early contenders for the next CEO job—had entered the elevator at 570 Lexington Avenue, an art deco skyscraper that was GE's New York headquarters at the time. The speechwriter was in the elevator when Jack and his colleagues entered, and Welch, in his always social and gregarious manner, smiled and asked, "What's the matter Bob? You look exhausted."

Welch's outrage grew as he recalled the incident. "You know what he said to me? He said, 'Jack, when you are carrying the intellectual weight of this company around on your shoulders it can wear you down.' Can you believe he said that? Can you believe that arrogant bastard? Manager of CEO Communications? Bullshit. *I'm* the manager of this company's CEO communications."

That conversation not only did much to frame my view of myself and my place in the world, but also was a key reason for my rare and almost cockroach-like survival during the two decades I worked for Welch. In the few interviews I did for business magazines, I would always minimize my role, describing myself as a mere "word assistant," or "dictation-taker," for a man who never read someone else's thoughts and words as if they were his own. I would panic when anyone approached me after Jack had enchanted a crowd to say, "Bill—that was terrific. You wrote that, didn't you?" I would loudly assure, for the benefit of anyone within hearing range, "No. That's all Jack. I helped him a little, but that's all him," which was essentially true. One day, Rosanne, who today is Jack's assistant and still my old friend, said, "Bill, Mr. Welch knows you never take the credit for his talks, and he appreciates it."

To do otherwise would have meant sudden career death and oblivion.

But the poor, sixty-ish "Manager of CEO Communications" was humbled sadly in the closing days of an otherwise great career. He walked in my office one day in the late spring of '81, practically in tears. "Bill, I'm writing for the wastebasket. I give him draft after draft and he just kind of laughs and dismisses me. I can hear the speech hitting the bottom of the wastebasket as I walk out of his office."

This writer, like so many sports figures, stayed around a season too long.

I stayed around too long, as well—but I *had* to. I was only 57 at the time, and despite 22 years of GE service, was ineligible for immediate pension and other benefits. I had to wait for them to "shoot me."

And they did. Decently and fairly, in the tradition of "Generous Electric," at least for people who work "around the flagpole."

I left the execution chamber, called my wife, and went up to see a friend of mine, GE's treasurer, Jim Bunt. My execution had been telegraphed for months, and I had told Jim that, before I signed anything, I wanted him to look at the deal.

More than once I've witnessed Welch listen quietly to a volley of seeming non sequiturs, oblique financial metaphors, and passionate but off-the-wall statements from Jim—who would then depart for a smoke, leaving Welch laughing quietly and happily shaking his head at this aviary of odd ducks he had assembled. "Anyone who thinks GE is a bunch of conventional uptight stuffed shirts needs to spend 15 minutes with Jim Bunt," Welch once observed.

Despite his strangeness, Jim Bunt is a brilliant financial brain, who would never have been allowed to run a business at GE, but was trusted by

Jack to analyze any proposed deals—particularly in financial services—and render a verdict. He had a gift for sniffing out fecal matter in a balance sheet; a thumbs-down from Bunt on a deal usually doomed it. He would have needed about two hours on the spoor at Enron, Worldcom, or Tyco to figure them out.

At our Boca dinners we would eat the Jack-dictated swordfish, chicken, and veal, but Bunt would wave his away and order a gigantic cheeseburger and fries, a huge glass of milk, and an ashtray. He'd then *smoke* his way through dinner while we laughed and shook our heads. He wore an enormous diamond pinky ring, and his attractive second wife is as quirky and interesting as he is.

But Bunt could give you a "shot" as well as anyone, including Welch. And he would nail Welch as well. Bunt was also fearless, even if it meant butting heads with Jack.

Once, at a meeting of his corporate executive council—a quarterly assembly of the top 30 or 40 people in the company, Jack was pounding away on costs—mostly travel and living—but particularly on air travel. After outlining ambitious, and compulsory, air travel reduction targets, he paused momentarily to hear a loud voice from the back of the room, asking: "Does that include the G-4?" referring to the Gulfstream IV, at the time the largest of the GE jet fleet, and for all intents and purposes "Jack's plane."

The room quieted at this death wish Tourette's Syndrome outburst from—who else? Jim.

Jim later told me that he didn't know why he yelled that out; but he felt bad about it, and addressed Jack as they stood at the line of Crotonville urinals during the break. He quoted himself saying to the effect of "Sorry about what I said, Jack." And Welch, pissed, and pissing, stared ahead at the wall, as guys do, and in a quiet voice said, "Jim, I don't care what you say as long as you keep on doing what you're doing."

So, on that February 2000 morning when I got "shot," (Jack departed six months before), I strolled over to the third-floor corner office of the West Building and said, "Jim, they just pulled the trigger this morning. You were gonna tell me your view on the deal."

Jim didn't tell me what he thought of my deal that morning. Instead, the diamond pinky ring waved off my request, and he said, "Sit down, Mr. Big Shot Communicator and Presentation Expert (he actually *did* say things like this); I'm going to make a presentation to you; and tell me what you think."

"You and a couple of other guys around here have been bragging for 15 years about having everything you own in the stock market and how you hold every option up 'til the day it expires; and how much smarter you are than people like me who have been telling you that you need to get out of at least half of what you've got in equities. And *diversify*."

He then walked me through a series of stock market charts and the various component industries, and asked, after each chart, whether I thought that market sector deserved a higher price/earnings ratio—than its average at the moment.

Again and again I answered "no," or "probably not."

He then said, "You need to diversify—now. You can keep some GE, but you need to move out of a lot of your equities."

He continued, "I'm not telling you anything I haven't been telling everyone, for years, including Jack, who thinks I'm an asshole. I'm just asking you whether you want to be a retired guy and go online every night and watch your family's money melt away, because it *could*, if this market blows up. The whole market, including GE, could take a beating. The market is overvalued. I've been saying it for years and *everybody* thinks I'm an asshole."

We never got to the subject of my package that day—or any day—because I thanked Jim for his well-prepared presentation, and walked over to the East Building, thinking, the entire way, of those poor retirees who took all their nice gains and principles out of the '90s mutual funds and traded them for dot-com magic beans. Many were now girding their shriveled loins for second careers at Wal-Mart and McDonald's.

After the Bunt presentation, I spent the next hour in my office, online and on the phone, switching more money than this Brooklyn-born, B minus, modest achiever ever dreamed he would see. I moved most of what I had out of stocks, including my beloved GE, and into boring, low-risk stuff. I paid off my mortgage. I put three college educations away.

I went home that night and told my wife that while I knew that GE was the best, most solid company in the world and that while I thought the Dow was pretty solid, maybe Jim—as nutty as he was—might be right; and we couldn't afford to be wrong.

GE, at $42 that day, was bouncing off $20 within a year, and the market was in the commode.

As my so-called retirement party neared late that summer, Jim asked me if I had paid attention to his presentation. When I told him that I had gotten out that day, he said, "Hey, you owe me a drink."

I think maybe I owe him a *couple* of drinks.

But now, with my desk cleaned out and my closed-door sessions with the HR undertakers scheduled, which would take place in a section of the East Building known, appropriately, as "Packageland," the subject of the retirement party reared its depressing head. I had been to scores of these parties during my career at GE. Some, like Jack's at the Crotonvile campus, were the hottest ticket in town. I remember ordering a Gordon's gin at Jack's party, thinking what an idiot I was, tossing it, and getting into a serious regimen of Château Lafite, while talking with CNBC's Sue Herera, the nicest lady on business TV; and listening to how impressed *she* was that I was a speechwriter—and Jack's speechwriter to boot. Later I switched to the bar white—Château Montrachet—as the dinner program began, and ate hummingbird tongues—or whatever—as a series of hilarious video tributes to Jack played on the big screens in the Crotonville dining room, featuring a host of major-leaguers including Jay Leno and Conan O'Brien.

I think I set my wine and canapés down on Andy Rooney's head.

My favorite video tribute to Jack was by Triumph the Insult Comic Dog from the *Conan O'Brien Show*, who, peering out at us in contempt with a cigar in his mouth, said, "Look at this crowd of GE executives and celebrities at Jack Welch's party. I haven't seen so many parasites since my last stool sample."

I remember telling Jack, just before we all staggered off for bed, how important being invited was to me. He was warm and gracious. It was a great party—a real celebration—which is what retirement parties *should* be.

Part II

I Can't Deal with this Anymore

My first big GE company meeting, in September of 1980, was also the first time I encountered Welch. He was a superstar, the boy wonder, an object of intense curiosity. For the many who had had unpleasant dealings with him in the past, Welch was an object of dread.

The race for the chairmanship was nearing the finish line. The field had been narrowed to three vice chairmen: Ed Hood, John Burlingame, and the mercurial, stuttering maniac, Jack Welch. "The fact that this man is even an officer in the General Electric Company, much less a candidate for chairman, just astonishes me," I remember some old fart saying; and his was, by no means, an isolated view of Jack.

Jack arrived at the next big meeting, this time as Chairman-elect, in the first limo of a five- or six-car motorcade, moving pompously around the circular driveway to a stop at the front of the hotel. I was there, and told him a few years later, that I thought the spectacle was obscene. He didn't disagree. It turns out that ground transportation had sent a *white Rolls Royce* to meet him at his jet—and he had angrily refused to get in. A modest black Lincoln was hastily called, and away he went. Jack never avoided luxury, but instinctively loathed the type of ostentation that would, years later, contribute to the downfall of several of his CEO colleagues.

Jack would move about quickly, usually with six or eight pals, radiating noise and energy like a thundercloud, whether emerging from the golf course (where he was a single-digit handicap), holding court at the Black Catte, or roaming from private meetings to scheduled events.

I was in the meeting room with three or four other speechwriters and staff, rehearsing the GE speakers for the next day. The Welch entourage came flying through the lobby doors, strolled up the long aisle of chairs, and parked themselves three or four rows behind me. The rehearsing speaker, who was droning through his slides on the stage, spotted the intruders and dialed up his intensity. He may have even said, "Hi, Jack." Welch conversed in his stentorian *sotto voce* for a while, as his compañeros leaned over, solicitously, to hear his acidic commentary, and strange, indescribable sounds I called "whale noises." Jack and his boys stayed to hear the speaker slog on for a few more minutes before I heard, "I can't deal with this shit anymore," which signaled the posse to get up and leave.

I wasn't sure I liked this guy, but he left me curious; he was the antithesis of everything I had encountered in my four short months at GE. He was 10 or 11 years older than I was, but he was a "kid," like me; or rather like the kid I *thought* I still was: wild, profane, and passionate. Over the years, and to this day, I marvel at the courage Reginald Jones showed in picking a successor who was nothing like himself—perhaps the *least* like him; a character the likes of which had never been seen at GE.

Jack Welch's refusal to "deal with this shit anymore" carried implications far beyond that day. After playing the game for 20-plus years, wasting money on "hats," slides, airplane rides, and bullshit meetings, it dawned on him that he *didn't have to* deal with it anymore. More importantly, under his command, no one else should have to deal with it anymore.

Power may corrupt, but it also can liberate, and he began to instinctively conceive ways for us to free ourselves from the corporate crap that had enslaved and bored GE, not to mention the entire capitalist organizational structure, for more than a century.

Jack ran his first meeting of general managers about 10 months after he took over. He had announced at the end of the final Jones-era meeting that we would leave the Belleview Biltmore and move to the five-star Boca Raton Hotel and Club in South Florida.

Welch quickly changed the agendas from the ridiculous, posturing, pretentious "Vision" extravaganzas they had become into what I would describe as "success stories with messages attached."

People who believe the legend of "Neutron Jack"—the maniac, bull in a China shop, Tasmanian Devil caricature, who upturned the tables and chairs of a boring, stolid company doomed to either breakup or hit the scrap heap—do not understand the GE of the early '80s.

Reg Jones was arguably the best CEO in the country at the time, and certainly the most honored. GE's management practices were the toast of every business school in the world and its management team was the prey of every recruiter in town. Indeed, GE used to annually publish a book that they would hand out at the Boca conference, filled with the pictures, titles, and bios of each attendee—but were forced to stop when the book became a headhunter's menu.

GE was profitable, competitive, and had the healthiest balance sheet in big business. Jack has always been quick to admit that GE was not some foundering wreck that he'd grabbed the wheel to save. Although Jack hated the analogy, GE was like a ponderous supertanker, slow to change direction even after violent spinning of the wheel.

But on day one of the Welch era, the wheel at least began to turn on *communications*. There would be no more "visions," especially visions like those offered up in Reg Jones's last meeting—onanistic fantasies that would supposedly unfold over a decade. Anyone who even *claimed* they could see four or five *years* into the future was now considered a bullshitter. The mass liquidation of the strategic planning apparatus, which was built around a five-year view, would begin within a year.

Welch's rejection of the Jones-era long range vision planning was especially apparent in the restructuring of GE Capital, a backwater business started during the depression to finance appliances consumers could no longer afford. After a leadership purge, GE Capital would soon grow, largely because it operated on the idea that no one could know what was going to happen in financial services *three months* from now, much less three years. It began to become, in the mid-'80s, the "place to be" for Welch-style, frenetic, instant gratification–loving people like Larry Bossidy and the ineffable Gary Wendt. And that whole crowd laughed at anyone who pretended to know what was going to happen three *months* from now in financial services, much less three years. Jack couldn't "deal with this shit anymore."

And you needn't, either.

Mike's Big Day

It was a warm and sunny afternoon in the mid-'90s. I had just run several miles and worked out in the GE fitness center, which I did as often as my schedule would allow, then finished a quick lunch in the cafeteria, and returned to my office, where I needed to kill off some boring administrative work. Before long, I could feel the velvet fingers of "the rack monster," as we called it in the Army, tugging downward on my eyelashes.

GE's corporate headquarters is a very quiet place. When the glass office doors are closed, it is completely silent, with the exception of a nearly subliminal buzz that we were told long ago was white noise piped in to keep the inmates sane.

The halls and open areas, with Dilbert-like cubicles, are equally quiet, ever since the last of the IBM Selectrics were abandoned for Wang word processors in the early '80s. The third floor of the East Building was the quietest of all—the holiest of holies—the abode of The Chairman.

When I first walked the hallowed third floor hall in 1980, I noticed that the few people who were summoned there would tread softly and cease talking as they passed by the unmarked office of Reg Jones, GE's legendary chairman. I suggested that perhaps a sanctuary lamp could be placed next to the door (this was my Catholic background speaking), and the candle lit when the chairman was physically present in his office. The sublime quiet ended on the third floor in April of '81, when Jack assumed the throne.

Working with armored vehicles at the Pentagon taught me an interesting lesson about the difference between high- and low-pitched noises: high-pitched noise, such as that made by an Abrams tank, does not travel as far as the low-pitched noise produced by diesel tanks. You already understand this principle if you live in an apartment with thin walls; your idiot neighbor's stereo doesn't transmit the treble but the bass is annoyingly clear.

But the rules of physics apparently didn't apply to Jack. His high-pitched voice—and his alone—could be heard from virtually any point on the floor. Shouted telephone conversations, on or off speaker phone, were audible from hundreds of feet down the hall, even in other offices. Bloodcurdling shrieks rang out, followed by the deeper, barely audible defensive murmurs of the business leader doing the rope-a-dope on the speakerphone. The communication would end with a series of commands, and a dire description of the disasters that would befall us, and him, if the victim did not move faster or more decisively.

When the call ended, there would be a between-rounds pause for a moment or two, followed by a shout to "Helga!"—or later, "Ro!" (his sainted secretaries): "Get that bozo on the line."

If the "spankings," as we called them, were administered in person, the victim was almost never heard. I recall an early speechwriting client of mine, Executive Vice President Jim Baker, a godlike figure in my relatively young eyes and a sector executive, being brutalized by Jack in the hall. I scooted down the hall and headed toward the elevator, away from the violence, as if veering from a gory car accident in my lane. As the elevator doors closed I heard, "You're in deep shit, Baker!"

When he needed to bounce something off one of his closest confidants and friends—Larry Bossidy, Dennis Dammerman, Ben Heineman, and others—he eschewed the phone and ran down the hall, barging into their offices, usually holding the letter or the bunch of papers that had set him off. He would apologize politely, but perfunctorily, to the four or five or 10 people who were making a presentation to Larry or somebody, people who would then flutter away like pigeons to permit Jack privacy as he bounced some things off Larry or Dennis.

The privacy was, of course, illusory, because even after the frazzled secretary closed the electric door to the office, the deaf could hear the conversation down the hall. "We've got to get rid of this fucking idiot. Do you want to do it, or should Glen do it?"

The briefers would then take their briefcases and overheads and return to Erie or Louisville or Schenectady, with a "Jack story" that would last a career.

So the third floor was an exciting—and at times terrifying—place, at least when Jack was in residence.

But the *second* floor—my floor—was a quiet, lulling place that warm afternoon. I sat and did some writing for a half hour or so, but the lids were starting to drop. Sun was streaming through the floor to ceiling windows in my office, and little specks of dust floated in the rays.

"You know what?" I thought, "I can just swivel the chair around so the back of my head is toward the glass door and potential witnesses, put my feet up on the credenza behind me, hold a yellow pad like a prop, stick a pen between two fingers, and maybe catch a five-minute nap. Maybe ten. No more."

And so I did, or began to.

Ahhh. The arms of Morpheus were reaching, beckoning me, when the GE work ethic nagged at my remaining consciousness, reminding me that whatever I had been working on *had* to get done by close of business. I didn't have time for a nap. So I swiveled back around, sighed, and began scratching away with my Flair pen.

Less than two minutes later I received unquestionable proof of the existence of a God who cares about me—because, without a knock, my office door flew open and Jack appeared, like Kramer on *Seinfeld*.

Had he caught me asleep he would, in fact, have found it hilarious—but he would have broken my shoes about it for the rest of our lives. It would have become my trademark descriptive anecdote, as opposed to the ten or twelve others he kept in his holster.

He had appeared to fetch me. "Bill, this kid Mike Fraiser has been running a project on best practices and how we might be able to use them. He's doing a pitch for me over at the Guest House and you need to hear it."

So off we went and walked along the outside podiums of the East and the West Buildings, and then across to the exotic wedge-shaped Guest House and Conference Center, which had been blasted into the side of a rock hill, requiring that you enter the building from the roof, and take the elevator down.

Jack burst into the conference room with a nasally "hi" to Mike Fraiser and the team that had been obviously alerted by phone that we were on the way.

We slid into chairs, and I got my first look at Mike, this kid Jack liked so much. And he *was* a kid: barely 30, if that, with red hair. My initial thought was that he was a dead ringer for Opie, from the old *Andy Griffith Show*.

Welch's body language signaled "let's get going," so Mike did, and with none of the ass-kissing pleasantries that most GE executives hate, he launched into the results of his study and the work he and his team had done over the past few months. No smiles, no small talk. His manner said, "I'm a serious man with some important things to say that you need to listen to, and act upon, if you agree with them."

Mike's pitch was on best practices—a familiar phrase today, but one, at the time, I had never heard. Mike described how the very best practices by the best companies and institutions in the world might be identified by GE. Those practices could then be spread quickly across the Company and put into operation. Implementing this strategy would strike a deathblow to the curse of vanity that has long infected big, old, successful companies like GE, where only in-house innovations stood a chance.

More importantly, the adoption and embrace of best practices as policy within GE culture could dramatically increase the *speed* at which the company moved and attacked.

Welch was preoccupied with GE's "speed"—this was also a source of his early exasperation. Jack arrived from, and pretty much created, the plastics industry, where innovation came at a breakneck pace; he was driven crazy by the slog-through-the-muck pace that he saw at GE.

In many respects, being considered ponderous and glacial was a reputation relished by the old crowd. GE cherished its image as a "supertanker," which, even after the wheel had been spun, still required miles and miles of water to shake off its inertia and begin to turn. I found this imagery interesting, and actually used it in something or other I gave to Welch—albeit for derogatory purposes. I thought he was going to have a baby when he read it—he told me he never wanted to hear it again.

Years later, Welch was interviewed by Mark Haines on CNBC, who ticked off the standard change-related business clichés about quickly evolving markets, globalization, electronic technology, and the like. He then asked Jack how a big old company like GE—a *supertanker*—could adapt quickly enough. There was a pause in the interview after which Jack shouted, "You mean a *cigarette boat!*"

Perhaps Haines remembered that GE owned CNBC and that he was lower in the food chain than the animated interviewee who sat across from him, because he suddenly seemed to *accept* cigarette boat as an accurate depiction of this 100 billion dollar behemoth—an absurd exaggeration. Even CNBC's Sue Herera (one of Jack's favorites) couldn't have gotten the super-tankers analogy past him without an eruption of some magnitude. It embodied all the qualities he detested in the "old" GE.

Speed was his need, and Mike Frasier sold it to him that day in injection form.

After a volley of compliments to Mike and his team, Jack and I headed back across campus toward our offices. I couldn't shut up about best practices, and how it could transform the company. Jack agreed, with staccato shouts: "Yeah. Absolutely." But what he *really* wanted to talk about was something other than best practices. He wanted moral reinforcement on the star he had just decided to create. "Was that the best pitch you've ever seen?" "Unbelievable." "He really grew in that job." "This guy's ready." "Unbelievable."

It may seem hard to believe that I wasn't able to see it at the time, but I was watching Welch's finger hit a career liftoff button. Within a couple of months Fraiser was named President of GE Japan; and from then on it was nothing but upward. Today, he is President of Genworth Financial, a huge spin-off of a GE insurance and financial services business. He was actually mentioned in the late '90s, as a possible Welch successor.

Not long after Mike Fraiser's presentation, GE accelerated its processes—in some cases dramatically—by adopting best practices, including Wal-Mart's "Quick Market Intelligence"; a cycle-time reduction technique called Quick Response, from some appliance company in New Zealand; Toshiba's "Half-Movement" design philosophy; American Standard's "Demand Flow Technology"; and Caterpillar's "part standardization" discipline.

Amazingly—and dead against the old cultural grain—GE also adopted thousands of big and small best practices from its *own* employees, as part of its "Work Out" initiative.

I spoke, a few years ago, at one of Mike's business meetings and asked him if he knew, that day at the Guest House, what an upper deck home run he had hit. He said he thought that it had gone well, but not as well as it had turned out.

I said to myself, as this unfolded: "Most of them simply don't get it, do they?" Some of the best and brightest understand instinctively how crucial to a career the ability to do a great pitch is; but others in "the brightest" category—particularly engineers, scientists, environmental people, and lawyers—*do not.*

Around this same time I took a trip somewhere with Larry Bossidy, a GE vice chairman, for whom I was also "doing" speeches. I brought up the subject of a guy named Steve Rabinowitz, who had been made a GE vice president (a "made man" as I used to say) just a few weeks before. Rabinowitz was a brilliant guy—in manufacturing, as I recall, but not known for his people skills. He had been placed on the Boca meeting agenda by Jack, probably at Larry's behest. Steve showed up at Boca with a pretty good pitch, and he and

I worked together to sharpen it and simplify the appalling engineer-style slides, which were Dilbert-esque, unreadable, and bafflingly complex.

When the big day arrived he did a fine job, delivering a reasonably useful message for that period. Shortly thereafter the wand came down upon his shoulders, and the gold bars of officership appeared. He became a vice president in a company where a corporate vice president was a huge deal; there were probably only 130 or so VPs (out of 300,000 employees) at the time.

Larry Bossidy is one of my favorite people, and some of my favorite memories of GE are times I spent with him. I still occasionally write for him. He came from a small, not-pretty town in New England where he worked in his parents' shoe store. The legend is that his mom made him turn down a pro baseball offer—the scout was literally at the front door pleading to come in—because she wanted him to be the first in the family to go to college.

I am not a big small talk guy with people who play in a different league than I do; I defer to rank, as I did in the Army. But I have always refused to kiss ass, and I have observed over the years that ass-kissers fill the legitimate big players with disgust. So whenever I traveled with Jack or Larry or a couple of the other "shooters," after catching up on discussions both useful and interesting to both of us, I tended to withdraw into my own world and let them move into theirs, typically by catching up on my e-mail (or just plain mail, back in the pre-Internet days).

So I pressed Larry about Steve Rabinowitz's recent promotion, since he was Larry's guy. "Tell me Steve didn't get to be a GE officer because he did a great pitch at Boca. Is that why he got it?"

"Yes, that's why he got it," Larry said.

I was stunned, and asked, "Are you kidding me?"—so he qualified his answer: "He didn't get it just because of one good pitch—Boca was like a final exam. We knew he was good, but we had to see if he could *transfer his ideas and practices to other people in a useful way; and he did.*"

He continued, "When you talk to these clowns at Crotonville (which I did two or three times a month), tell them they are going *nowhere* in the General Electric Company if they can't do a great business presentation. You can't be a leader if you can't stand up and present, and we are only interested in leaders."

He suggested that I be put on the Boca program to talk about this, which would have been okay with me, but, pondering the idea as he spoke, I realized that it would be impossible for me to convey this critically important message in 15 or 20—or even 30—minutes.

I fell prey to a typical attitudinal conceit, a root cause of presentation disasters: the belief that what you think is so important is also considered to be so by the audience.

The best presentations I've done in my life—including my father's five-minute eulogy—are ones about which people I respected came up and said: "It was great, but it was too short. I wanted to hear more."

All first draft presentations are too long and should be cut. Second, third, and fourth drafts should be cut further.

Crotonville High

It was widely understood that I was business illiterate. I couldn't even read a balance sheet, and was bored by most of the non-combative stuff, the nuanced minutia people spent their days worrying over in Fairfield. And I hated what Welch himself called "buzzwords, jargon, and terms"—words he understood but refused to use. But he felt I should at least know what they meant. I was flying somewhere with Welch and Joyce Hergenhan, to whom I reported, and Welch said, "We've got to send him to a 'big time' course at Crotonville."

So I set off for Crotonville, in the summer of 1986—as a "kid" of 42—to learn about *leveraging* and *return on total capital*. My wife, who was caring for our eight-month-old with an "Irish twin" on the way, was thrilled. We had recently moved into a fairly small, under-maintained ranch house on a little river in Easton, Connecticut. It was a fixer-upper, and I had neither the skill nor the interest to use a hammer.

Despite the splendor of Crotonville in late June, the 30 of us spent our days in a small, windowless amphitheater called "The Cave," insulated from bird noises and the beauty of the campus. Ram Charon, who later co-authored, with Larry Bossidy, two of the best business books I have ever read, ran the course.

Ira Magaziner—later of the Clinton administration—who reminded me of what Ichabod Crane might look like on methamphetamines, was one of the guest lecturers.

Jack came and spoke to us, as he did with every class at this level, and I glowed while he gave me several good-natured shots during his pitch. In 1986 he was on the cusp of stardom. The stock had achieved liftoff, the old guard had been sent off to green pastures, and a cocky bunch of managers with Welch DNA were ascending.

I was with a group that was arguably the craziest bunch ever assembled at Crotonville. There were a few other competing classes of more junior people on the campus for a few weeks during our course, and each evening gallons of beer, animated arguments, and good-natured insults were *de rigueur* at the "Rec Building." Within two weeks, firecrackers had been thrown into an enemy classroom. Food flew in the dining hall.

On one occasion the thirty of us, each armed with paper balls, assembled quietly outside a class in session. Someone gave the *go* signal, and we burst through the door, running in front of some Harvard geek in mid-lecture, and firing at the enemy class in the amphitheater while they shouted, laughed, and threw whatever was at hand at us. We disappeared as quickly as we had appeared, out the opposite door, slamming it behind us, the room in shambles, leaving the speaker whey-faced, and on the verge of shitting his pants. We were advised, half-seriously, by the manager of Crotonville, to "tone it down," after, I guess, the Harvard geek had threatened never to return.

We were given the same "tone it down" message a few days later after one of the class clowns returned from nearby Ossining with several porn video tapes. The big screen was electronically deployed from the ceiling of "The Pit," the biggest amphitheater on campus—made famous by Jack, who loved it—and our class and some members of our enemy classes, fueled by beer runs to the Rec Building, threw popcorn at the screen as "Big Mamma Jamma," a 350-pound lesbian contortionist, displayed her flexibility. The two "girls" in our class, almost as wild as the worst of us, shook their heads and took a pass on this particular evening's entertainment.

When I told Welch about the things that went on during our Crotonville class, he laughed and purred, because he perceived, correctly, that the juvenile, *Animal House* behavior was a welcome symptom of the high-spirited *joie de vivre* that was spreading across his company. Our behavior reminded him of his early days in the plastics business—and that was just fine with him.

The memories of our class, despite the behavior, fared well in their subsequent careers, either with GE or elsewhere. Welch and Bossidy already had their eyes on a few of my classmates. A few made VP. I didn't. I shouldn't have.

Prior Planning Prevents Piss-Poor Performance

Two presentations, in particular, knocked me off my horse of conventional corporate presentation philosophy, and turned me into something of a monomaniac in my thinking on how business people *must* learn to communicate with one another.

Aside from being an immature, cocky bunch, we were politically astute and understood the rings and hurdles, such as whose ass might be kicked with impunity, and whose ass might require a chaste little smooch. That did not apply to me. I was politically unconscious, and really did not need to keep anyone happy but Welch, Bossidy, and Joyce, to whom I directly reported.

One of those presentations was by a GE senior vice president named Jim; a Jones-era holdover, but one with a good reputation and, perhaps more importantly, Jack didn't hate him. Welch had already become a powerful booster of Crotonville, and had told the businesses he wanted their best and brightest sent to the courses as opposed to the "hacks" that could be spared for a month. He also told his business leaders that he wanted them at Crotonville, whenever asked, to speak to the classes, and it was expected that they do a good job presenting.

So Jim walked in, an impressive looking classic GE senior VP. He took off his jacket, and flipped through a stack of overhead transparencies he had brought with him. "Give me a couple of minutes to look at these. They've been in the file cabinet for months. Jeez. Some of these are dusty," laughing as he said this, not looking at us slouched in our seats inside The Cave, while flipping through his charts (or *somebody's* charts).

Impatient murmurs and annoyed body language rippled through the room. I remember whispering to the guy next to me, "Screw him. He obviously doesn't think we're worth a shit if he won't even look at his charts in the car on the way down. This is all he thinks of us?" I could see others quietly mumbling as well, totally turned off by his casual and dismissive approach to us.

Would he have pulled a "these charts are dusty" routine in front of Welch and the senior leadership of the company?

I don't think so.

I doodled and wrote myself some unrelated notes while the generally affable Jim cruised through his pitch and left. A couple of us flamed him on the speaker evaluation forms. Maybe he learned something from them or maybe not. Maybe he didn't even read them.

There is one simple message you need to understand from this: No matter how important or unimportant your audience is—whether they are aspiring ninth-grade writers (to whom I have spoken), big shots, or customers—never, ever, convey the impression that speaking to them is a duty, a pain in the ass, or something other than what you would rather be doing at the moment. Appearing nervous is fine. It conveys to the audience that you care about how well you perform in front of them; that they matter.

Fred's Bad Day

After Jim's pitch, we began to get increasingly critical of presentations as the sweet month of June wore on. A few were excellent, or "pretty good." Some were just boring or useless, but we took notes and asked questions anyway, either to show off, or be polite and show interest.

But the presentations that were *really* eating away at us were those given by our own classmates.

The Crotonville regimen was a full day of lectures from GE people or business academics, with a break at 5 p.m. Dinner was about an hour afterwards, and at around 7 p.m., we would reassemble in The Cave for no other purpose than to hear two of our classmates, each night, make 10-minute presentations on their businesses. Being a "corporate weenie" with no connection to any particular business, I was given a pass; I didn't have to pitch.

While a couple of the presentations weren't too boring, they were *all* mostly useless and too long, averaging more than 20 minutes. There were a few good-natured shots from the audience and some laughs; but we were all friends by now, so we endured the boring show-and-tell pitches so we could get out of there at a reasonable hour. Afterward, we would make calls to our demoralized home fronts, fire down a few beers, and prepare a business case for the next day (Crown Cork and Seal sticks in my mind), and watch the Yankees on the Rec Building TV, before succumbing to "the rack monster."

So the innocuous show-and-tells continued until the night of "Freddy"—not Freddy Krueger of *Nightmare on Elm Street* fame—but something even more terrifying: *Fred the GE engineer.*

Fred walked into The Cave carrying *two* (!) slide carousels for his *10-minute* pitch!

Panic gripped the room. People actually got down on their hands and knees and theatrically crawled behind the desks toward the exits. Cries of "Oh my God," and "We're Doomed!" rang out, along with a great deal of laughter, including some nervous laughter from Fred, who was (and I assume still is) an awfully nice guy.

Fred got started, and we settled back politely. His pitch was about the chemical plant he ran, or assisted in running. As I recall (in nightmares), it involved slide after slide of banks of pipes: what each pipe held, where the pipe led, what its contents converted into, and on and on, into the balmy night.

The 50-minute mark came and went; and we realized, with horror, that Fred was still finishing his *first* slide carousel. Another carousel remained.

Some amusing *sotto voce* comments, including threats of suicide and murder, along with a few obscenities, issued from the chafing crowd.

It was at this point that Steve Bennett—a future GE VP and now CEO of software giant Intuit—fired "the shot heard 'round GE." From the back of the room, Steve rolled up a ball of paper from a legal pad and yelled, "Fred, shut up!" as he threw the paper ball toward the presenter, missing Fred, and hitting the screen filled with Fred's color-coded chemical pipes. Fred laughed nervously and continued: "This green pipe leads into the red pipe which contains the…"

Tumult simmered below the surface for two or three minutes, and then we all began rolling up yellow legal pad sheets into balls of our own, and firing away. Fred gamely darted around the front of the room with barrage after barrage of paper balls hitting him, hitting the screen projector, hitting the walls. He began shouting with great urgency, "C'mon guys, I just have a few more minutes. See, this red pipe goes through this oxidizer and…"

Then it got nasty. The entire class, even the women, stood to gain leverage, shifting their target from the screen to Fred; specifically, Fred's *head*.

Fred dribbled off through an ankle-deep sea of paper balls and found a seat.

I enjoyed that pitch—at least the end—probably as much as I would have enjoyed the Sermon on the Mount.

Fred didn't enjoy it though. Over the remaining one or two weeks, he barely spoke to any of us again.

I told my wife what we did, and she said she felt sorry for him.

Screw Fred. *We* were the offended parties.

We were denied what few creature comforts we would have rather enjoyed that evening by some self-absorbed nut of an engineer, who wanted to waste the ticking moments of our lives telling us about his factory's pipes.

The paper ball became a popular tool for providing immediate feedback during the rest of our summer days at Crotonville and, incredibly enough, a tradition at the school that lasted for a year or two afterwards.

Outsiders, from Harvard or Wharton, or even visiting lecturers from GE, were exempt from the fusillades, because no matter how irreverent we thought we were, no one was ever going to fire a yellow paper ball at an outsider, or a GE officer. But the students were fair game, and the few remaining evening presentations improved dramatically. Presenters were motivated to avoid overly long, self-absorbed data dumps by the distinct possibility of yellow legal pad barrage, and—despite the laughter that accompanied the assaults—the humiliation of knowing that your presentation was lousy, boring, and useless.

It was during that time, in the mid-to-late '80s, that tolerance for bad business presentations ended—not because my class threw paper balls at bores, but because Jack was running the show. And if George Bush the First didn't have to eat broccoli, Jack didn't have to sit through another 20 years of ghost-written, self-serving crap from gasbags, at the meetings and briefings that occupy much of a senior executive's day.

He had decided, in a vague and not-yet-focused way, to make communications—oral and written—a critical lever in the operation of the company.

No one, as far as I know, has ever stressed communications to this degree at a Fortune 100 company. Most start-ups and young companies place a heavy emphasis on communications, otherwise they get prematurely sclerotic and die before their teens. Only big fat companies have the financial cushion that allows them to waste their people's time.

When our BMC course came to an end, I emerged as something better than that the business idiot I'd shown up as, 28 days before, and received a plaque and class picture to prove it. I was finally able to read a balance sheet (well, sort of) and I now understood some aspects of business that were mere buzzwords to me before, such as inventory management, depreciation, and calculating market share. It was time well spent—typically first-class, top-shelf GE in every respect—with the exception of the student presentations, which I found troublingly banal. I knew the fate that awaited several of my classmates if they dared put on a slide show of colored chemical pipes for Jack Welch.

Near the end of our course, the whole class was put on a bus and sent to a great Italian restaurant in Westport, Connecticut, about 40 minutes from Crotonville. The few husbands or wives of class members living in the area were invited, and an abnormal—even for a GE group—amount of booze was consumed. We kissed our wives goodbye in the restaurant lot and stumbled back onto the bus for the ride back to Crotonville, alternately breaking each other's shoes and promising to stay in touch, in those days before e-mail.

One of the class members, a Japanese man from a GE Capital business in Tokyo, was falling-down, knee-walking drunk, happily cavorting in the aisle of the bus and laughing and shouting incomprehensibly in a language that was neither English nor Japanese.

I recall doing a Mae West impression from the back of the bus and asking, "Is that a torpedo in your pocket, or are you just thinking about Pearl Harbor?" The bus driver almost crashed.

The next day, picking and puking our way through the slow motion fog of hangovers, we completed course evaluations, and did other easy stuff. Some of us failed to make it in from the Residence Building and others retreated back to it to sleep. I was not in bad shape at all, and grabbed the den mother of our class—a GE manager and member of the Crotonville faculty, and told him how great I thought the course was, how impressed I was with the faculty, and how impressed I was with the intellectual level and leadership traits of most of my classmates.

But then I unloaded on my classmates' presentation skills and the fates that would await them if they dared to stand up and spew some of the stuff they did for us in front of the "new cats" that were now running this company. I told him that Crotonville had to restyle the course to better prepare the students for the new GE—Jack's GE—and include presentation skills as part of the courses. They were sending lambs off to the slaughter if they did not, at least, make them aware of how critical this art and skill was to their careers. He agreed, and, in fact, had approved of the radical paper ball therapy for bad presenters that we had introduced. But then he said, "Why don't *you* tell them the importance of this, and how to do it. If you tell them, they'll believe it's Jack's message. If I bring in some consultant, he won't have the credibility."

That pretty much shut me up. There was another BMC class starting in a month, so I agreed to do it. And so began 15 years of crack-of-dawn drives down the Merritt, "Hutch," and 287, to talk to virtually every mid-level-to-senior class at Crotonville. I would then jump back in the rental car and be back at my desk in Fairfield by 10:30.

Triumphs, Train Wrecks, Coronations, and Jack's Biggest Miss

Each time I arrived at Crotonville, I would wander around the dark and quiet classroom building, run through my notes, try phrases and thoughts on myself, and get "psyched" up to the point where it didn't appear as if I did this a dozen or more times a year.

My presentation evolved rather smoothly after 40 or 50 late-night hours of thinking, jotting notes, writing, and rewriting. I reasoned that if I could make these people at least understand how *important* effective business communications were to GE, they would recognize the importance of communications to their careers. If I could get them to buy into a few simple principles of communication that I knew worked and to be true, I could change their lives.

My first pitch was a success. Despite my nervousness at the start, I loudly intimidated and harangued the BMC class in the same Cave where we had tormented the bad presenters.

I told the paper ball story, well aware of its dreaded implications for me if my pitch failed. I growled at them. I pleaded with them. I described the triumphs, train wrecks, disasters, and coronations I'd witnessed resulting from the best and worst pitches I'd seen. I implored them to look in the mirror that night and ask themselves, "Do I have a good pitch? And, if the answer is 'maybe not,' they would need to ask themselves, 'What do I plan to do to get better?'"

I finished, sweaty and high as a kite, and took a big round of applause from the crowd—and a few good-natured paper balls. They liked it because they knew I was not at Crotonville to kiss my own ass or deliver some boring report, but because I desperately wanted to make them believe in some simple things that I knew to be true.

My perception—both then and now—is that younger, thirty-ish managers tend to see my point that the ability to stand up and present, powerfully and persuasively, is one of the two skill sets you absolutely must possess if you are to move into the upper echelons of GE.

The other skill, of course, is what you do for a living: finance, engineering, HR, or law. The ability to present well will get you nowhere if you don't have a story to tell or insights to share. And, naturally, if you don't "make your numbers"—whatever that phrase may mean in your world—you're toast.

But if you lack the ability to deliver a galvanizing presentation, your talents will effectively be hidden under a bushel basket, and you will be labeled a bore, an idiot, deadly, and much, much worse; all words I have heard Welch and Bossidy use to describe people who weren't *that bad*, but who just weren't *that good*.

Welch told me, long ago, that he had never encountered an IBM guy who had joined GE who wasn't good. But he had never seen one who was *really* good. My observation was that they presented themselves as passionless, white-shirted techies, in contrast to the leadership corps of fanatics he was assembling.

Even his friend, IBM CEO John Akers, during the period in the early '90s when it was in a tailspin and headed so low that GE seriously considered acquiring it (!), mystified Welch. I had asked him what the problem was with IBM, and he said, "I don't know. Akers says all the right things. Everything he says makes sense. But nothing ever happens."

GE could have had IBM, *as a GE division*, but GE perceived IBM's condition as more parlous than it turned out to be. Jack was on a roll when IBM came up on the screen, but he was also aware that if the acquisition failed, it would have wrecked GE. So he backed off, showing the conservative side for which he is rarely credited.

You're Going Nowhere at GE Unless...

The audiences who heard my rants, for the most part, agreed with my message on the importance of business presentations. Unfortunately, when they returned to their work environments they too often sank back into the morass of day-long droning meetings, "homicide by PowerPoint," data dumps, and the mumbled reading of eye charts, and feeling, as Pat Sajack once described, as he did his one thousandth episode of *Wheel of Fortune*, that their brain cells were dying one by one.

Not all of them backslid into presentation mediocrity, but many did, often because their bosses didn't *demand* that they present well.

It's difficult to say how many students dramatically changed their presentation styles as a result of my talk, but I would guess it was between 30 and 35 percent. Although I wish the number were higher, it was certainly worth my time and effort.

There's another audience segment to which I speak, albeit a fairly small one. They are the "naturals"—people who instinctively know how to communicate and instinctively understand its importance. They listen to me and nod their heads, but I'm not telling them something they don't already feel in their guts, and know how to do.

Mark Vachon is an old friend of mine, whom I first met on the Boca Raton golf course. Mark was in his mid-thirties at the time, in finance, very personable, and fun to be around. He also had a reputation for being highly ambitious and very political. Anybody at GE who is going anywhere has at least one of these characteristics—but Mark had both, and was resented for them by a few of his peers for wearing them too visibly on his sleeve.

A few years after meeting Mark, I was invited to speak to a couple of breakout sessions at a GE global finance meeting in Georgia.

Golf was involved. I went.

In addition to doing my breakouts, I sat in the back of the room for the general sessions. In the front of the hall—which was set up like a school room—sat the murderers row of GE finance: the top financial officers of the best financially managed company in the world—the CFO, controller, treasurer, VP's of finance of the bigger businesses, Bob Nelson, who was Welch's financial analyst and a VP, and others, 10 or 12 in all.

And, one by one, the junior presenters mounted the podium, moved into the limelight, turned on their projectors, and augered into career oblivion. One disaster followed another: boring, overlong, poorly prepared, obviously unrehearsed, self-absorbed, useless. They seemed to get progressively worse. The finance guys in the 200-plus member audience kept turning around to me, laughing and shaking their heads and pointing at the ridiculous, unreadable visuals, as the speakers broke every rule I had suggested they not break in my sessions just hours before.

An NBC guy got up, so I thought that maybe with the NBC theatrical flair he might be a bit better. He "cratered"—horribly—rambling, ill-prepared, stupidly unfunny, and incoherent. The pitch was described later as "a holocaust." I'm not even sure he knew how bad he was. He had to be gently encouraged to finish up and get off by the CFO in the front row.

Then I noticed that my new friend, Mark Vachon, was on the program, a speaker or two later. I was horrified by this point and even a little depressed at watching several hours of this debacle from the heights of the back of the amphitheater. It was like what Jonestown must have looked like from a helicopter as the suicides began.

I thought to myself, as Mark approached the lectern, "Let's see just how ambitious and savvy this guy is, and if he *really* understands how important it is that he 'knock this out of the park'—as Jack says—in front of this crowd."

And he did. A triumph. I don't pretend to remember, today, anything that he said, but I do remember saying to myself, "He understands; he 'gets it,' and he's going places."

Mark walked off that stage knowing he did well, while the others limped off with holes they had shot in their own feet; some of them, intelligent people, just stupidly unaware.

You're going nowhere *in GE unless you can do a great pitch.*

A few years and promotions later, and Mark Vachon became the VP of Investor Relations, with an office 100 feet down the hall from mine. The job was traditionally seen as a pre-retirement sinecure, but Jack elevated it to being one of the fastest routes by which a 40-year-old could become a vice president.

A company that was in the midst of a five-split stock run and that was creating millionaires by the thousands does not put anyone but the best in the analysts' faces. And the indispensable, *sine qua non*, going-nowhere-without-it ticket to this job? The ability to do a great pitch! Bore a stock analyst or a portfolio manager, and you represent a boring stock.

Before Mark, there was another "kid," Warren Jensen, who later left GE for Delta to become their CFO, and after that Amazon, and then elsewhere. I used to hang around with him, as well—at golf and a little bit socially. Warren would often half-seriously brag about how good his pitches were, knowing my fanaticism on the subject.

I finally called him on it, and we took one of the GE Citation jets down to Washington so I could watch him pitch to a group of analysts and financial reporters in Washington. He was very, very good, even with the added burden of having to deal with some obnoxious jerks that I suspect were mainly there for a free lunch on GE.

I told Welch a few days later that I had seen for myself Warren's presentation skills, and that they were real. He gave me a look that seemed to say, *are you stupid?* and asked, "Do you seriously think someone could get the job of telling our story to the analysts and be a shitty presenter?"

I guess not. I *know* not.

What jobs are you disqualifying yourself from because of poor presentation skills? These skills are fairly easy to acquire, and involve the architecture and effort in the presentation itself, rather than theatrics and what color dress you wear.

How to Succeed in Business by Really Trying

Sometime during the mid-'90s, I reported up to Jack's conference room for a meeting with Larry Bossidy and Bill Conaty—a Senior VP and top HR manager.

I don't remember what the meeting was about, but I *do* remember we could not get started because Jack was enthralled, in love, and would not shut up about, some guy who had presented to the Corporate Executive Council at Crotonville the night before. "He was unbelievable! Who is this guy? How great was that? Holy shit!" Then Conaty chimed in, "After this guy did his pitch, three of the business leaders (of the 12 big GE businesses) came up to me and asked, "How do I get this guy? I want him."

Well, one of them got him. Within a few months of his presentation, this "kid" had an offer, and a big, new GE job down South.

I never met him but I later asked at Crotonville what had happened, and was told an amazing story; amazing if you're a business communications nut, anyway, or a fan of Machiavelli.

There is a scene in a movie I haven't seen in 30 years, *How to Succeed in Business Without Really Trying*, where the main character, J. Pierpont Finch, devises a plan to work his way up from the mailroom to the executive office. One of his ploys involves hearing the CEO mention to his secretary on a Friday evening that he would be stopping by the office in the morning to pick up his golf clubs on the way to a match. Finch, armed with this intelligence, shows up at the office early Saturday morning with an array of equipment: dozens of cigarette butts, yards of calculator paper tape, paper coffee cups, and all the detritus of an all-nighter. He strews the evidence all over his desk and the floor, and poses, in his rumpled, stained shirt, as sound asleep and snoring, face down, on a pile of documents.

When the boss walks in, he's visibly impressed with this tableau, and Finch's career progression accelerates.

Our Crotonville student—and new hero—showed up for the class, checked in, went to the reception with his classmates, and, knowing that the class would have to present to Welch and his top 30 people, immediately and aggressively lobbied to do the pitch himself. Most of the students wanted no part of it, so the competition was not fierce. By week two he had the job, and by week three he was ready.

He rehearsed and rehearsed, and nailed it. He hit a home run and parlayed that into a bigger job. Ineffably careerist? Of course. Smart? No—he was *brilliant*.

Most Crotonville students would rather undergo a colonoscopy than do a presentation to an audience like Welch and his crew. The amount of work involved is endless. The tension is unbearable. You lose weight and dream about it as the day approaches. Your classmates, who help you put the pitch together, each want a plug for their part in the project; "Show them this analysis. Mention that we interviewed 60 customers; that we went to seven plants in three countries. Make sure they know how much time we put in on this."

If you wind up "honking everyone's horn," talking about each part of the project, and blowing about how hard you worked, you will wind up with an overlong, unfocused "kluge"; an abortion; a disaster.

Refuse to do it.

In most situations like these, in GE, as well as other companies, they can't make you do it. If it "feels" bad, looks tedious, has no point, and you hate it, just say "No"—because even though the big shots who hear your pitch will understand that it's the product of a committee, it will be your face, voice, and name forever associated with the disaster.

Never, ever, make a presentation you do not feel is excellent—a home run. If you don't spring up to the podium because you can't wait to do it, something is probably wrong.

Love—or Hate—at First Sight

Bob Nelson, a GE finance guy and VP, once made a comment to me that was chilling in its implications: "I can tell five minutes into a pitch whether somebody's any good or not." Note that he didn't say "whether he's a good presenter or not," or "whether this pitch is useful or not." Bob was suggesting that he could tell whether any presenter has any value to the General Electric Company, and, by implication, to the world.

And Bob was perhaps being generous with his five-minute allowance. Jack Hilton, the late New York communications consultant who did a fair amount of work for GE, would often prep GE interviewees for *60 Minutes* appearances. He once told us of a study he had done that concluded that the analysts and portfolio managers in New York make a preliminary judgment on a new CEO within *90 seconds* of his or her maiden appearance before them.

Very early 2002. Thirty Rock. Studio 8-H of *Saturday Night Live* fame. Big projected CNBC market ticker on the screens. The Dow, including GE, wobbling and sinking in the aftermath of 9/11. Jeff Immelt walked up to the lectern for his first solo pitch to a major-league analyst group. TV screens wink off, and he begins. Mark Vachon, VP of Investor Relations, and I huddled in the back of the room, hearts in our mouths, as Immelt began. Five minutes later we were beaming and doing silent high-fives. Jeff had seized control of the room and established himself as a serious individual with important things to say. There was no "gargling," no "background," and certainly no jokes at a venue 40 blocks or so from the rubble that was the graveyard of thousands of our countrymen.

He absolutely *had* to do well; and he did, and, as I recall, the market and GE settled down, at least for that day.

Welch, among his faults as a manager, tended to jump to early conclusions about the value of an individual—either positively, as with Mike Fraiser or the Machiavellian Crotonville student; or dismissive, quick to label an individual as "an idiot," "dumb," "boring," or "a bullshit artist." Typically, these judgments were based on the victim's or anointed one's communication ability.

But ameliorating his predilection for snap personnel judgments—a serious flaw in a business leader—was his ability to reverse these judgments, if appropriate, as more data emerged.

Some of the instant superstars in his early tenure were men in their thirties or early forties who were canonized by Welch from the stage at Boca as leaders "moving toward the highest levels of this Company," and other fulsome pronouncements. They sat there modestly beaming, bathed in the envy of most of the 500 of us who weren't canonized, or at least beatified, that day.

And then, a year or so later, an HR large-bore revolver, with a soft-nosed bullet, was fired, and the late "saint" was carried from the premises on a bier made of cash, and laid to rest beneath a dismissive tombstone that read: "Screwed up. Didn't make his numbers." Or even: "He was awful."

For a while it almost became the GE version of the curse of the *Sports Illustrated* cover: getting a "kiss" from Jack on the stage at Boca.

On one occasion, I boarded a Challenger with the boss to go somewhere, and another superstar's name, one with whom I was barely familiar, came up. Jack nearly swooned as he described the virtues of this very young executive, a European of indeterminate nationality with an impeccable aristocratic, semi-British accent.

"He's unbelievable. He's going to take that business to a new level. He told me he wants me to give him a million bucks (a pretty big deal in the '80s) and, you know what, Bill? I just might give it to him."

Fast forward one year to another plane ride I took with Jack. In the interim I had worked closely with the precocious and extortionate starlet, and had even flown to Paris to help him with a major speech, representing GE, to a big-time European audience. I actually liked him a lot and began to regale Jack in the plane about how well he did with the speech, and how great I thought he was. Unbeknownst to me, however, the page had turned, and a scowling Jack ended the conversation with a dismissive hand gesture and "Ahh. He's a kid. He's just a kid." The business had badly underperformed and, shortly thereafter, another pistol shot rang out.

We used to call these people "meteors"—a brilliant but brief flame in the sky that then flares and winks out. I thought Icarus was perhaps a more apt metaphor: executives who flew too close to the sun got their waxed wings melted off, but that was considered a bit arcane, so we stuck with meteors.

I actually kicked the "Icarus syndrome" around with Jack once, and it didn't seem to offend him. He allowed that that was "just the way he was."

Icarus and meteor syndromes were never too big a factor in my life, since I never got very far off the ground, and, as a speechwriter, I could never really hope to. But I was given a few "kisses" from the Boca stage by Jack, and nevertheless survived. One kiss came in the mid-'80s when Welch told the assembled multitude that I represented the type of "candor" toward which he was trying to move this company.

I can't emphasize enough that an opportunity to make a presentation in front of people who can make or destroy your career or your company is one that should never be avoided. It should be sought after and seized upon. But you must deliver! You have just pushed a big stack of chips forward on the table, and God help you if you don't have the hand to play. If you don't have a good story, feign a heart attack and don't show up.

But don't ever, for a moment, believe that you are not being judged—consciously or unconsciously—by everyone in the room, including your peers, your own reports, and those who can advance or retard the throttle on your career.

And they are making those judgments within minutes.

The View from the Bowling Alley

What did I do to produce Jack's belief that I represented "candor"? I simply laid out for him, in our conversations, some views I had heard from here and there about whether he was being fair or mean; or whether his initiatives were "hula hoops" or "flavors-of-the-month," phrases that drove him screaming up the wall.

I'd tell him that I had talked to a Crotonville class—something I now did constantly—and that they thought that a particular initiative was bullshit. I never, *ever* mentioned a name, nor was I ever asked to.

I once remember telling him that there were 35 guys in an upcoming class, but no women or blacks. Welch ripped the phone from the cradle and called Crotonville to shout at the manager about why we weren't doing better on this score.

I loudly and angrily proclaimed "shit!"—for Welch's benefit—as he made the call, because I knew I would be seen as an informant, and a rat, by Crotonville people, and would have to go mend fences with them the next day.

Jack has a way of drawing things out of you that you wish you'd never said.

Welch knew I "swam with the fishes" at several levels of the company. I worked with his vice chairmen and with all his business leaders, as I ran the general managers and officers meetings, spoke at Crotonville, and got a feel for their perspectives. I was friendly with most of the secretaries, and the security guys, one of whom, Marcus, I badgered for years to get M80s for me for the Fourth of July, but he never did. I even bowled in the blue collar GE league.

Jack also "lived" at Crotonville and spoke to virtually every mid- to upper-level manager that came through, in a genuine effort to stay in touch with what was really going on in the company, although I suspect that he was never really sure that he was getting the *real* troop-level view on every issue. So he was all ears, and would interrogate people like me whenever he got the chance—providing me with the occasionally irresistible opportunity to torment him.

He and I boarded his G-4 on one occasion, buckled up, and, as we taxied, he turned to me with a friendly grin and asked, "So, Bill, who's screwing who?" He meant at GE's headquarters in Fairfield, as well as among his business leaders in the field.

This was a rare opportunity, and I seized it, shaking my head dramatically and saying, "There's an awful lot of stuff going on, Jack. You wouldn't *believe* some of it—but I can't give you names."

"Why not!?" (loud and excited)

"I just don't think it would be right. Some of it is going on right under your nose."

He got louder, but was laughing. "Tell me! Or I won't pay you!"

But I stood my ground, and he laughed and called me a few names.

The fact was, the level of fooling around and bad behavior at the senior levels of the company was fairly modest, with some celebrated exceptions. An officer back in the '80s, who rode a Harley with the Hell's Angels, wound up in the slammer on IRS-related stuff. That was one.

Then there was the legendary "stairwell incident" in Fairfield, which may or may not have even occurred, and some other stuff of the type that should have a bar code on it because it goes on at every company—big and small—around the world.

Welch especially liked to pump his subordinates about what people were thinking, because he needed the reassurance that what he believed in passionately (which was mostly everything) was bought and believed at every level of the Company.

One of his rationales for selling off low-performing and sometimes ancient company businesses was that their sale would be good for the employees of those businesses. Air conditioning, for example, at GE had become something of a backwater. When we sold it to Trane it became part of the major focus of that company; so employees in that division were now "in the center of the action." The same rationale was behind the sale of the TV receiver business to the French company Thomson.

One of the most controversial and resented divestitures was of the housewares business to Black and Decker. Housewares made small appliances as opposed to stoves and washing machines; items like toasters, electric potato peelers, and that famous duo—vacuum cleaners and fans—known affectionately as "old suck and blow."

Now Jack was selling it all.

And Wall Street approved.

Jack loved the approval of Wall Street, but the Irish in him craved the approval and affection of the divested employees, as well. He wanted to believe they were *thrilled* at being divested. One Wednesday morning, shortly after the housewares sale to Black and Decker had been announced, he asked me what my "bowling guys" thought of it. He knew about them—most of whom were hourly manufacturing workers from Bridgeport—because I had given him other feedback from them. I would then go back and tell them, "I told Welch what you said about why the Japanese are kicking our asses, and he agrees." They couldn't wait to get home that night to tell their wives and their friends at work the next day.

On the subject of the sale to Black and Decker—I told Jack that these now-former-GE "bowling guys" had been talking about it at the alley just the night before; and that one of them had summed up the general view by saying, "We're just slaves that have been sold to a new master." I didn't want to tell him that, but I had to. His face fell with disappointment, and we moved on to a different subject.

I would often come up from the graphics department, located on the service level—in the basement, along with the mailroom—with a chart, or a speech reprint that Jack needed, and he would ask me things like, "Are they comfortable down there?," "Is it clean?," or "Do they need anything?"

I would bring him down to graphics or into the back room of the GE TV studio and he was unfailingly gracious and friendly to the whole staff, calling them by their first names, and asking them to call him "Jack"—which, of course, they seldom did.

He told me one day, very early in the '80s that one of the things he found scary about his new job was that he might fail in being "fair" to people. All through his early days in plastics, and even as a sector executive and vice chairman there was always at least one man above him to tell him if he was mean or shitty to someone, or some group, and he would then be told to "make it right"—guidance he needed and reluctantly wanted.

Before that—and this is not pop psychology—he had his mom.

Now, as CEO, he had no one above him to perform that function, and he relied on the people with whom he worked, even people at my level, to keep him "fair." And we tried, and even if the feedback made him surly and cranky, as it sometimes did, he always listened and usually "made it right."

Executive Vice President Frank Doyle was also the head of all "relations" for the company—company, public, employee, union, and the like—as well as the man who made believe he was going to throw my retirement speech into the pool. Frank was also Jack's most trusted advisor on "fairness."

Sometimes Welch would be "trying something out" on a couple of people in his conference room, and would get agitated, and mutter, "I just know that goddamn Frank is going to say this is the wrong thing to do."

That "goddamn Frank" wasn't even in the room, but Welch felt the hot breath of his judgment on his neck.

Over the 20 years he eventually developed a very keen sense of "fairness" himself, and didn't really need Frank, or anyone else, to guide him. He has referred to his own father as "passive" and "a good man," but seldom spoke of him at all, certainly compared with his mother. But once, in describing some move the Company was contemplating making with some employee population, he said, "That's simply wrong. My father would have had his whole union out in the street if his bosses did something like that to them. It's just wrong."

One year I received a copy of a union flyer that was prepping the membership for contract negotiations with the capitalist oppressors and jackals who were threatening their livelihoods. It scorned the GE negotiations team and its auxiliaries as "a bunch of overpaid managers and their flunkies," which was probably a fair description of our group. I sent the sheet up to Welch and asked him to clarify whether I was an "overpaid manager," or a "flunky."

I didn't like delivering some of the views that were out there, but I did. And, as the new manager of the Boca meeting, I had achieved instant credibility and status when Jack, in his closing remarks at the meeting in one of the early years, said that, "Bill represents the total candor that everyone in this Company needs to be moving toward."

Welch's intolerance for bullshit lasted throughout his entire career. Bill Woodburn, now of a Credit Suisse–related private equity group, but a senior GE officer for much of his career, recounts, with awe, the day he and Dennis Dammerman, then a vice chairman, along with several other very senior GE people, sat as Welch listened to a presentation by 20 (!) investment bankers pitching a mega deal that amounted to a hostile takeover of a financial services business.

Jack stopped the presentation.

"Stop the bullshit. I'm 65-years-old and I've seen everything. I've had bullshit coming at me for years and I know it when I see it coming my way. This is bullshit. Stop it."

He was laughing as he said it, but the message was not humorous.

Bill Woodburn told me, "The air changed in the room."

The bullshit stopped and candor reigned for the duration.

My advice to you, therefore, as the CEO of a company or institution, or head of a division, who wants to take the first step toward improving your internal and external communications, is to insist on total candor in every presentation, beginning with your own.

After you've told someone to "stop bullshitting or get off the stage," just once or twice, the word will spread like wildfire and your communications culture will have moved a giant step forward. The political stuff, the bragging, the spinners, and bores (we will get to them), won't go away entirely, but the liars will be banished from the podium, never to return, until you, yourself, bullshit your people or tell a lie.

And you must never do that.

The Bogus Boca Presentation

After Jack had established "absolute candor" (everything he did had to be "absolute," or some adjective denoting passionate commitment), I *never* heard a barefaced lie from the stage at Boca. A couple of egregious spins and distortions of reality made it into the presentations, but since every presentation had to be sent to me to review with Welch, they were unceremoniously ripped from the womb of the script before the meeting.

Often, the speaker—usually a company officer or leader of one of the businesses—had barely reviewed the presentation that had been put together for him by his or her staff, and now found him- or herself being torched by Welch on the phone and told, "get the bullshit out of that talk. That's not the way it is. Here's what you need to say…" And then Jack would essentially dictate the elements of the next draft.

One such incident in the '80s involved the GE factory automation business. I had written speeches for a GE executive vice president named Jim Baker who ran the sector that included the factory automation business (robots, numerical controls for machine tools, computer-aided design equipment, etc.). I coined the phrase, in one of Baker's speeches, that American manufacturing—then beleaguered by the Japanese and Germans—faced three choices: it could either *automate, emigrate,* or *evaporate.*

The phrase was a hit. It was picked up all over the world—*Newsweek, Time,* even on T-shirts. It got me noticed, and in the running to be Welch's writer. And I was suddenly able to go on a lot of great trips to California and Virginia business locations; so refreshing after the dreary rust-belt venues of old-line GE.

But this enormous factory automation market we had envisioned for the electronic equipment, which would refresh America's factories, never really materialized. *Human* productivity measures became the path the country chose, correctly, I think, in retrospect.

But in the '80s, GE spent billions on acquisitions, production facilities, and model factories for a market that never approached our expectations. Welch cornered me once at a GE officers meeting in Phoenix and asked me, good-naturedly, "What was that slogan? Automate, or escalate, or whatever it was? How many billions did you cost me with that bullshit?"

Well, it wasn't bullshit, and we *were* true believers; it just never happened. The problem we had with that market was that we were competing against the Japanese—specifically against a great company named Fanuc—in things like numerical machine tool controls, and we were getting beaten on price, quality, and features.

So we lost in that campaign, ran up the white flag, sold off the Silicon Valley stuff we had acquired—whatever was left of it—and followed the old maxim: *If you can't beat 'em, join 'em.* We agreed to a joint venture with Fanuc to sell numerical controls out of idyllic Charlottesville, Virginia, naming a Japanese Ph.D. as CEO. It came time at the Boca meeting to explain why the company had disassembled and divested most of the factory automation business and slid much of what was left into a joint venture with an archenemy, Fanuc.

I remember laughing out loud when I received the proposed Boca presentation. The gist of it was that, as our strategy evolved, we spotted an opportunity to partner with Fanuc, a great company that was a perfect fit for our U.S. marketing strategy in factory automation; and so we constructed a win-win arrangement with the Japanese.

This pitch was analogous to one that might have been given by a Vichy France functionary explaining that his part of the country saw an opportunity to "partner" with their old friends and competitors, the Germans, in 1939.

It was a lie. The 500 GE managers would *know* it was a lie. So we sent it back to its authors with an angry phone call from Jack instructing them to *tell the truth*, which was that we got our asses kicked, and saved what was left of our business by going in with the Japanese.

Some time later I was lecturing in "The Pit" at Crotonville to a mid-level management class on the subject of business presentations. Part of my talk was on the subject of candor, and Exhibit A was the story of the disingenuous GE/Fanuc presentation that these people had tried to slip by us onto the Boca agenda. I told them in lurid and dramatic detail about the angry phone call from Jack to the business leader.

As I gave my presentation, which was about an hour long (too long), I looked around the room of 60 or 70 people, and read their faces, for the immensely important performance data faces provide.

I kept returning to one man's face because of the agitation, squirming, and what I perceived might be real anger. He seemed to settle down after my three- or four-minute "candor" section, but the negative vibes continued to emanate from him.

Afterwards—a few days afterwards—the manager of the class at Crotonville sent me the Presenter Evaluation sheets, which every class member filled out.

All were complimentary of my pitch, except one.

To the question that asked, "What, if anything, struck you, or stuck with you from this presentation?" was the following response, written in an angry, scrawl: "The gratuitous, vulgar language and the nasty denigration of senior GE business people by this presenter."

Fine.

But the next question was, "What was your most important take-away from this presentation?"

And the answer: "That you can be the speechwriter for the Chairman of GE and still be a pig."

"Whoa!" as we used to say, "Don't hold back. Tell me what you *really* think."

It turned out, as you might have suspected, that this person was the one who had helped put together the bogus Boca presentation. He probably had been torched by his boss after he was flamed by Jack, and was probably happy, when, later that year, he was sent to Crotonville to get away from it all, only to have this opinionated corporate weenie, who he probably viewed as the source of his problems, come in and rehash the whole mess.

I had his evaluation form made into an overhead and used it at future Crotonville classes when I alighted on the subject of candor.

The bogus Boca presentation wasn't his fault, really, or rather it wasn't his fault alone. He was responding to vibes, or relayed vibes, from his boss at the business, and had produced what essentially was a lie.

I always tried to get Jack to use, in his speeches, the honor code of West Point: that a cadet would never "lie, cheat, or steal, nor tolerate those who do." I'm not sure he ever did use it—I think he may have a couple of times—but that summed up his, and our, view at GE as the '80s wore on. If you lie, dissemble, or "head fake" from a GE podium to your mates, you're outta here.

Jeff Immelt, the current GE CEO, feels the same way. His view, which he has expressed over and over, is: "One strike and you're out."

GE is the cleanest company I've *ever* heard about. I've never heard of anyone even suggesting something even slightly illegal be done.

I know of five or six people who ripped the company off via expense accounts or minor embezzlement, but they were all caught and fired. Some were actually escorted down to the front gate by security after the GE parking stickers were removed with razors from their car windshields. I actually suggested at one point that one of the edges of the laminated GE "values card" be sharpened and tempered so the miscreant's card could be confiscated and used to remove his parking sticker before his removal from headquarters property.

Another piece of advice to HR that was ignored...

On occasion, I had put some fairly funky and extravagant stuff down on expense accounts. Did I really need those few bottles of Dom Perignon with my speechwriters to celebrate my first successful Boca meeting? Or those company-funded golf shoes from the Boca pro shop because I had forgotten mine? Probably not. But I never *lied* about it; and I never once had the gimlet-eyed auditors question anything on my expense reports.

Died and Went to Headquarters

I joined GE in the fall of 1980 and was stunned by the opulence of life at corporate. I actually had my own office, after seven years sharing a bay in the "D-ring" of the Pentagon at a shabby metal Korean Warera–desk, with typewriters and adding machines clacking and clattering. I now had a credenza, some chairs for visitors, and a rug. The ridiculously cheap subsidized meals in the cafeteria were as good as any I had ever had in restaurants.

The two fortress-like white buildings, which gleamed in the sun and overlooked a Connecticut glacial valley, had three lakes at the foot of the hill. In warm weather, I would skip lunch, run four or five miles, finish up at the one lake that was only partially visible from the buildings above, strip off my shirt and sneakers, and jump in, swimming around and observing some big fish in the cool water.

Then, back up the hill, I'd shower, and get back to my cool, quiet office refuge, my yellow legal pad, and my Flair pen.

Less than one year earlier, acting as what we used to call a "horse holder" at the Pentagon, I accompanied the Assistant Secretary of the Army for R&D and a three-star general, in a rattletrap, kerosene-smelling Huey helicopter, to a contractor's (Westinghouse, I think) radar development facility near Baltimore.

After a few boring presentations, lunch was announced, and everyone sat around the conference table eating turkey sandwiches out of the boxes that were passed around the table with the cans of warm 7-Up. After lunch I performed another of my assigned horse holder functions by taking a dollar from my pocket, putting it in the box and going around the table, collecting a dollar from the general, and a dollar from the Secretary; and handing the three bucks to the company functionary. That's the way we did it, and the way we *had* to do it. This is probably the way it *should* be done, with lunches for public servants, although it seemed asinine at the time.

To arrive at the wondrous world of Generous Electric was a bit of a pleasant shock, especially for a not-overly-privileged Brooklyn kid.

One Saturday shortly after I joined GE, my parents drove up from Franklin Square, on Long Island, and I gave them a tour of my new corporate domain. They were both children of the Depression; my father was a gunner's mate on a Navy destroyer in WWII, and a clerk at New York Life Insurance in Manhattan for 35-plus years.

They walked with me through the silent buildings on this quiet Saturday. My mother marveled at the thickness of the carpets. I told her what I had been told my first day: "Your shoes never wear out here; it's just another perk." My father pressed his nose, literally, and maybe figuratively, up against the full-length glass doors of the closed employee store, surveying the displays of small appliances, light bulbs, radios, and other electric paraphernalia. His question: "But when can you come here? You can't just leave your desk, can you?" My father was a brilliant but modestly educated man, who was pretty much chained to his desk and his pen, with the coffee and donut guy pushing a cart around the floors signaling "break time," a few times a day.

I explained that we could pretty much do whatever we wanted, as long as we delivered what we had to deliver, and that as "professionals," we pretty much had the run of the place. We then moved another 10 feet down the corridor to a large open bay with two large "blue tube" GE TVs facing in opposite directions with clusters of plush chairs in front of each. Since it was Saturday, the area was empty, and the TVs were off.

"What's this?"

"It's the TV room for the secretaries."

"What?"

"It's for their lunch hours. They get their food from the cafeteria and bring it down here to watch their soaps."

(Laughing) "Why do they need *two* TVs?"

"Because they like different soaps, on different networks, and this way they can watch the ones they want."

That did it for him. He shook his head and laughed again, and after a few more descriptions of his Dickensian work environment at New York Life, we left the building.

I was proud and showing off a bit for my parents, and they were proud and happy for me.

My mother, typical of her generation and of the Irish, had been distressed and disapproving when I announced I was leaving the Pentagon to go with GE. She would never push her views on me, but agonized with my brother, Richie, the homicide detective, on my career move. She asked him,

"Why would anyone quit a great civil service job, with security and benefits, talking with Senators, going to the White House—and move to Bridgeport?"

Bridgeport was where I was living, and it was, and still is, a city held in low regard by New Yorkers since before the war. But Bridgeport was but a stone's throw from GE and had condos with rent prices I could afford. I was making about $40,000 at the time.

Bridgeport was justifiably regarded as run-down and corrupt. Its public officials—particularly the mayors, have been known to have their tenure interrupted because of other, more pressing, commitments—like prison, for one of them.

When I first joined GE, I was regaled with the famous visit of our former chairman, Reg Jones, to the Jimmy Carter White House.

Reginald Jones, the CEO, was British-born, eloquent, intelligent, and refined to the fingertips.

At the White House cocktail reception Jones stood with a small group of important people, including the Mayor of Bridgeport, whom he had never met, and who, apparently, had no idea who Jones was.

"What do you do, Reg?" asked the Mayor, pleasantly.

"I'm with GE in Fairfield, right next door to your town."

"What do you do in Fairfield?"

"I run it," said Reg, modestly.

(Impressed) "You run the GE Fairfield office?"

"No, actually," he replied, "I run the Company."

(Loudly) *"The whole fuckin' company!?"*

Selling Hats to Each Other

If the eloquent Mayor of Bridgeport was impressed at the power and reach and wealth of GE, I was floored by the spare-no-expense extravagance of the business presentations—presentations I was expected to write within a month or two of joining the company.

In 1980, the final combat for the CEO job was being waged in the brain of Reg Jones, and the weaponry consisted of slide projectors and windy "CEO-sounding" speeches written by the members of the Corporate Communications group, of which, shortly after, I became a part. There was a stable of five or six speechwriters—"stable" being an appropriate word, because of the horseshit we produced for our clients.

The agenda for the 1980 managers meeting, held in January, about eight months before I arrived, will give you an idea of the kind of things we talked about. Jim Baker, a sector executive not in the running for chairman and a man for whom I would write, literally, fifty speeches over the next few years, read a pitch entitled "Strategic Directions for the Industrial Products and Components Sector in the 1980s"—a real stem-winder that one, I'm sure. "Strategic" was a word sprinkled into just about everything, like a seasoning. Strategic planning was the rage in the business world, and GE was widely regarded as the pioneer and foremost expert in strategic planning in world business.

No one would have suspected at the time that, within three years, the new chairman would vaporize the entire strategic planning apparatus and the entire highly paid and generally brilliant priesthood of practitioners. The products these very smart people produced were drop-dead gorgeous vinyl binders that attempted to capture five years of future within their covers—an undertaking Welch felt was impossible, stupid, and even dangerous.

GE was under assault by Siemens, Asea Brown-Boveri, Toshiba, Philips, and dozens of companies we had never heard of before. Inflation was in and out of control. Microelectronics was changing the world. And the strategic planners were supposed to be able to predict, for any business in the company, the way the world would work in five years.

Welch recognized the hubris and corporate arrogance he saw in the strategic planning function; but, as far as I know, never spoke publicly about it until he got his hands on the detonator a couple of years later.

But in 1980, "strategic" was the word. And if you were among the final three for the chairman's job, "vision" was *your* word. And if you had a "vision" of something very "strategic," you probably had the right stuff, as Tom Wolfe might say.

And so the final three candidates made their presentations at the last general managers meeting before the big decision was to be rendered.

Ed Hood, Vice Chairman, read "A Vision of the Energy, Technical, and Materials Businesses 1980–90." John Burlingame (soon to be another client of mine), read "A Vision of the Natural Resources and International Businesses 1980–90." And then there was John F. Welch, with "A Vision of the Industrial and Consumer Businesses 1980–90."

I remember remarking that if these guys are having all these "visions" they may be dropping acid, which drew me some blank stares.

I showed Welch a copy of that agenda about 10 years ago, and he said he "came close to throwing up."

"That's what we used to do," he said. "Sell hats to each other."

Larry Bossidy said of these meetings, often referred to cynically as "blow and goes": "We used to listen to 18 success stories and go home and wonder why nothing ever changes around this place."

The meetings were pageants, shows, and rituals, particularly during the two- or three-year campaign for the chairmanship. After Welch got his hands on the prize he vowed that this type of succession circus would never be allowed to distract the company again.

And, 20 years later, despite media attempts to *create* a circus, he managed to make the transition to his successor as smooth and non-distracting as possible.

In the spring of 1995 the media began to speculate as to when Jack was going to "bail" and who his successors might be. "Succession stories" seem to be their favorite brand of catnip.

Welch preemptively struck—sending a copy of one article to senior management with a letter that read, in part:

The horseshit has started!

Remember, reporters have to make a living and have to fill pages daily, weekly, or monthly. This is reminiscent of the late '70s when the same speculative stuff started. At that time it was both wrong and internally corrosive.

As I have told you, for better or worse, I will be around for several years and our collective job is to create the exciting, boundaryless, non-political atmosphere that has made us the most valuable company in the U.S.

He smothered that baby story—and several more like it—in their bassinets, and we got back to work.

Bob Nardelli, Jim McNerney, and Jeff Immelt, the candidates for Welch's job, were never required to inflict speechwriter "visions" on GE people.

• It had been made abundantly clear to them that the one certain way to achieve rapid self-defenestration from the succession train was to show up with a political, self-promotional presentation at Boca, at the officers meeting, or at the corporate executive council meeting. The line was tiptoed up to, once or twice, but never crossed.

Everyone in the room knew the rules.

But even more absurd than the pomposity and emptiness of the turn-of-the-eighties presentations, which were really campaign infomercials, was the visual circus that accompanied them: 12 slide projectors, run by a primitive computer called a "Roadrunner," firing images onto a single giant wide-screen comprised of three normal-sized screens. These shows conspicuously rivaled each other in expense and garishness.

When the field for the CEO race was even larger, in the 1978 era, one candidate went with a relatively modest single-screen presentation at one of the meetings, which sparked widespread speculation that he was "taking himself out of the race" because of the modesty of his visuals! The medium had become—as it has become today at most companies—the *message*, with the speaker and what he had to say relegated to being mere accessories.

Part III

The Russians Are Coming

GE's extravagance astounded me, coming from my days in the Army's Congressional office, where we supported a three-star general and an Assistant Secretary of the Army as they testified in support of the Army's billion-dollar research and development efforts. The case for the weapons systems we wanted had to be made in multiple hearings before four congressional committees—both the House and Senate Armed Services, as well as the Appropriations Committees.

Our audio-visual budget for this entire process was *$10,000*. We would throw a borrowed overhead projector and screen into an Army van and meet the general and secretary over at the hearing room.

I worked for a colonel. We would have, with us, boxes of "Reading Statements" and "Statements for the Record," that I had written. The statements "for the record" were sometimes 100 pages long, and I had taken to cutting pictures, out of defense magazines, of Russian tanks, helicopters, etc., that were the equivalents to the systems we wanted, and interspersing them with the text. I remember peeling off, from some kind of dispenser, a thin black border-tape, and clumsily trying to frame my pasted-on, cut-out magazine pictures, angling for help and sympathy from some of the lovely young secretaries in the "bay," some of whom I had hired, and was dating.

The standard operating procedure was that statements were "submitted for the record," and then other brief, "opening statements" were read aloud by the witnesses to begin the hearing. Questioning by committee members and staff then began.

The statements themselves were unclassified, although the hearings were "closed" because most of the weapons systems, and the intelligence information about the Russian systems we presented, were classified "secret," or sometimes higher—sometimes a lot higher.

Copies of the statements were piled on a table outside the hearing room for any of "the public" who wanted them. The "public" waiting for them to be put out were generally contractors—and "Soviets"—Russians.

The contractors—many of whom I knew, and liked—were just doing their jobs, and so were the Russians, for that matter—although I still hated them. One Russian in particular would inevitably wait near the hearing room for us to arrive, and once or twice, after my loud and angry questioning directed at no one in particular as to "why these bastards are even allowed in this building," I would sometimes pull a briefing book with a "Top Secret" cover sheet out of the briefcase I was carrying, wave it, and say, loudly, something like "Hey, Boris, how much will you give me for this?" "Boris," a classic blond Russian embassy toad, would look embarrassed and smile sheepishly. The colonel would try to keep from laughing as he told me, "Bill, you can't do this," and we would disappear into the hearing room and shut the door in Boris's face.

The hammer we used constantly to forge the case for our new weapons was: *the threat, the threat, and the threat*. The U.S. Army was lined up in Europe against a vastly numerically superior Soviet and Warsaw Pact force, which was now in the process of moving toward *qualitative* as well as quantitative superiority.

The Soviet T-72 was clearly a better tank than our M60, and they had another, even scarier model well into development. They had a true "infantry fighting vehicle," the BMP; and we had a lightly armored "battle taxi," the M113. We needed this tank. We *had* to have the fighting vehicle (and the missiles and helicopters). We even *had* to have a new helmet, and the one in early development seemed to be a version of the old "Wermacht" model, with the protective neck ridge. This helmet prompted a spate of hate letters to the generals, including one that asked why we were building "these son-of-a-bitch helmets." The general wrote a note on this letter and sent it to the secretary: "At least now we know what to call the new helmet."

In any case, I began to focus the presentations at these hearings *as much on the Soviet equipment as on our own*, and the successive generals and secretaries I worked for gave me a free hand, despite the fact that I was a lowly—by Pentagon standards—GS-14.

I made the statements simple and even exciting. I invented scenarios where the Warsaw Pact would send huge armored forces through the European Fulda gap, and how, as they slammed into the NATO forces, our new, desperately needed weapons systems would slow them up and eventually stop them—the attack helicopters picking off their T-72 tanks, the Patriot missiles clearing the sky of their MiG-23s, and our centerpiece, the XM-1, later named the Abrams, with its secret armor, accompanied by the Bradley Fighting Vehicles trashing and throwing back the commies in a satisfying and triumphant bloodbath.

We tended to downplay the most controversial weapon—the ace in the hole—in case the scenario went awry: The "enhanced radiation" warhead, media-nicknamed the "neutron bomb," which "killed the people but left the buildings standing." I could never have guessed that within a few years I'd be working for someone with "Neutron Jack" for a nickname.

I changed the way the Army communicated because in my first days of watching the hearings in 1973, I watched the eyes of the Senators and congressmen as they glazed over as the droning, soporific, jargon-filled, acronym-infested statements were read to them by men who had, at one time, led men in combat, killed the enemy, and been shot themselves—and were now reduced, with the weight of the stars on their shoulders, to acting like bureaucrats and politicians—because that's the way they thought you were supposed to present to the Congress.

I didn't buy it. No one likes to be bored; no one likes to have his or her time wasted, but that's what we were doing: boring people and wasting their time, and our time, in these stultifying rituals called "hearings."

How can we interest them? How can we win them over to a cause in which we *really* believe.

I focused on reaching Senator Robert McIntyre, a key R&D subcommittee member—a WWII vet—who, even then, was getting elderly, quirky, and cranky.

I began by radically simplifying our presentations. I was merciless with jargon, which spews from the Pentagon like toxic waste. Acronyms were outlawed unless explained. Boring "development data" were removed. I constructed these presentations with Senator McIntyre's face before my mind's eye. Within this paragraph I am about to write, what will remain in this man's mind when he leaves the hearing room? That view, often led to a big "cross-out" of what I had just written.

All the boring bureaucratic stuff about program milestones, overruns, and competitive bids was left to the staffers to address in the Q&A. Let them be the ones to read the questions and bore the senators. We wanted their hearts and minds. A man who saw combat in World War II would understand why you wanted a better tank than "the other guy"; would sympathize with your desire to defend your troops from air attack, move them quickly and safely across the battlefield, and allow them to kill a numerically superior enemy quickly and efficiently.

We didn't "neutralize enemy armor formations" in our presentation; we killed enemy tanks, shot down their helicopters and MiGs, and devastated their exposed infantry with exotic and lethal weaponry.

The general and secretary quietly signed off on the presentations I wrote, looking at each other and shrugging, while saying, "*I* like it, but do we normally talk like this to the Congress? Let's see how it flies." The first time I wrote the statement, I ran it by the Defense Department bureaucracy, which also, quietly, and virtually without comment, let it go. *They* liked it, too, I could tell, although they communicated their approval with smiles and body language, rather than words that could be quoted in a "who shot John" inquisition some day if the statement didn't "fly" on the Hill.

Hectoring the Hobbit

One Saturday, a bored Army driver took me to Annapolis to brief Senator John Tower, and waited for me outside the motel where the senator was "marking up" the budget. I knocked and was admitted by one of the staffers, a friendly guy, and he asked me to begin right away.

Senator Tower was in shirtsleeves, *sans* tie and seated sideways in an overstuffed chair. He would hole up in a motel each year to "mark up" the budget free from phones and lobbyists. The senator had no shoes on, and one leg was over the arm of the chair, with his sock slipped down and dangling three or four inches off his toes. He was cordial, southern, maybe a little bored. He thanked me for coming and asked me to tell him "why we needed this tank." Were the Russian tanks really as good as we had been saying? "Or is this all Army bullshit? This is a lot of money."

I began, strongly, by saying, "The Soviet tanks *are* better, Senator." Then I began to describe the Soviet and Warsaw Pact formations, emphasizing their massive numerical superiority. Next I focused on the T-62s and the newer T-72s that would soon comprise the majority of their tank force. I had spent maybe a $150 of our $10,000 audio visual budget on some good color close-ups of the tanks, and they showed up well on the white motel wall. There was no screen. They did have an overhead projector that I nervously fooled with until I mastered it.

"Notice how 'low' their tanks are, Senator," I told him. "It's much easier for them to hit our higher-profile tanks than for us to hit theirs. Theirs are just closer to the ground."

"Why can they make theirs so low, and we can't?"

Perfect! I had set this up beautifully; and he bit.

"Because, Senator, the Soviets have such an enormous manpower base they can restrict their tankers to just short people—five-feet-five or shorter. Since they have an unlimited supply of short people to use, they can build flatter tanks that are harder to hit."

I really hit my stride, and facing a chart of an array of Soviet tanks on maneuvers on the motel wall, I said something like, "So, Senator, what we face in Europe are about 250,000 *midgets* riding around in modern tanks;

and if we are to hit these shrimps we need a tank with the fire controls only the XM-1 will possess…"

As I blew through the second or third ad-libbed "midget" or "dwarf" reference, I noticed one of the staffers on the periphery with a faintly rueful smile, and his head lowered as if cringing.

Then I heard the drawl: "Well, son, I guess if I was in the Soviet Army I'd be in the tank corps." I turned around. He had delivered himself out of his chair and stood up, in his stocking feet, and appeared to be about four feet tall. He looked like a hobbit.

I mumbled something apologetic as the little feller padded across the room to the coffee pot. I tore through the rest of my presentation and got the hell out of there, wondering if the fate of Europe and the American army had just been sealed by an idiot Pentagon bureaucrat who didn't take the time *to learn the height of his target audience before he began ad-libbing cracks about very short people.*

Late Monday, after sweating it out all day at the Pentagon, the colonel came in and said that the feedback had been great from Tower's people and that they thought my pitch was very valuable.

Then he said, kind of laughing, "I didn't know you had never met Tower. I guess you didn't know he was a little on the 'short side.'" He said Tower's staffers were still in hysterics about it.

Never ad-lib in a presentation. Any ad-libs you would like to make should be carefully constructed in advance and rehearsed. Never walk into a room without knowing everything there is to know about an audience. Never make references to physical or other human characteristics without knowing those of everyone in the audience.

Better still, avoid them altogether.

Movin' On, Sideways

So I left the world of the $10,000 AV budget and joined the world of "Generous Electric," which was spending as much as $10- to $25,000 *per presentation* at its big corporate meetings—and there were typically 15 to 20 presentations per corporate meeting.

I adapted to this new lush environment like the proverbial fish to the proverbial water. My first General Managers Meeting was at the Belleview Biltmore in Florida; thus the meeting was known as "Belleair." The top 500 GE managers flew in, in two shifts, for the meetings, because of the limited capacity of the hotel. The 250 would listen to the two days of speeches, play golf, and then clear out in time for the next 250 to fly in. At that time we would do it all over again. At the end of each day, the staff, writers, and audiovisual people would make the long drive over to our quarters—which was the Sheraton Sand Key Hotel (later famous for the Jim Bakker trysts with Jessica Hahn). I was just as happy to be at that hotel rather than the Biltmore—probably the largest wooden structure in the world. GE would hire "fire marshals" to walk back and forth on each floor of the hotel, all night long. Some of the attendees had a hard time getting to sleep with the endless approaching and departing footsteps outside their doors.

As staff, we stayed, of course, for both shifts of the meeting, as did all the speakers and the CEO.

The Chairman's speechwriter was at the apex of his career. Reg Jones's speechwriter's title, in addition to "Manager, Chief Executive Officer Communications," was "Conference Chairman." He was clearly a big player and was treated with deference by all the lower level speechwriters and communications managers, as well as by the business people, all of whom knew he was the pen behind the "Industrial Statesman" that was Reg Jones.

He outdid himself with the speech he wrote for Reg at the final meeting. Jack Welch had been picked as Chairman-elect in December 1980—a few weeks earlier—and would take over the Company in April of '81, so this was Reg's farewell to his managers. It was moving, touching, and hugely support-ive of Jack. At its conclusion his voice broke with emotion as he said, "I predict a great future for you," and he strode off the stage to a thunderous and heartfelt standing ovation.

I was moved, although I was brand new and had never met Reg. The first crowd of 250 went home and the next crowd came in; and two days later Reg delivered his closing oration for the second time—with his voice breaking up at exactly the same place.

Speechwriters are a more cynical group than the average population because we see "how the sausage is made." The staff bar, on closing night, featured several boozy renditions of "I predict a great future for you," as well as speculation whether or not Jones's speechwriter actually placed a prompt in the speech text ("choke up here") just before the last line. Reg's speechwriter didn't attend the staff bars and dinners, as he was an "attendee"—a status it would take me another seven or eight years to achieve.

I wrote five of the presentations for that meeting. *Five.* And I got rave reviews on all, particularly from my boss, who had hired me and now felt his judgment vindicated. I was "the hero of the conference," he confided to his colleagues, as the second martini disappeared.

I forget four of the pitches I did, but the one for the head of the locomotive business became the stuff of minor legend. The slide house I worked with sent a photographer out to snap some shots of a GE locomotive pulling a train through the Aspens in Colorado. The theme was from the standard corporate playbook: the business was rebounding now, and we have a great team in place (read: *I'm* in place), and within three to five years our numbers will top x dollars and x ROI and blah, blah, and my team (meaning me, again) will deliver for the new chairman (this was one of many kisses at the meeting delivered with laser-guided precision onto the chairman-elect's ass).

As he finished my remarks, the locomotive guy walked the long way across the stage, with a loud locomotive whistle following him, stereophonically, the whole way. It was my idea, and the "sound guy" did a great job.

The crowd loved it.

I found later that Jack *hated* it.

And, despite the praise I was receiving, something bothered me about these presentations. I wrote them with only months of GE experience. How could I *possibly* have anything of use to say to a crowd that probably averaged 20 to 25 years of business experience? All I had done was take a pile of puffy factoids from the businesses, spun them, with admittedly pretty rhetoric, and spent a ton of money on dazzling visual and sound effects.

I wondered, to myself and sometimes aloud, why someone from, say, the consumer electronics business, or jet engines, or appliances could possibly give a damn what the locomotive business was going to do in three or four years. What did they carry out the door from that speech that survived the trip to the men's room other than the impression that it was "well-done" or "impressive"?

Everyone remembered the locomotive whistle, or 'horn,' as Jack later, more accurately, described it.

But what was the point? What was gained? What was learned?

At the Congressional hearings, the senators or congressmen or staffers walked out the door with a clear message from the Army: either you fund this helicopter or tank and let us get it quickly into the hands of the troops, or you may allow our army to be defeated by the Russians and your children condemned to live under Communism.

At GE, Executive VP Frank Doyle would tell me, just a few years later, that what you needed to present—particularly to a decision maker—was a "yessable proposition"—one that, when-and-if the nod of approval was given, allowed you to grab all your papers, turn off the projector, thank the audience, and "get outta Dodge."

That's not what we were doing at Belleair. We were spending, roughly, two million dollars to stage a series of "shows" which were "puffy" (Jack's word), often disingenuous, self-promotional, and wasteful of everyone's time. The real messages and learning, the useful communications, took place at the dinners, the cocktail receptions, and on the golf course—*anywhere but the meeting room.*

Death to Strategic Planning

At a key speech early in his career, Welch decreed he was not a fan of strategic planning. Jack then went on to quote Helmuth von Moltke (Moltke the Elder), of the Prussian General Staff, to the effect that strategy was not a "lengthy action plan," but rather "the evolution of a central idea through continually changing circumstances."

I have no idea where "von Moltke" came from; this was two years or so before I started working with Welch, and I would bet my firstborn that Jack read as much of von Moltke ("the Elder," keep in mind) as I had—which means about a page or two of his greatest hits.

But his imagination had been captured by the absolute truth of what von Moltke said regarding planning. Any military plan drawn with more than the broadest of brush strokes tends to begin disintegrating when the first shots are fired.

Intense combat is insane chaos. I planned and participated in a few 200- to 300-man Montagnard and Vietnamese operations in Vietnam in 1968–1969; and despite intense planning and intense briefings, the whole structure seemed to dissolve when the first shots were fired—sometimes even when *no* shots were fired.

I planned one operation early in my tour in Vietnam in which *I* fired the only shot that hit anything. I had four of my second lieutenants in a hooch at our camp as I laid out a plan—an insanely complex plan in retrospect. I talked on and on, pushing a grease pencil across a map of territory in which we believed a large enemy force would be found. I enthusiastically described how we were going to kill them all.

So absorbed was I in laying out this plan that I picked up a captured Chinese officer's pistol from an ammo box that served as a nightstand next to a lieutenant's cot. I waved it around, using it as a pointer, and then—unbelievably—picked up the full magazine that had been next to it—talked some more, inserted the magazine into the pistol—and *jacked a round into the chamber*, with no one seemingly noticing. I then continued to gesture with the weapon until I pointed it at a plastic coffee cup held between the knees of one of the lieutenants, and shortly thereafter *pulled the trigger*, blasting the cup out of his hand and spraying coffee all over everyone in the room. Luckily, the bullet missed anything organic.

An embarrassed silence followed.

The lieutenant still has the cup.

But how mesmerizing was my pitch that the four or five of us never even noticed this idiot loading and aiming a pistol around a group sitting around a map on a big box?

Thank God instinct had guided me, and I never pointed it directly at a friendly human.

But despite all the details and work and enthusiasm invested in my plan for this operation:

1. the helicopters landed at the wrong landing zone;
2. the radios didn't work;
3. the distances the units were supposed to travel to link up were simply impossible to traverse as planned, because of the terrain; and
4. the enemy didn't show up for the farewell party I had planned for them.

The only plans that work well are those that put the *best* of leaders in charge of the *best* people, striving toward von Moltke's central idea; with alternative, fallback objectives again, broadly defined.

Everything I *still* believe on this subject was shaken profoundly by the events of 9/11. The fact that four terrorist teams *could* have planned and executed one of the most severe blows in history against a nation is inexplicable given the things that could have gone wrong for the plotters, or gone right for our country. Some gathering clouds or fog in the clear blue sky might have saved the lives of thousands.

I sincerely ask God to "bless America"; but in some quiet moments wonder where He was that day.

So long-range planning—*visions*—were out at GE. In fact, Jack went on to dismantle his entire staff of strategic planners. And while Jack's first big outside speech got mixed-to-unfavorable reviews, the speechwriters and communications people got the message, kinda.

Blubbering on the Stand

The next phase early in our communications revolution was engineered totally by Jack and was what I call the "Perry Mason period."

In the new GE world, one might actually see a manager appear on the stage, and, in somber tones, outline how his business (not him, exactly) had screwed-up—lost a big customer through bad quality or service, or mishandled a price increase. The explicit message, disseminated by Welch, was that it was okay to describe this disaster for the benefit of the general managers, so that they might avoid replicating this type of thing.

The Perry Mason scenario that I whimsically half expected was that the presenter would break down on "the stand" and start sobbing his guilt. Jack would then rush up to the stage and either say, "Go thy way and sin no more," or "Bailiff, take him away."

It got a little tedious; consumer electronics managers were describing how they were being death-marched by the Japanese on cost; and how their efforts to cost-compete had wrecked their quality. The slides depicted knobs dropping off cheap GE radios—and not a lot of hope was offered. Not a lot of *anything* was offered, really. It was a confession.

But it was closer to reality than "visions."

The visual communications circus, however, continued and, until I ran the meetings, actually grew more garish and expensive.

The visuals at the major company meetings, in the pre-PowerPoint days of the '80s, had reached a point where the 12 slide projectors I described would fire integrated images onto three screens dominating the entire stage. The sequencing was so complex that no human could "pickle" all the projectors. That was done by the computer that responded to the one click from the human operator by cycling all 12 projectors.

But I quickly came to hate them.

I just found it all wasteful, useless, and pretentious.

The speaker—the so-called leader—up on the stage seemed to me a mere bit player—an emcee—a background figure with startling images behind him, speaking over or around loud stereo sounds assaulting everyone's ears.

And the complexity of these things meant disaster was always lurking behind the curtains.

I went to a Consumer Sector meeting in Marco Island, Florida one black day, stood in the back of the room with our VP of PR, a Brit named Len Vickers, and watched as two, big, expensive "shows" cratered. In one, a short video clip had somehow thrown off the resumption of the slide show.

The computer lost it.

Cacophonous sounds filled the room and bizarre images flooded the screen; the curtain was closed and the "business leader" making the presentation walked off the stage. He was tethered to the crap on the screen, and *couldn't actually stand there and say what he had to say without it.*

Two or three presentations later the unthinkable struck again. This time it was claimed that someone had pushed a hotel elevator floor button and sent a "phantom cue" to the computer controlling the slides.

All of this—accompanied by shouts, screams, and the F word from backstage—was enormously entertaining to the audience, perhaps more so than a successful execution of the actual show might have been.

I stood in the back of the room, pale and cold in the air conditioning; and shaken and sad for witnessing the human misery and failure that had unfolded before me.

I resolved then that if I ever did get control of the communications at this company I would relegate the AV nonsense to deep background; and that, as a presenter, I would never, *ever*, cede control of my destiny to some tourist in double-knit pants pushing an elevator button.

From Grunt to Flunky

In another year or so I had become the Manager of Executive Management Communications, a cacophonous and uncommunicative title for someone who is supposed to communicate. My new responsibilities, however, included running the two big corporate meetings—Boca and the officers meeting—while also managing the stable of four speechwriters, and continuing to write speeches for senior executives other than Welch.

At this time Jack was auditioning speechwriters for himself. I was transitioning into my new job, and was, as I remember, not too unhappy that I had seemingly failed my first audition. I still didn't *know* Jack, and continued to hear a series of stories about what a mercurial maniac and consumer of people he was.

On the other hand, I was content to write *30* or *40*(!) speeches a year for other big shots, manage my writers, run the meetings, and move into my new office in the East Building. I had been promoted to the "Executive Band," and I was handed my first partial incentive compensation (bonus) check by my new boss, Joyce Hergenhan. Jack had hired her away from Consolidated Edison—ConEd, which Welch referred to, kiddingly, as a "popcorn stand"—to be GE's VP of Public Relations.

My first move, as meeting manager, was to get Jack's backing in ending the ridiculous visual circus.

I explained to him that I was only going to have *one* slide projector available at the show, and *one* screen, and no video extravaganzas. GE jet engine people were particularly fond of impressing their colleagues with presentations which they felt distinguished them from the more boring businesses.

Frank Doyle, head of Relations for the Company, and my boss's boss, told me, thoughtfully, "You know I could watch them shoot those frozen turkeys into the jet engines all day. It's very interesting. But I don't know why they're always showing it to me. What's the point?"

I agreed, though I never got around to asking Frank why he found bird-strike testing such a turn on.

Welch, incidentally had to be the most responsive CEO in America to notes sent to him. A short time later the "visual circus" note I had sent to Jack came back with a quick note from him saying that he would back me up. He is a hopeless mail junkie and loved to get short notes telling him something he needed to know, or asking for a "view." Often the notes would be returned just a few *hours* later, with his distinctive scrawl all over them, with underlining and exclamation points. Often, notes sent to him resulted in a phone call, so a note was never sent up to Jack if the writer had already scheduled a tee time.

As the years wore on we could tell when he was uncomfortable with something we had asked, but did not want to give a flat "no" to, by the mere *lag* in hearing from him. If we did not get a note back the next day, or a call, and had established by asking Helga, or, later, Rosanne, that he was in the office, we already had a partial answer: He's uncomfortable.

I was called up to see Jack two months before my first officers meeting, and told, "We're not doing that old stuff anymore. These people are going to talk about what *we* want them to talk about, not that 'vision' bullshit they used to talk about at Belleair."

Over the next few weeks I would be called up to see him, and further additions and changes would be made to the program. I would then retreat to my office to hammer all the slots together to include time for Qs and As and coffee breaks; and make sure the whole program would be done by noon, in time for the players—I'm sorry, the officers—to be fed their box lunches and be on the tee by one o'clock.

As the weeks moved on, Jack kept encountering more "vignettes" or stories he wanted relayed to the officers. He kept calling me up or sending me notes to add this or that to the program. Soon we were arriving at the proverbial ten pounds of speeches in a five-pound bag.

"We can't fit all this in," I told him. He grunted. "Unless," I said, "we get them out of bed earlier."

"Yeah, *yeah*," he brightened, "Let's do it. Get them in there at 7:30. That gives us another half hour." He loved this idea, which I'm citing as Nobel Prize material, because, in addition to making more room on the program, it sent a message *by itself* to his officers: the intensity level is being turned up in this company and we are going to *work harder*.

There were about 125 officers at that time, and, sure enough, three or four with panic stricken faces would tiptoe into the room at 7:50, praying not to be spotted.

They were still on Jones time, and this was *Jack* time.

I still have the program from that meeting, and some of the pitch titles suggest how far we had already progressed from the "vision" days:

- "*Responding to Change in Information Services*";
- "*A New Tool for Global Competitiveness: the GE Trading Company*";
- "*Staying on the Leading Edge: GE Credit Corporation*"; and
- "*Rethinking a Business: Motors*".

You get the idea. These were show-and-tell sessions designed to raise before his officers issues he saw as most important to the company, with solutions that he had already proposed or approved. There were no surprises for him or me because each presenter had been specifically told by Jack the tone and substance of his pitch, and the script had been reviewed by us a week or two in advance.

Despite my ignorance of many of the business issues, I was starting to get where he was coming from as far as the all-important "tone." I could ferret out the arrogance and smugness he hated, and point it out to him to be changed. I did not have the credibility to just change it myself.

My first Boca meeting was less than three months later. Most of the presenters were at the general manager level of the company. There were about 500 attendees—a mob.

I've estimated that at his first meeting Welch probably couldn't stand about 25 to 30 percent of the people in the room, and shortly after they began retiring or otherwise disappearing. By January 1985, he probably hated only 15 percent, but still considered the general manager population one that needed to be talked to more simply and directly than the officers.

And there were still many he didn't want to "shoot," but really couldn't stand. At Boca we all took random tickets from the staff giving our table numbers for dinner. This was done to break up cliques and business flocking. Jack didn't exactly take a ticket. In fact he "designed" his table and its denizens, including the exact seats in which they were to sit.

I needled him on this subject on more than one occasion, only to be shot down—only semi-angrily: "Why should I have to wind up sitting next to that asshole (fill in name) if I draw the wrong ticket?"

"Yeah, so why should *I* have to sit next to him?" Then the look that screams, "You don't really understand, yet, that *I* can do things *you* can't, do you?"

But in preparing the meeting, rather than have me harangue the speaker-victims over the phone, he would have me pass along his guidance to them, and make a date with them to come to Fairfield and do a demo of their presentations to him *in front of his desk*. Not all of them, but most of them, and particularly the ones he wasn't sure would get across exactly the point he wanted them to make.

So I would be called by the receptionist to come down to the lobby and greet the often grim and pale-faced presenters, and bring them up to Jack's office, as they schmoozed me in the elevator with stuff like, "I think I've got what Jack wants in here. What do you think, Bill?"

"Yeah, maybe, but don't be surprised if he makes some changes."

I'd usher Joe or Manny or Tak or Roger into the office, and Jack would rise to greet him, pleasantly enough, but with an anxious edge to his manner. "So, did you do it the way I said? Are you showing how connected the lab is getting with the businesses? Did you put that stuff in…? Okay, why don't you just run through it for me," he'd say, as he grabbed all the paper charts out of the guy's hand as he sat down.

The victim would then begin reading his script as Jack flipped through his charts, making whale noises, or occasional approving comments like "good, good, *perfect.*"

Then more reading, interrupted by impatient sounds, and about seven minutes into the 15-minute pitch, a cut-off: "Charlie, you've got some good stuff in here, but you're missing *your main point*. Here's what you gotta tell these guys so they understand we're not going to do that same old tired shit that doesn't work in that business. Here, write this down…" I'd hand Charlie a pen and Jack would begin dictating; then after a minute or so, dictating would become too tedious and Jack would begin writing whole sentences and paragraphs on Charlie's charts, as the sweat ran down Charlie's face.

After 45 minutes or so, Jack would say, "Perfect. It's gonna be *perfect.* Just make sure you emphasize that stuff about being connected. Here! Here! On *this* chart. Not that one! No subtlety. Use these exact words," pointing to those he had written on the correct "Charlie's chart." "Perfect. It will be great. Thanks for coming in. See ya at Boca. Thanks. How's Edna? Everything okay? Did you get rid of that asshole, (fill in name)?"

And I would lead Charlie back down to the lobby with his head swimming. And he would typically say, "Well, that was a good session. He kinda changed everything I was gonna do, but I think I got it now. What do you think, Bill?"

And I would say, "Yeah, I think it's gonna be terrific. Run it by me when you do your next draft, and I'll run it by him, and it will be really good. Have a good trip back."

And then I had a half hour or so to do all my other work—a situation which was starting to eat a *really big* hole in my stomach—before the parade of "Vans," or "Genes" arrived, like little kids with their term papers, to have them rewritten by the levitating, stuttering wizard behind, over, and around the desk.

One point he wanted made I remember clearly and just mentioned. It was that the corporate R&D people—engineers and scientists—needed to form close long-term relationships with their counterparts in the businesses. Welch hated the "hobby-shop" mentality that often creeps into business labs; the gravitation toward "pure research" rather than what he and I called "combat engineering": *focusing everything on winning in the marketplace.*

GE used to brag every year about how many patents came out of its labs. Welch found that a complete bore; and said his view of the lab would be shaped by how many "cars with out-of-state plates"—from the various GE businesses—would be found in the Schenectady lab parking lot, with their drivers inside the lab, demanding help, "solutions," and the technical edge that would assure them a win.

To illustrate the type of relationships he wanted, he had put some senior engineer from one of the embattled businesses on the program to explain how his relationship with corporate R&D was helping him win—or at least survive.

So I fetched the speaker from the lobby, and was introduced to his companion, a nerdy looking scientist type from the lab. He had *not* been invited by Jack or me, but had been brought along, like a security blanket, to offer support as he entered the dragon's lair two floors above.

Jack looked quizzical as the scientist was introduced by the business guy, but became increasingly animated, excited, and happier as the pitch was delivered to him—with the business guy turning periodically to his partner and saying things like, "Isn't that right, Larry?" or "Do you want to add to that?" or "Larry's been spending more time out at our place (Ft. Wayne, I believe) than he has at the lab." Welch was *thrilled,* and declared that they should *both* be on the Boca program, doing what we used to call a "Frick and Frack" or a "Heckel and Jeckel," alternating comments from two lecterns on opposite sides of the stage.

And they did a terrific job at the actual show, nervous as cats, but very effective in getting Welch's message across.

For a week or so after their rehearsal, Welch would spontaneously break out in chuckles and actually act out how the business engineer "would hang on to Larry"—the "lab guy." And he would illustrate by grabbing on to whomever's arm he was talking to. "That's *exactly* the kind of relationship I'm trying to get across to these people. Not wandering around the lab playing with chickenshit that doesn't mean anything, but out there with the businesses."

So, Jack starred at his first real Boca meeting as an Edgar Bergen character, sitting in the front row, while 18 or 20 Charlie McCarthys got up and did their speeches. The riot was that if, for some reason, one or more of the speakers couldn't get to the meeting, Jack *could have done his pitch for him!* After all, he wrote it. He could have stood up for two days and delivered, if anything, a more impassioned, more effective summary of every "point" to be made—with few, or none, of the increasingly annoying visuals in the background.

And this, in essence, is what he did at the end of the program, as he moved toward his CEO-level oration—his "close"—which was usually fiery and spectacular.

He would begin by zipping through the two days of the program, touching upon, and underscoring, the one or two points from each speaker that *he* wanted to make sure his managers took away.

Sometimes what I call "homework assignments" were given. For example, he would say, "So, by October, I'd like to have the businesses come in and describe, in detail, how they are strengthening their ties with the R&D lab (or the audit staff, or whomever) and what *concrete, quantifiable results* this has produced so far. With no bullshitting."

"Next, as Gloria described, supplier costs can be reduced, and she mentioned some ways that can be addressed immediately. We have got to get costs down, and then whack at them again and again. So, in July, please come in and tell us the progress you have made, the results that progress has produced, and any ideas we can *share* on how we can do even better."

Five hundred people were writing furiously.

Think they did that when the speakers had speechwriters who expounded their flatulent "visions"?

And Boca didn't end with the meeting and the homework assignments. A few days after the meeting, when everyone was back home, somewhere around the globe, the letters and faxes would arrive from Jack that usually read something like, "Great meeting. I think we've got some real momentum going. A couple of points I think need emphasis as we head into the New Year..." or "On cost reduction, I enclose a copy of the CEO letter in the Toyota Annual Report, the gist of which is *we will cut costs as we have never cut costs before*. Please read every word. This is what we are up against. Great meeting. Big things lie ahead. We've got the greatest team in world business..."

Almost always, these follow-up notes were carefully *handwritten* in black Flair-pen, not to save work for Helga or Rosanne, but to make the statement that these are *my* views, *my* thoughts; not Lane's nor anybody else's.

And at the bottom would be the flamboyant "Jack"—as if the recipient didn't know from whom it might be coming.

The domination and orchestration of company meetings may sound like the machinations of a control freak, a meddler, an autocrat, or dictator. That is precisely what I am describing; but it is also the picture of a leader, and how a leader can capture ownership of his key meetings and his organizational communications, virtually overnight. These meetings were Jack's megaphone, and everyone knew it. Do the people who attend your key meetings know whose thoughts and views they are hearing?

The Marionette Meister

This stage-managing of company meetings might sound prehistoric, old-fashioned, tyrannical, repressive, and dictatorial. Maybe. All I know is, it *worked*.

We quickly dumped the "Q&A" at the large Boca meeting. This exercise was one in which I, like my predecessor, stood in the front of the room just below the lectern, and received questions written on 3x5 cards that were collected by the better-looking secretaries who ran up and down the aisles as the cards were handed down the rows.

The questions were either pure ass-kissing or annoyingly tendentious: "Why aren't we putting more money into 'large transformers' or 'switchgear'? They are 'our legacy'." A question like this marked the anonymous questioner as a member of the undead, lurching spasmodically down the tracks behind the train that had pulled out of the station several years ago.

I'd sort through the 3x5 cards and hand Jack the ones that weren't either stupid or too sarcastic. I gave him the tough, coherent ones, however, and he struggled to maintain civility as he answered them. Later he would say something like, "I bet that asshole, Joe Somebody, asked that one about switchgear."

Half the time he was right. It was Joe. While we just dumped the Q&A at Boca, the big meeting, we kept it up at the Officers Meeting, the 125 people with one attended by the self-confidence and personal career options to sound off. This created only a few unpleasant scenes, and many *real* conversations.

I am not implying that Welch was intolerant of what is annoyingly called "pushback." He simply could not restrain himself from delivering a sarcastic "shot" when the questioner's argument was, in Jack's view, patently stupid or implied an inability to change, or to look forward.

You, as the leader of an organization, a business CEO, a head of an audit staff, finance function, or any entity that you wish to function in accordance with your views and principles, need to seize control of the "meetings" as soon as you walk in the door.

Blow up any you find wasteful, and then run *the rest.*

You need to decide the points you want made at the meeting and then pick the presenters best qualified to make them. Do not leave this to your "communications person." You do it, and then have him or her help you fit these into time slots. None should exceed 10 minutes without a very good reason. You should open and close the meeting, and speak as long as you need, using the disciplines I will shortly offer for your consideration.*

Once you have an agenda you are enthusiastic about, speak face-to-face, or by phone, with each speaker. Have your "communicator," and any-one else you may need, with you.

The gist of your desires for the pitch—the "big points"—cannot be relayed efficiently to the speaker by your communicator, and print or e-mail are toneless and no good for this purpose. The warmth of your voice and your passion needs to be downloaded into your speaker's brain and heart. You speak to every one of your speakers and tell them what you want them to say.

Sounds "bossy"? Well, aren't you the boss?

In the early days Jack and I, and maybe Larry Bossidy, would sit around the speakerphone and Welch would—after a few laughs and greetings, and inquiries about family (all of it 100 percent sincere, believe it or not) get to the point. "Look, Ralph (or Gary or Sandy or Rick or Walt) here's what I want you to tell them at Boca…" and, further instructions such as, "Don't get sidetracked with all that technical bullshit nobody knows what you're talking about (ha-ha). This is important. You need to talk to them at 100,000 feet. Don't get bogged down. Do a good job and let me see it in a couple of weeks. Send Bill a copy. Thanks. See ya."

Jack always sat in the front of the Boca room with his vice chairmen, the CFO, and others and left the enforcement of attentiveness to me, or my predecessor, in the back.

I would walk up to a *Wall Street Journal* reader and say, "If you are going to read that paper you might want to go outside the room. The light's a lot better out in the lobby."

I took this approach with maybe a handful of people over the years, and almost all would close the paper, redden, and look at the stage. I did not like doing this. I had not made a friend of someone senior—sometimes, very senior—to me, but they weren't going to mess with me with the nuclear option I had available.

Once, in the fairly early days of the laptop, I politely kicked the CEO of a newly acquired company out of the room for noisily pounding away at the keyboard on something unrelated to the meeting. I mentioned to Welch that I had done this, without giving the name, and he demanded to know who it was. Uncharacteristically, I told him, and he smiled faintly and said, "Well, that asshole's not going to be around here long anyway."

And he wasn't.

But you should sit in the back, with your mike, and boom out, on occasion, some enthusiastic endorsement of a point the speaker is making, or a clarification, or emphasis, if you feel the point is not being made with sufficient impact or passion. Welch did this very frequently at the 150-person officers meeting, and, the 40- to 50-person quarterly corporate executive council meeting.

I don't think it's "boorish" to interrupt; and if it is, who cares? Every ear in that room will be focused on what you have to say—much more so than on what the speaker was saying.

Never be surprised, unpleasantly, by anything said in a presentation at your meeting. Review every script and every chart a week or two before the meeting, and mark them up, enthusiastically praising and putting exclamation points next to things that you like, and crossing out stuff you don't like, with reasons given: "Boring," "Off the point," "Too much detail," "Too long," "Bullshit." "Sally, can you make this point with more passion?" "Pound this home." "Can't read this. It's too busy. Why not just say it?" "Great chart. I'm taking a copy of this with me to the board meeting (a Welch innovation)." "Not necessary." "Unreadable; too busy." "What's the point?" "Get rid of this." "Are you kidding? A nightmare." (All Jack comments.)

Drafts that are totally off the mark, or have been slapped together by underlings, need not be marked up. A phone call should be made: a firm, serious, or volcanic shouting phone call, depending on your persona, explaining why this pitch is unacceptable, and what, once again, needs to be said. Offer to remove them from the program if they are not comfortable with your guidance.

I once received a script from a GE Officer located "offshore," as we used to say. The script, written by the guy himself, read as if he had smoked a huge "Euro-doob" before hitting the keyboard. It wasn't a bad try, but it was off the wall, and just wouldn't make much sense to the Boca crowd. I couldn't even edit or rewrite it. This guy was close to a hand-pick of Jack's. I told Welch what I thought, and had him read it, or the first few pages of it. Jack's phone was off the cradle within minutes for a call to the guy's boss.

"We made this guy an officer because he performs. Did we make a mistake? Did you see this Boca shit he just sent in? It's nuts. Makes no sense. You wanna talk to him, or should I? We need a whole new pitch with the points I told him I wanted. Yeah, yeah. Have him talk to Bill. Okay." Tone change; voice lowered. "How are you? Things going well? How's this goin'; that goin'? How's GM lookin'? Are you tracking blah-blah? Great. How's Sue? Workin' out? Great. Terrific. See ya."

And, in a week, a new draft appeared on my desk, right on the money, and it was a hit at the show.

Have your paw prints all over your meeting.

Jack moved the corporate officers meeting from the Arizona Biltmore in Phoenix back to our Crotonville facility near the Hudson, because of the added four or five hours of travel for our European VPs; and because he had fallen in love with the atmospherics of "sharing" that The Pit had come to symbolize. Arizona was too much like a "show."

I had rented, at the Biltmore, a series of consoles that were put in front of every officer at the meeting. One could key them, with a red light appearing, and speak, in a conversational tone, with everyone else in the room. They worked very well in the fairly large Phoenix meeting hall, so I had the audio-visual people rent them again and set them up in The Pit at Crotonville. Mistake.

Welch enters The Pit last, which is the signal to begin the meeting, strides down to the lectern to "open"; explains the change in venue—does his usual great opener, and walks ten rows back up the little amphitheater to his seat.

The next speaker, a vice chairman, is teeing up the day's program when Jack notices my "console" in front of him on the schoolroom-style desk, and says loudly, "Who put these things here? Oh, I know. Somebody misses Phoenix," gesturing over his shoulder at me.

Then, as the vice chairman gamely tries to continue, Welch, grumbling, pulls the console out by the wires and drops it over the front of the desk, out of his sight. I signaled the AV guys to kill the entire system, and then sat there fuming until the coffee break about two hours later, when Welch strode up the steps toward the door, looking at me. I said, "What's the matter with you? What are you, anti-technology?"

Welch just laughed dismissively and repeated that I was "missing Phoenix."

Was this a big, black eye for me? Not really. Jack didn't fault people for trying new things—even if he hated them.

The bigger point of this little incident is how totally committed to communications this man was, and how compelled to control its atmospherics. I would guess no other CEO in global business would have even noticed my consoles in front of him, nor cared about them if he did. This company was being moved dynamically—by communications: *Welch's* communications—and he began to wrap those reins even more tightly around his fist.

We had one very senior player in the company when Jack took over, who was smart, handsome, deep-voiced, personable, tough, and a very good golfer. He was one of Jack's boys. Welch, in one of his earliest messages, stressed his belief that a business must be "number one or number two" in its marketplace, or should be "fixed, closed, or sold"—a view that created consternation in some of the old, small, mediocre businesses around GE.

Jack passionately and forcefully made his case for this view in his closing remarks at one of the very early corporate meetings. Golf followed, evening came, and the closing dinner was climaxed by the witty and hilarious remarks of Jack's friend, whose job was to make people laugh—or so he thought. In one of his Boca finance pitches, after a year in which we had successfully used investment tax credits to negate the entire company tax bill, he announced, dramatically, "We've beaten taxes. Now we're going after *death*."

What followed at the closing dinner was a series of martini-fueled references to Welch's hair, about which Welch was very sensitive.

I recall snickering as I sat across from him at his desk while he "took a call." There was a videotape in the middle of the desk entitled "A Thinking Man's Guide to Hair Loss." I was going to suggest we watch it together, but with three small children and a big mortgage, decided not to. The hair commentary by the speaker dissed Jack, something that a leader should not tolerate.

But then the speaker committed the truly unforgivable, by weaving into the sports-award presentation what he thought were hilarious references to being "number one or number two" in whatever prize—golf, fishing, or tennis—that was being awarded.

I was at the meeting, as staff, but not at the dinner, so I did not see Welch get up from his table and stride furiously out of the room, but I was told that he did.

The hair stuff he could have lived with, but not the cracks—even the funny ones—poked at a serious message about the Company's future.

The joker was gone before long.

Micromanage your meetings if you want to change the way your organization communicates with itself.

If people joke that the speakers are 10 or 15 of your puppets—fine. Perfect. You are, or should be the marionette meister. Don't let one idiot get up on stage and, as I put it, "fart in church," disagree with, or God forbid, ridicule some principle or strategy you are trying to embed in the organization. It's death to your meeting and to your leadership. Do not allow it to happen, and you should execute anyone who does it. It's that important. Tolerate—even encourage—contrarian views in Q&A and discussion, but not on the program.

And don't tolerate public sarcasm or cynicism. Speak with the infidels, reason with them. Listen to them; they may deserve to be listened to. But it is your ship, and you must set the headings. If you don't you are a "figurehead, an empty suit."

Forget having an "outside speaker" at your meetings. Save yourself several grand, and eliminate the distraction. I say this with touching selflessness, because I've become an "outside speaker" myself at $15,000 a pop.

Forget hiring a "motivational speaker." It's usually obvious he stuck a CD in his ear before he got up. Everyone loves to hear the "message," but it's virtually forgotten after lunch. Unless you know exactly what the speaker is going to say, and are sure it reinforces your message, don't do it. It's a distraction.

Jacking Up the Commo

Communications *did* start to get better at GE after a year or two of "the Jack Man," but several unpleasant scenes still had to play out.

One of the keys to change was that Welch immersed himself in business data. A man who had spent most of a 20-year career in plastics now began to dig deeply into appliances, financial services, engines, turbines, and medical systems. And blessed with a God-only-knows-what IQ and a built-in bullshit detector, he was, within a year, capable of energetically jumping into any presentation made to him, and—unbelievably—adding value or wreaking destruction on the bullshitters or "feather merchants," as we called them at the Pentagon.

Woe betide the feather merchants. I went with Jack to Crotonville many times, or was already there, sometimes speaking, when he came in. I would then park in the back of the room and watch, as, in the pre-casual days (Crotonville had been "casual" for years), he would take off his suit jacket in The Pit, talk about the company in inside baseball terms: "I talked to Ted Turner (or Greenspan or Volker or Bush), this morning, and his view is…"

He'd talk for 10 minutes or so; sometimes place an overhead of a newly beloved chart or two he had lifted from someone's presentation on the machine, then turn it off, and ask: "So what's your view?"

Forty hands would go up, some with questions they had probably rehearsed in their rooms for a week. Some had real insights. Others would affect some *faux*-querulous position: "Jack, you say you want the businesses to work with and be supported by Corporate R&D; and yet we have had this problem with our fan blade on the CF-6 engine (totally invented conversation, but representative) and corporate gave us no help…"

Typically, there would be a pause as the questioner would anticipate Jack saying something like, "I'm going to look into that and get back to you in a couple of days. Thanks for the input. I appreciate your frankness."

What they got was often a snarly homily that went something like, "That's not the problem. That's bullshit. That fan blade (or locomotive or X-ray tube) is failing because of shitty manufacturing. I talked to Brian (or Walt or Ralph, the kid's *uber* boss) this morning, and you guys simply haven't figured out a way to beat (Siemens or Philips or Toshiba). In fact, you've screwed up this… and that. And the failure rate on that tube is six and a half times the industry standard. Don't give me this bullshit about this being CR&D's fault. Was it their fault your manufacturing processes in Evendale (or Lynn or Schenectady) are so far behind your competitors that *BusinessWeek* put us at the bottom in two or three customer surveys? Blaming the lab is bullshit."

At this point the questioner would begin to comprehend that *this guy knows more about this than I do.* A sickly panicked smile would cross his face, and I, in the back of the room, would stage-whisper to whomever was next to me, echoing the *Hindenburg* radio commentator, "Oh, the humanity!"

Don't Dive. Swim!

Later, in the '90s, when fools continued to attempt to look smart at these sessions at Welch's expense, I would whisper, "I see dead people," as the carnage began.

You couldn't get away with the bullshitting anymore, and the reason you couldn't was that Larry Bossidy, Ed Hood, our CFO, Dennis Dammerman, and most of the business leaders, immersed themselves in the data and the issues, got their hands dirty, felt the problems and failures, and swam in the currents of their businesses, rather than presiding over them in "executive" fashion, skipping over their surfaces like flat stones.

One of the more significant "I'll get back to you" disasters was the case of Ed Russell, who ran the company's superabrasives business, man-made diamonds. I knew Russell, vaguely, and he and I once spent a pleasant October afternoon bobbing around on a yacht in the Hudson River, firing shotguns at balloons or cans off the Indian Point Nuclear Plant (try doing that today). We were the only ones who had picked the "yacht trip" as our recreational activity, after the first day of the corporate officers meeting.

Jack has told this story in his first book, and I am not into "twice told tales" in *my* first; but Russell showed up with his boss, Glen Hiner of the plastics business, and laid a fatal egg. I'm not sure what violence, if any, took place in the meeting room, but the next day Welch sent a note to Hiner that went as follows: "Russell has to go. He made a fool of himself in July and yesterday he appeared totally out of it. Imagine a presentation to you and me and he had no numbers and, more important, knew none. I don't want to fool with this fellow much longer but will respect your end-of-year timing."

You need to spend much of your days in what is now, trendily, called "deep dives" on the factory floor; or kissing an angry, arrogant customer's ass; or having the lab people explain to you why they can't solve "this problem." Because, if somebody like Welch—or Larry Bossidy—dove deeper into your business than you had—you were in trouble—or would be in trouble today, I hope, under Jeff Immelt. Two or three questions would take them to your exposed underbelly, if your knowledge was based on "talking points," and the fourth and fifth questions would be bayonet thrusts into your gut.

Jack Welch was not just a "deep diver," but a top-to-bottom feeder, a catfish, someone who would paddle his way, teeth-bared, through the kelp in some Godforsaken industrial town where GE inevitably had a business, and surface to hit you—in front of the leadership of the entire company—with a neutron bomb. Like this one.

Welch, at Boca:

"Just last Thursday I had lunch with the president of one of the fastest growing retailers in the country. Turns out our system wasn't 'available' in December to deal with him.

"He said, 'How could you not ship me stuff? Why would you let your competition in the door? I'm growing 60 percent a year and you're not shipping me stuff. Were you meeting some internal goal? Some measurement? Are you out of your mind? I brought the other guy in.'"

Then Jack said, dramatically, and with real feeling:

"You hear that and it makes you want to die!"

This was the Boca meeting, so there were probably a couple dozen people from lighting present, all of whom took this one between the eyes and wanted to slither under the chairs and out of the room. The complainant Jack quoted was the head of a new company called Home Depot; and the problem was some ridiculous bureaucratic "GE internal goal"; probably some inventory management target.

I think "deep dives" is a patronizing way of condescending to focus on the real mechanics of the business and its relationship with its customers.

Welch would visit, say, Louisville, Kentucky (appliances); go to his meetings, and then go hang out with the *union* leaders at the plant—the "enemy"—argue with them, laugh with them, and listen intently to what they had to say, the reasonable and the unreasonable. Before his regime, doing such a thing would have been considered unthinkable, and a sign of weakness.

There were a bunch of union guys on the floor at medical systems in Waukesha, Wisconsin, as well, whom Jack made a point of hanging out with every time he visited the business, asking them how their savings and security plans had grown since the last time he saw them.

He did all this while in the process of breaking the backs of the UE and IUE, and making the union presence at GE a weak and increasingly vestigial one.

This swimming at every level of company operations and affairs was not a "deep dive." It was part of his compulsion to be on top of, and conversant with, everything GE. And he had the mental capacity to do it almost effortlessly.

You, as the boss, need daily immersion in the "grunt stuff" if you are to claim that you really run your operation. "You've got to smell the shit," they told all the lieutenants at the infantry basic course. If you don't see what the men see and understand what they understand, you're kind of a fake, a figurehead, a guy walking around with the trappings of an officer taking salutes but knowing you're not a real leader.

Part IV

Restuffing Guts

In January 1968, with my usual perfect timing, I arrived in Vietnam and was assigned to the first special-forces camp to get hit by the North Vietnamese in the Tet Offensive. Like many new officers, I was not sure how good I was, or if I was any good at all. I was terrified—not of being killed—I was sure I was bulletproof, but of screwing up, showing indecision, or worse: getting some of my guys killed.

At one point, we were fighting from behind tombstones in a Vietnamese cemetery and "smelling napalm in the morning." The Vietnamese company I was advising, two American sergeants, and I had been stopped in our tracks and pinned down while assaulting a village that had been taken over and fortified by the North Vietnamese.

Then, crawling around among the tombstones, I saw the pathetic spectacle of a Montagnard striker—one of ours—writhing on the ground with his intestines out and dragging in the dirt. It had been a shrapnel hit from a grenade or mortar round. "He die," said my Vietnamese radio man, quietly and with certainty.

I don't know why, but I felt so bad for the guy that I slithered over behind the tombstones and bushes, and got to him. He already had that gray face (Caucasians get it even worse) when blood loss and shock signal that death is on the way. Rounds were breaking the sound barrier over our heads and kicking up dirt between the tombstones. I said, "Screw it," and called a couple of Vietnamese strikers over. We picked up his stinking, slimy, dirty guts and stuffed them back, as best we could, into his abdomen and his shirt. Then we dragged him back behind the tombstones. Then, even further back out of contact, and got him taken to a Vietnamese hospital in a truck.

And you know what? One of the Vietnamese told me, about a month or so later, that he *made* it. He lived, because of—or despite—having his giblets stuffed back into his body by a couple of filthy, garlicky strikers, not-to-mention a sweating, dirty, "round-eye" lieutenant.

The point of this is, from that moment, no one was ever going to tell *me* that I didn't know what combat was like. No general or no sergeant. I felt the guts. And I smelled the horrible sweet smell of the rotting North Vietnamese I had called the napalm in upon.

And I survived. And my two American sergeants survived. And we won. They pinned a Combat Infantryman's Badge on my chest a month later, and I growled with pride. I still wear my old 'Nam field jacket, with my airborne wings and CIB. I should feel like an old fool pushing around a shopping cart at the Stop & Shop with my wife—but I don't.

You gotta smell *it* in the field; in your operations, if you have pretensions to leadership.

Welch talked for years, in the early days, about *self-confidence* being the indispensable ingredient of leadership.

I nodded. I agreed with it theoretically, but never really grasped it until later, as *the* key attribute of a leader. Some are born with it; some develop it; some fall on their faces, their self-confidence undeserved.

But I've never seen a real leader without it.

Welch listened, increasingly less politely, to a presentation made to him by a "dweeb" whose relatively small company GE had just bought. The BS detector was on, and picking up significant readings. The guy was serving up an air-ball, garnished with generalities designed to satisfy the gullible, had a millimeter-deep knowledge of his own business, and after three or four attempted deflections of an increasingly scary Jack Welch, went down in flames and vituperation in a scene that causes most people who were present to cringe when prompted to recall it.

Once, when I was swimming in the nutty, wonderful, piranha tank of the business management class at Crotonville, the head of one of the units was scheduled to speak to us. Instead, in walked a newly hired head of "Planning." Her boss probably had a higher-priority engagement than speaking to us, and no doubt told her, "Fill in for me. Here are my charts, you can just follow them." She was pleasant enough, although apologetic that she was new to the business. We "students" were tolerant enough until someone interrupted her to ask what some technical phrase on a chart she had just thrown up, meant. She said, "Um, I'm not sure. Is there anyone in here from plastics?"

There was, and he explained her chart to her and to the class.

That pretty much did it. She went through the motions of reading her way through the overheads as the 30 of us doodled, read the *Journal,* hit the restrooms, and administered the *coup de grâce* at the end—silence when she asked if anyone had questions. I believe there was some perfunctory, sarcastic applause that followed.

I felt terrible for her, and even mildly angry at her boss, whom I knew and liked, for doing this to her and to us.

What should she have done? Refused to do the pitch? Not possible. Not done in GE. You do what you are told, if you can't get out of it. What she *should* have done is walked in the door and announced that her boss had asked her to do his pitch and she had said yes, but since she's only been with the company six months or so and had no desire to make an idiot out of herself, what she would like to do, without charts, is bounce some of her early observations on the strengths and weaknesses of this business off the 30 consultants in front of her, and see if they buy those observations, hate them, or can add to them. "Observation number one: plastics, long reputed to be the number one marketing business in this company, is in my observation not that good, and can be better. Here's what I mean…" Off to the races, yelling, loud arguments, laughter, stimulating ferment. She would have gotten rave reviews and been dragged to the Rec Hall for beers afterwards.

She didn't get the raves or the invite. In fact, she didn't last more than a year or so at the company. She was incinerated in the written class evaluations. Not by me, because I felt bad for her.

Never allow yourself to be pushed onto the thin ice you will instantly feel through your shoes, by questions that are getting "outside your expertise."

And never, ever, agree to do someone else's presentation under any circumstances. I have never seen someone do so and walk away better off than when he or she walked in.

Gentle Meddling

On another road trip I took in the mid-'80s, this time with Welch, we had gone with Carl Schlemmer, the head of the locomotive business, to see the president of a U.S. railroad who had a pending order out to bid for 60 to 100 locomotives. General Motors was our other competitor, and Schlemmer had brought Jack in as the heavy artillery to try and help him land the deal. The problem, which became apparent after the meeting with the railroad president, was that he was intent on squeezing the vendors so hard that the margins on the locomotives were going to be razor thin. Carl had soured on the deal and wanted to walk away from it, but Jack didn't want him to. But he wanted to *convince* him, rather than order him. As we reached cruising altitude on the way back to Pennsylvania to drop Carl off on our way back to Connecticut, Jack was all over him to take the order. He was soft, warm, Irish, almost tender: a side of him that I had not, at that point, yet seen. "Carl, wouldn't you like that big order for your factory? Wouldn't it do great things for the place? Look at how much capacity you would fill. Think about it." Not an order, either explicit or implied, but an intrusion into a level of operations that a business school professor would probably define as *meddling*.

Carl took the deal because of Jack's urging—and his factory in "dreary Erie" hummed along.

Analysts, and even business reporters and portfolio managers, gave up trying to score points or catch Welch in a contradiction or get him with a "gotcha." He knew far more about the business in question, and *the industry*, than they did; and, after several years, they deferred to him on some issues rather than get spanked publicly by him, and look dumb in front of their colleagues.

Besides, they *loved* the guy.

See the Enron movie, *The Smartest Guys in the Room*. I was struck by how Jeff Skilling explained why he discontinued a conversation he was having with a woman from *Fortune* sniffing around this "black box" of a company he operated, with the excuse that he was "not an accountant," and therefore really couldn't answer her questions *as to how Enron made its money!* The GE Board would have fired anyone *the next day* who said anything so asinine. No one I have ever known could *imagine* Welch demurring on a question because "he wasn't an accountant" or a metallurgist or an aeronautical engineer or an insurance expert or a bond trader or dredging expert or—whatever. A Jack of all trades. Larry Bossidy left GE to lead Allied Signal. He grasped it in his bear-like embrace, learned it to its roots, sniffed out all its bullshit, fired the bullshitters, made it his own, and *ran* it. Years later he wrote *Execution*, the best business book I've ever read. Its central point, in my view, was the *imperative* of micromanaging, meddling, kibitzing, and knowing how everything works from top to bottom.

Doing so partially explains, in my view, Welch's success as a leader and GE's success under his tenure and beyond.

Handle the dirty guts of your business or operation. Doing so will give you the confidence to walk into meeting rooms immune to fakery and with no need to engage in that activity yourself.

Called on the Carpet

The early Boca desk rehearsals that Welch conducted with the victims I brought up from the Fairfield lobby were loud and intense, but not nasty, and always administered with an anesthetic of praise for how "spectacular" the final pitch was going to be after the speaker put in everything Jack wanted him or her to say.

Being a full-service CEO, he even helpfully scrawled out charts for his presenters—levitating, hovering, and stuttering as his puppets visibly sweated and tried to figure out what these hieroglyphic-like fragments meant, and how the presenter was going to explain them to his "visual people," when he didn't even understand them himself.

The pale, perspiring one in the elevator on the way to the lobby would sometimes implore, "Bill, I don't know what he means by this chart," holding out the Jack scribble with an x- and y-axis and some arrows and numbers and cryptic word fragments. I would comfort him by telling him that I didn't know either, but would find out and get back to him. And I would, after biting a bullet and telling Welch, or writing him a note to the effect that "we didn't really understand what he meant" by this or that. After some pyrotechnics, implying stupidity on the speaker's part, and possibly on mine, I got some agitated people in Ft. Wayne or Cleveland or Schenectady comfortable with the pitch they were supposed to construct, and then made Jack comfortable with it when it was done.

And it always went off well at Boca and was garnished, in his closing remarks, with effusive praise by the one who created it: Jack.

Presentations to Welch, whether at Crotonville Management School or at reviews at businesses or at corporate, immediately became less boring, but often less pleasant. It was soon apparent that the old GE corporate civility, where a droning bore or dissembler worked through his script and was thanked regally, by the boss, was over. Civility was no longer a corporate virtue. Spatters of career blood began to fleck conference room walls. Horror shows in the field were reported. A friend of mine, a VP, described a scene at a presentation to Welch in the field. Shouts and imprecations ripped through the presenting team early in the pitch. "They ran the white flag up," he said, "and he still kept going. Pounding away. It was *not* pretty."

He did homework and research on the subject of the presentations—and was briefed by his trusted finance VPs—and would drop nuclear devices on presenters for putting a "pretty face" on some operational pig they were minimizing or allowing to slouch in the background.

Mark Vachon, his Investor Relations VP, told me Welch would always focus on confronting head-on some abscess or other that might affect GE's stock, preferring to "take the hit" with a frank and candid exposition to the financial analysts, rather than "spin it" and build up what Mark referred to as a "hair ball" that would have to be expelled some day from the corporate guts. Candor ruled his presentations. He built up immense credibility by allowing it to guide him. And when he *really* had a "good story," they would believe it and run for the phones.

The image that consistently presents itself to me in situations where disastrous pitches were made to Welch, is of a gazelle or antelope run down on the African veldt by a lion. The animal struggles to escape for a few moments with the lion's teeth in the folds of his throat—and then goes limp, not yet dead, but in resignation, instinctively knowing the pain would abate and the end would arrive more quickly if it did so.

"Going limp with resignation" during a cratering pitch to Welch was an acknowledgment that, "yes, I screwed up, my pitch was poorly prepared, not well thought out; and I wasn't forthcoming enough or on top of the subject or the numbers. But I now understood the problem, thanks to Jack's comments, and will do better in the future."

That approach usually produced a reduction in the noise and savagery of the assault; and sometimes, even mildly conciliatory warmth. *Sometimes.* That's why my friend was in awe as he described the occasion that the lion continued to rip and tear even though the presenting team of gazelles had exposed their throats and gone limp.

After Jack changed communications at GE, no one ever dared to lie or dissemble again, at least at the corporate level, as far as I ever saw. I'm pretty sure they never did it at the meetings I ran.

And they weren't afraid of *me.*

There is a 150-yard winding corridor running through the east and west buildings of GE headquarters in Fairfield called the "GE Gallery." It houses some truly spectacular exhibits, borrowed from the Hudson River School, and other classic scenes and portraits. There is also a lot of modern Motherwell-type crap that Welch liked. One exhibit, around '85 or so featured beautiful and accurate paintings of wildlife. One of the larger works was a ferocious great white shark—lips rolled back and teeth bared á la *Jaws* facing the viewer. Someone had written on the frame, "Jack Welch." A security guard, who *observed* the graffiti writer (who didn't seem to care if he had been observed), told me that it was an executive vice president of GE who had been eviscerated after a pitch to Welch—and had been "sent home," a Jack euphemism for removal.

The intolerance for vacuous and useless presentations was zestfully adopted by Welch's lieutenants, at least at Corporate. Larry Bossidy, a new vice chairman and Welch's soul mate, simply would not tolerate fools or foolish presentations. These he shut down, curtly and rudely, but with little of the violence and volcanics of Welch. Ayn Rand wrote a book called *The Virtue of Selfishness*. I've often thought that Larry should have written one called *The Vice of Patience*. He demanded the "point" of the pitch be evident very early on and grunted or made darkly humorous comments if things weren't moving quickly enough in some productive direction.

I took a couple of knee-buckling shots in my career at GE, and one of the best came at the hands of Frank Doyle, our Executive VP, resident Irish intellectual, and (partial) Welch emergency brake.

One of our business leaders—from the motors business—had done an *avant-garde* presentation revolving around rethinking a 100-year-old business, and examining high volume segments to see if they are the source of its best margins. Often, he contended in his presentation, some of the biggest product lines were a drag on profitability and a distraction from focusing on some lower volume areas where we were making real money.

I—once again a business idiot with three or four years in the company—was thrilled by this pitch because it was about a best practice applicable to many. It was a teaching and sharing vehicle. But I was surprised by one negative reaction to it: Larry Bossidy's.

I told Frank Doyle that this was the kind of pitch we should *always* be doing, and the way we should all be teaching and helping each other in the future. I told Frank that Bossidy's view of it was, "That pitch was basically for low IQs." And then I said, "I don't understand; I thought it was terrific."

Frank's comment as he left the room: "I guess that sort of proves Larry's point."

The comment was meant to produce a laugh, and I did just that as I stood there shaking my head while extracting the *rapier* from my liver.

"I wouldn't let him manage my fucking bowling alley," was Jack's review of a pitch at Fairfield one day in 1984.

"Either you know more than you're telling me or this is a complete air ball." The "air ball" was thrown up by Zöe Baird, who some may remember as Bill Clinton's first nominee for Attorney General. Zöe was a senior GE lawyer, a decent and nice lady and, as I understand, a good lawyer as well. And even though Jack liked her, she did not present well, or "do well with Jack." Had Zöe not run into "a nanny problem" that derailed her AG nomination, I've often surmised that those children incinerated at Waco would today be well into their teens or beyond.

Corporate lawyers rank up there with engineers and environmental people as among the worst presenters. I was invited to speak to a group of GE lawyers at Crotonville and asked the leader of the group, a vice president, what I could possibly tell a group of people who made their living communicating well about presentations. "Isn't that how you all earn your money? By arguing cases in court?," I asked.

Her answer was, "Bill, you're thinking of *trial* lawyers; people like Clarence Darrow and Johnnie Cochran and people like that. Corporate lawyers are among the worst. They're horrible. They can't talk to business people without boring them, confusing them, or making them hate them. They need help."

More Change via Negative Reviews

Woe to the presenter whose pitch was not up to Jack's standards. Here are a few typical reactions.

- *"The first thing we're going to do next week is fire that poor, pathetic, low-energy _____ " (a string of obscenities so awful I wouldn't want my mother to read them).*
- *Entering a room to meet with me, along with Larry Bossidy, and saying, "Larry, I didn't want to be rude to him, but he was wasting our time." "Rude" was the euphemism of the day, and I had a vague vision of the EMTs trying to pull some maimed wretch out of a smoking crater next to a conference table.*
- *His capsule reviews of presentations he had just listened to were amusing, if one didn't think too hard about the career wreckage they represented:*

  "That was bullshit."

  "What a bore."

  "He did a hammerhead; a total hammerhead." People have asked me what that word means, used in that context. There are two meanings I can think of: one, an aerobatic maneuver; and the other, a species of shark. No, this is a proprietary "Jack word" whose meaning I don't know. I only know it was not a compliment when used to describe a presentation.

Another Jack favorite was "noodle" used as a verb, as in "Let's get together tomorrow and noodle this pitch"—meaning, obviously, think it through. The problem with "noodle" arose in his stuttering days, when the word would take two or three seconds to finally exit his mouth. The problem for the addressee was what to do with one's eyes until Jack finally got it out. "Business," believe it or not, was another word he had a terrible time with, leading me, in my early carefree, cynical years, to question "how can he run something he can't even pronounce?"

The effect of the stuttering, in combination with his ferocious demeanor in the early years, could be frightening to behold.

If he hated the conclusions or recommendations being presented to him, there would be a lot of animation and interruptions and shouting—but it was all the healthiest ferment and give-and-take—especially if the presenters rallied and fought back with data and intelligent argument. That made for an exciting day, and it never closed without him reassuring the presenters that while he thought their conclusions were—all said with a friendly face and voice—"insane" or "bullshit" or "nuts," they had done an absolutely *terrific* job; he appreciated all the time they had put in; and that Jim or Sue (their bosses, sometimes in the room) needed to know what a great job they did.

Most of the failed pitches to Jack, from my viewpoint, had flaws in their preparation—or lack of preparation. There was a lack of thought or what Welch considered a lack of seriousness—he detested even a hint of "flippancy." Don't fall into this trap.

Takes One to Know One

John McLaughlin and his whole McLaughlin Group, whom GE sponsored on TV on Sunday mornings, were "invited" (told) to do a version of their show after dinner at the GE officers meeting in Phoenix one October. McLaughlin, Joyce Hergenhan, and I had a few beers poolside at the Arizona Biltmore the day of the pitch. John, an erudite ex-Jesuit, has body hair like an orangutan. After a few beers he told me he might hire me as his speechwriter since he heard I was so good. I had just recently crossed the six-figure threshold, so I told him, smugly, that "he couldn't afford me." After a few more beers I pointed at his chest and shoulders and informed him that it was "too hot to wear a sweater at the pool."

My point was to outline what Welch wanted from John and his group: a half hour of not-recorded-for-broadcast *McLaughlin Group*; a "show" for the 150 or so GE officers after dinner. Welch had told me several times to "make sure he doesn't go on all night." I emphasized this to John, who verbally patted me on the head, and with endearing Jesuit pomposity told me "not to worry."

But I *did* worry, and I had the staging crew make up some very large signs that I would wield at the back of the hall. One read "10 minutes," another "5 minutes," then "2," "1," and finally a larger-than-life size authentic looking traffic STOP sign as my last signal. I showed them to John, who found them amusing, and gave me another Jesuitical "don't worry" verbal head-pat.

Welch asked me as the dinner wound down, if I had John "under control," and I said I did.

Dinner ended and the *McLaughlin Group* show began. The bickering about Reagan-era stuff was very good.

They were good enough that I let them run for 30 minutes before holding up the "10 minute" warning. The "5 minute" went up on schedule, and I could see in John's eyes that he saw it.

Finally, I raised the STOP sign and began waving it in the back of the hall, walking back and forth. We were at the 50- or 55-minute mark at this point and I finally noticed Welch, with his tablemates, laughing and pointing at *me* and my sign. I almost flipped them off, but continued to try to do my job and shut these people up. I considered for a few seconds having the audio visual people kill their mikes, but that is not something GE does to guests.

Finally, they stopped. It had been a fun night—although too long. I cornered Welch on the way back to the rooms and said, "I'm sorry; this guy told me he wouldn't run long, and I could see you laughing at me for waving the stop sign." Welch was still laughing and said, "Bill, don't worry about it. He's just an Irish bullshitter."

A more brutal and dangerous review of a presentation occurred at the officers meeting—now at Crotonville—in the '90s.

A new vice president at one of the businesses had done his pitch, which was familiar to me since we had rehearsed it, and I had heard him do it at the Boca meeting nine months earlier. It was great then and okay now.

Welch strode up the aisle toward the back of the room as the coffee break was called and said to Larry Bossidy, ominously and loudly, "Larry, did we make a mistake making this guy an officer? He put no time in on that pitch, no new thoughts. That was the same speech he gave at Boca. I think we made a mistake." Twenty officers probably heard this. They were *supposed* to hear it.

I found out that, happily, the presenter recovered from this disaster and has done well ever since.

Never get up and do the same pitch over and over. Never do it twice in front of the CEO or senior people who can influence your career. The core speech can be the same, phrased differently, but there must be evidence of intellectual growth, new data, new anecdotes, new thoughts, or you will be labeled a tired hack regurgitating past glories and dancing to golden oldies. Old is sneered at.

"Same old" is death.

Dead Man Talking

At Crotonville, GE's beloved management school, Welch tried his very best to restrain his volcanic nature. While he had taught many courses, he had never attended a course there since it was opened in the '50s. I think he was secretly proud of that. We've all heard self-made gazillionaires brag that they never went to college. Dr. Welch was probably like that about Crotonville, although he never bragged because that would have implicitly denigrated Crotonville—which he loved. He spent *billions* on it, and its training programs, over his tenure.

Crotonville is no picnic, particularly for the senior classes who, in the '90s typically spent three weeks or so studying some particular issue of direct interest to GE. Some of the classes lucked out and were assigned Western European problems. Others spent their time in Eastern Europe, Russia, or industrial Mexico.

One of the first Crotonville class "report-outs" to Jack and his Corporate Executive Council was a total disaster—because of mistakes that eventually prompted me to write this book.

A young man from India, making the presentation on behalf of the class, could not seem to get to the point. I live and die with anyone on the podium, and with increasing angst, and then horror, I got the impression that he was simply not well prepared.

Jack *jumped in* on this guy's pitch and tried to get it back on track, even offering observations to support what he thought the speaker was trying to say or should be saying. The presenter didn't get the message, but everyone else in the room glumly and silently did. His frozen smile became even more fixed as he meandered through streams of trivial data and methodology.

Welch, after asking four or five questions designed to get the disaster back on track, finally flopped back in his seat with a theatrical gesture of resignation, and fooled around with his mail or some papers in front of him until the poor soul dribbled off and left the lectern.

Afterwards, I said to Welch, "That didn't go very well, did it?" And his reply was, "It was a *disaster*. He got lost in detail, grinding us through the minutia. It was awful."

I never heard of the guy again. How could he blow the career opportunity of a lifetime?

After witnessing the disaster just described, I decided it might be a good idea if I spoke to the classes after they were a couple of weeks into their project and get them focused on the direction they should be moving mechanically, and in their approach, to make Jack happy. Please understand that this was not an exercise in toadying or ass kissing. Neither Welch nor I ever suggested the *answers* the class was supposed to supply, but rather the *kinds* of things he wanted them to tell him and his Corporate Executive Council—which included the CEO of every business in GE.

I would call Welch up, or go see him, after giving him, by note, a little time to think through what he wanted to tell me. And then I would fly to wherever the class was to tell them what "Jack was looking for." I had enormous credibility, because people knew who I was and what my job was, and because I would start most of the pitches by saying stuff like, "I'm only going to take 20 minutes or so of your time, but I've seen probably 40 or 50 of these presentations—good, bad, and ugly—and I know what works and what doesn't, particularly with Welch. And I just spent a half hour with him yesterday talking about, *specifically*, your class and what he wants to walk out of the room having learned after your pitch next week."

Talk about having their undivided attention. They knew I was there with no other agenda than to make sure my GE brothers and sisters won. And none of the students I *ever* spoke to fell on their asses after I spoke to them.

Make sure what you plan to present is spectacular. Try it out on smart people. Get help from somebody who has presented to this individual before. Ask an opinionated jerk like me for a view and some help. This may be the only chance you get to pitch to this individual, and you need to walk in the room loaded for bear and knowing you have a great pitch.

"Stop Construction Today"

Take the time to find out where your audience is "coming from" and its desires. In other words, what do they want to hear from you? Pick up the phone and call the big shot himself (or herself) before you go in. Why is that unthinkable?

Welch had various ranges of accessibility, but I guarantee that if some 35-year-old business management class presenter called him up and said, "We've got a ton of data on this study, but the class is split as to whether you are interested in what geographic areas we need to focus on in Mexico, or whether we should raise or lower our presence here. We only have an hour with you guys and we don't want to miss the target. What are you looking for?" that person would have received a response. An approach like this would produce enormously useful data that would, more often than not, change an entire approach to the talk and guarantee its success. Often the presenter would realize he was 180 degrees ass-backwards from where Welch wanted him to be. I used to do exactly that on the few occasions I got stuck in the logic flow of a speech I was doing for him. After explaining my frustration, he would erupt with clear, incisive, and sometimes spectacularly elegant phrasing, and a 10-minute phone call would save me days of wandering aimlessly through my own rhetoric.

Sometimes this technique of "smoking someone out," while inevitably effective, proved scary, particularly in the early "violent" Welch years. Jack was named Chairman of the National Academy of Engineering (NAE) in the mid-'80s, a very prestigious appointment. But it was a group for which, I suspected, he had little affinity or affection.

His maiden speech to this group was coming up, and I couldn't get him to focus on it. He kept telling me to "work" with Fred Garry, a VP and pretty much the top engineer at GE, a job that ceased to exist after he retired.

Fred and I "noodled" this speech on several occasions, but really couldn't get anywhere without knowing what Jack's view of the group was, and where he wanted to take them. Fred had some views on what *he* would like to say, but felt that they might not be anywhere near Jack's views—which remained a mystery.

So I decided to put a stick through the bars of the tiger cage.

I was walking by the office of Joyce Hergenhan, my boss, and spotted the Chairman running around and waving his arms in front of her desk. I waited until I saw what looked like a break in the action, and barged in.

Jack lit up—he liked me, or so I thought—and went into the, "How are you? How are things going?" Then the shift into high gear: "How's the NAE speech going? You and Fred come up with anything? It's only two or three weeks away. You got anything?"

I said, "Well, we'll come up with something soon, but we both kind of think (and here the stick went through the bars into the cage) that *you really don't know that much about engineers as a group, and don't have any views that we might make into a speech. We'll do some shit for them that you can read.*"

The last part didn't get across, because the *you don't have any views* part, piggybacking on the *you don't know that much about* line set off a spectacular explosion, at God knows what decibel: "NO VIEWS? YOU DUMB SHIT!!! I'll tell you what my views are on these people. They're a bunch of academics puttering around in the lab doing 'pure' research shit that nobody cares about. We're getting our asses kicked by the Japanese, and they don't have a clue what's going on in the marketplace. They need to get out of the labs and into businesses and help them win…"

The tirade continued, and then slowed as I eased my way out the glass door past a row of pale secretaries with their hands folded and eyes downward, and scooted down to my office, about 60 feet down the hall, past more people scattering or closing their doors as if an air raid siren had gone off. I plopped into my chair—after shutting *my* door—and began writing "bullets." *I had the speech*, and I wrote bullets for five minutes or so until I looked up at the noise of the door opening to see the little bastard sheepishly saying, "Bill, I hope you don't mind if we get a little 'loud' around here sometimes." I had a big grin on my face, and said, "Don't *mind*? This is *exactly* what Fred and I have been trying to get out of you for weeks."

Then I asked, "What did you mean when you said they should 'get out into the businesses'…?" He plopped down in one of my chairs; I hit the tape recorder button, and a pretty good speech was born.

Some of the engineers who were dumped upon during it didn't like it, but they got the point.

The secretaries and some of my colleagues all expressed condolences after he emerged and went back upstairs; but I had a *great* day, and had learned—or relearned—something that I had always instinctively believed: Don't talk about anything you don't really care about—care passionately about.

Some of the guidance Welch gave me to pass on to the Crotonville classes is useful to most anyone in similar situations; for example, "reporting out."

He always told me to tell them to drop the "how hard we worked" section of the presentation, which would regale everyone with how many factories they visited, how many other-company executives they interviewed, how much data they accumulated. He would say, "I *know* how hard they worked and this was not a fun trip, but just tell them to tell us what they learned and their views on *what we need to do.*"

One of the several BMC classes dispatched to Mexico to investigate a specific issue returned to make a presentation to the Corporate Executive Council—once again at Crotonville. One of the findings they presented was that one of our power systems factories, currently under construction in the Monterey area, was simply not a good idea because of rapid worker turnover and other factors, mostly demographic. Bob Nardelli, then head of power systems, later CEO of Home Depot, and now, Chrysler, was asked by Jack, from one side of The Pit, "What should we do about this, Bob? Doesn't sound good, does it?"

Jack then said, outrageously, "What does that 'guinea' on the other side of the room think?" referring to Paolo Fresco, Vice Chairman and Jack's best pal at the time.

Paolo, as I recall, agreed with killing the project, and a couple of the class members, while shocked or perhaps amused by the crudity of the ethnic slam, added some concise, reinforcing comments. Nardelli went back and forth with them and noodled it with Jack; and then Jack said, "We'll stop construction today. Shut it down."

A huge investment, tens of millions, stopped on the recommendation of a class at the company's management school.

On to the next issue.

That's the way a fast, communicating, learning company works: calling "automatics" after powerful, data-based presentations from respected managers.

A pitch along the lines of "A Vision of GE in Mexico 2000–2010" would not have produced action. In fact, it would have been impolitely ignored.

I've never heard a GE pitch criticized for being too specific. "Too complex," often, but never too specific.

"Conclusions people can walk out the door with...!"

When I went to BMC in the mid-'80s we would spend almost the entire three and a half weeks holed up in the campus classrooms "drinking our own bath water." At the end of the course, a vice chairman would fly in, and the helicopter would shut down long enough for him to listen to our esoteric and gaseous recommendations. He would pat us collectively on our heads and praise us for our "contribution." I forget what the contribution of my class was, aside from raising the bar of rudeness and bad behavior. He would then hop back in the chopper, and the class would head for the Rec Hall and a beer.

Crotonville really works for GE. The drama of a plant being stopped in its tracks based on the recommendations of a bunch of "students" sent a message across the management of the company: "They listen to and act upon what we say, so we can't get up there and bullshit with a 'What I Did on My Mexico Vacation' pitch." Every presenter is a valued consultant, or should be.

Jack's views, which I recorded, made into overheads, and showed to the classes the next day, were:

"I want conclusions people can walk out the door with. Not a lot of details."

"What are other companies doing?"

"How fast are we going, in their opinion? Fast enough? Too fast?"

"If not fast enough, how do we make it go faster?"

"Where do we need more resources?"

"Do we have the right people?"

"What should specific strategies be?"

"Do they think there is a serious enough commitment across the businesses?"

"How important is it perceived in the organization?"

"I want specific recommendations. Add an officer? Buy two companies? Name those companies."

Every Biopsy Doesn't
Have to Come Back Positive

Welch sent another BMC class off on a quest to see if we were "missing anything" in post-Soviet Russia. The class spent a few weeks in several grim, polluted, industrial cities with Stalinist architecture, and came back scratching to find something positive and opportunity-oriented to present to Jack and his henchpersons.

I spoke to them two or three days before they gave their presentation; and I spoke to Jack the day before I spoke to them.

"If there is nothing for us in Russia or if there are a lot of problems doing business there, it would be a big hit if they just gave us their most candid impressions. That's hard, because a lot of times people think if they tell you 'it's shitty' they get a bad grade on the presentation." The class exhaled with relief when I threw that Jack quote up on the overhead. They went on to give a grim, candid appraisal of the opportunities in Russia at the turn of the century: Not here yet, maybe in a decade.

Welch loved them for their thoughts, the rigors of their hardship tour, and their candid advice to their company.

Don't feel you have to—or make your people feel they have to—put lipstick or rouge on any pig they are asked to evaluate. A well-done "thumbs down," must become, culturally, as big a hit as a wildly positive evaluation of an opportunity, and if they tell you it's shitty your whole organization must know that they will not get a bad grade for their candor.

Think of those presenting to you as consultants—highly paid consultants—because that's what they are, or should be. Demand useful recommendations from them.

Presenters, think of yourselves as consultants. Think of yourselves as receiving a nice check for what you are about to provide. Would you be embarrassed by or proud of, the value you were providing your customer?

I'm Okay; You're an A-hole

It was no longer "okay" at GE to do a lousy pitch, even if done at relatively low corporate levels. A culture of excellence was growing all through the '80s, and pathetic, boring, and pointless presentations stood out more and more.

Welch, as lead dog, constructed the paradigm of how a leader should listen and react to subordinate pitches. An NBC presenter, full of himself and his business as he wove a tedious tapestry of Hollywood crap and pretentious showbiz jargon, froze as he finally noticed Welch gesturing with one hand to "C'mon, move it, get going."

Then there was the high-pitched interruption—"Got it!"—during another ponderous snoozer. The presenter, in this case, actually looked flattered, momentarily mistaking the cry as meaning Jack understood his point. So he continued. After another 30 seconds of slogging with waders through the muck of his presentation, the eerie falsetto rang out again—more urgently and increasingly angrily. "Got it! *Got it!*"

The presenter, at this point, realized that "got it" meant that he was supposed to move on to other points of interest—if he had any. Smoke billowing from the cowling, oil on the windshield, and the altimeter winding down rapidly, he zipped through an abbreviated version of the rest of his badly prepared talk and crash-landed on the podium.

I visited Welch one time to work on something, and found him chuckling like a 12-year-old. He had just seen a press clipping that said George Stephanopoulos, a former Bill Clinton staffer, was being considered for a job as an NBC news commentator—NBC was now owned by GE. Welch had just fired a missile. He sent a fax copy of the news report to Bob Wright—President of NBC—with a clearly drawn cartoon of a human fist with its middle finger extended. There was no other message and no signature, which made it even more effective. He had done this "digital decision" drawing on other issues—large and small—hundreds of times. I think I once suggested he have a rubber stamp made of it, to save drawing time. He showed the Bob Wright fax to me and said, "Stephanopoulos! What do you think of that? Look what I sent Bob! Stephanopoulos! That liberal asshole!" I laughed in amazement at this, another succinctly expressed, major business decision (sorry, suggestion) and thought, "This has to be the most fun job in the capitalist universe, and I don't know of anyone in the world more suited to it than Welch. Or anyone who would *enjoy* it more."

Bulletproofing the Love-In

Jack spoke to my class, and two others assembled in The Pit that beautiful June, and announced that we were "reducing our presence in the defense industries"—or some words to that effect.

The reason we were reducing our presence—despite just having bought RCA, with its huge defense offerings—was that Welch hated the way GE was painted as sleazy because of some stupid "time card violations" (that were almost an inevitable part of defense-related dealings with the government). But also because of the protesters at the front gate in Fairfield and at the shareowner meetings. The protesters were the only negatives in what I used to refer to as "the annual love-in."

Years later, after two or three stock splits, the annual shareowners meetings became the most enjoyable event of the year. On one occasion the stock hit its *all-time high* on the morning of the meeting. Welch warmed up the crowd that day with a hilarious commentary on "the luck of the Irish."

The highlight of one of those shareowner meetings was an impassioned speech by a black minister to the GE board of directors seated up front. He warned the board that if they did not "pay this man (Welch) more, they were going to lose him to another company."

Yeah, right. Maybe to U.S. Steel or Union Carbide. Throughout this eloquent peroration, Welch wore a Cheshire-cat grin, occasionally glancing down at us in the "bulletproofing-for-the-board" section as I laughed and made stealthy puke gestures with my finger on my tongue.

At another meeting, near the turn of the century, when "CEO compensation"—or over-compensation—was the issue *du jour*, Welch began that chapter of the meeting with a deadpan pronouncement: "The next shareowner resolution addresses executive compensation. 'So-and-so' will speak in favor of this resolution." Then, after a pause as the irate shareowner approached the aisle mike, he continued, "This should be fun."

A couple of the board members for whom I was bulletproofing and I were in hysterics. Welch, with a barely concealed grin, focused his eyes where we were sitting in the front rows. The individual, who respectfully delivered a well-rehearsed view of why all of us, but specifically Jack, made too much money actually heard a couple of catcalls and "sit downs" from some of the shareowners, who were enjoying the rush of the orbiting stock price and didn't care how much Welch or any of his executives made as long as the stock kept moving.

Welch ran the shareowners meeting with an occasional surreptitious glance at his clock. The pace was dictated by the necessity to be out the back door and "on the bus" by about noon, and at the airport a half hour after that. The GE fleet of G-2s, Challengers, and Citations were filled in a highly choreographed boarding, before they taxied, one behind another, to the end of the runway. Some were headed for GE towns like Schenectady, Ft. Wayne, or Louisville. "GE-One," as I called it, and another G-2 had Augusta, Georgia locked in their NAVs.

The annual meetings were all east coast, and usually *south*east coast, affairs deliberately held at locations with three key qualifications:

1. cities where healthy GE manufacturing or service facilities were located, so the sites could be toured and shown off to the Board and local media by Jack;

2. cities that were "out of the way," that could seldom, if ever, be reached by a direct flight from pain-in-the-ass liberal fever swamps like New York or D.C.; which meant that only hardcore anti-defense hippies and nuns would make the multi-change trip; and

3. cities within less than an hour-and-a-half jet time from "the holy land," Augusta.

This was so the Board, among whose qualifications Augusta membership was very favorably viewed, could assemble at the first tee, put the ball in the woods, and be done by dark. Senior GE officers were invited to fill out the foursomes by Jack's invitation—the ultimate perk.

Welch, while in GE-One, would sometimes whip the pilots like a musher on the Iditarod. If the digital display in the cabin dipped below 500 knots or so, questions would be yelled into the cockpit, such as, "What are we doing, saving gas?"

On one legendary trip to Augusta (after I had returned, forlorn, to Connecticut, on one of the company planes despite Welch's *promise* to get me "on Augusta"), the board arrived and got in a round despite threatening weather. The forecast for later sounded worse, and Jack announced a road trip. Everyone piled into the G-2s and zipped down to Seminole, in Florida, another of the best courses in the country. They enjoyed a round or two under sunny skies with the boss monitoring the Augusta weather. The forecast indicated that it was clearing. And *voila!* Back into the planes, boys, and back up to Augusta for another round!

This type of obscene excess can only be justified by smashmouth business performance and warp-speed stock performance.

That we delivered.

But the bedraggled hippies and mannish nuns that demonstrated and hectored us at the shareowners meetings, and paraded at our headquarters gate, really *bothered* Welch. While we didn't dump most of the defense-related businesses to Lockheed Martin because of these irritants, I think it was a factor. He wanted GE to be loved by everyone.

Jack, while at Crotonville, said that he "was an altar boy" and a Catholic, and being lectured by these nuns about the incongruity of a company that brought "good things to life" while simultaneously making nuclear weapons components and—my favorite—Gatling guns, was "disturbing," and "got to him."

I had a different view. I had been educated by nuns for my eight years of grammar school and generally loved them. My Confirmation name is Vincent—in honor of Sister Agnes Vincent, whose signature I still have on one of my report cards, festooned with gold stars and nothing but As.

I peaked, academically, in fourth grade.

I am a nun fan and a reasonably devout Catholic. Still, I gagged at the sisters who showed up at our meetings. You expect nuns to be plain. But there was something about the nuns that showed up every year at our meeting that transcended plainness: these nuns were in their fifties, wore flowered dresses and earrings, had salt-and-pepper cropped hair, and legs that should have been covered, for aesthetics if not modesty.

Jack would usually defer to them, patiently addressing their allegations that GE was a "war profiteer." I would fulminate and reproach him for placating these two or three "nuns" who upbraided him at the meeting. I called them "commie bull-dykes" and other unpleasant names. Jack would ignore or silence me, citing once again, his lingering Irish Catholic guilt.

But the nuns always live somewhere in your thoughts and dreams, especially if you grew up Catholic in the '50s—as I did—or '40s, as Welch did.

One day Jack and I took the chopper from Fairfield and went to a convent. It housed one of our chief antagonists, a sister who was involved with

Catholic hospitals and was attempting to get GE medical systems equipment barred from them because we helped propel the U.S. Armed Forces airplanes and helicopters with our jet engines. Jim, a GE medical systems vice president, came in the chopper with us.

"Why are we kissing their asses?" I would ask. "Catholic doctrine doesn't forbid national defense or supplying the military. Why aren't these sisters teaching kids or caring for the sick like they're supposed to instead of flying around the country to shareowner meetings to harass us on defense or PCBs?"

I sometimes thought I saw a glimmer of agreement in his eyes before he gently told me to lay off the nuns; that he had to do this.

The helicopter pilots had a hard time picking out this convent, which was in a wooded mountainous area of, I believe, Pennsylvania; but we found it and set down. Jack and Jim set off to the nunnery leaving me and the pilots at the helicopter. The last thing they needed at this meeting with "Sister Rosetta Stone"—as I was calling her—was input from me. I have no idea why I was asked on this trip.

As I sat in the helicopter with the doors open on this warm day, I saw coming from the woods, two- and three-abreast, like woodland creatures, *the real thing*—'50s-style nuns in full habits, smiling and shyly approaching the helicopter, something that I guessed none of them had ever been near.

They had no idea who we were or why we had set down in the field near their convent. I told them Jack Welch from GE was here to see Sister what's-her-face. They smiled, having heard of GE, although obviously not of Jack. I wanted to take the eight or nine of them, in shifts, up for a ride, but the pilots were frightened by that thought and said something about "not having enough fuel." So I had them take turns sitting in the plush seats, offered them sodas, and even a couple of beers from the bar, part of the helicopter interior designed by Jack, a proposition they thought was amusing.

I told them about the Josephites, "my nuns" from my childhood, and that my cousin Peggy was a nun.

We had a great time, and by the time these warm, Godly women had gone back into the woods to "get back to work" somewhere, Jack and Jim had returned from their meeting with the nun-in-chief, which they said had "gone well."

We took off, and we saw several of the sisters waving from the grounds below. Jack was delighted that I had made some friends for GE—although we would never see anyone who looked like *these* nuns at a shareowners meeting.

By this time, Jack was tired of the nun stuff; and he turned to counseling our VP friend Jim, who was getting remarried in the near future.

The counseling focused on how you "pull this off" without World War III, and Jack's key point was to "make sure your children are at the wedding. It's critical."

I chimed in, adding, "That's a best practice." Jack, teaching and sharing, said, "Absolutely. A best practice. They have to be there…" I think I fired up one of the beers I had offered to the nuns, and the rest of the details of that nice day have long since gone away.

Part V

Death by Presentation at NBC

As the '80s headed for the '90s, the stock headed ever skyward, and with the cleansing of the Boca 500 long since accomplished, GE began, more and more, to assume the character and personality of its leader: aggressive, hands-on, mercurial, impatient, and loathing of anything that smelled of mediocrity, dishonesty, bureaucracy, or lack of a "110 percent" passionate effort. When any evidence of these surfaced during a presentation made at corporate, or to the Welch generation of corporate leaders, unpleasant things began to happen.

Losers are interesting—sometimes as interesting as winners—and can teach valuable lessons by their failures. One of our famous aircraft engines VPs, "Herman the German," said years ago that, "no man is totally worthless. He can always be used as a bad example."

But the "totally worthless" became an endangered species from the beginning of the Welch regime, and became genuinely rare—at least at corporate—in the '90s.

There were, I've read, and been told of, "mummies" in Jack's pre-CEO days. The mummies were people who would be hidden or put "under wraps" whenever Jack came to the site. Their humane bosses were trying to get them over the finish line to full retirement.

Or the mummies were people who were judged as smart and talented at what they did, but came across as idiots and "did not do well" when presenting to Jack. They were advised to "take a couple of days off," or do something "out in the field" when Welch came to town. Sometimes Welch would ask, "Where's Harry?" and would smirk or become angry when told where he had, in effect, been hidden.

Larry Bossidy had, if anything, a lesser ability to suffer fools than Jack. He, as my remaining readers may recall, rendered the "basically for low-IQs" verdict I recounted on the pitch I liked, and summed up another as "the most ridiculous shit I've ever heard in my life."

Larry is big and gruff, and capable of extreme curtness; but a very decent guy, with "meaty ears" (a description in a business publication that I found strange, and even gross). His rejections of idiotic presentations were more dismissive than angry; and not as confrontational as those of Welch or Dammerman—our CFO.

Dennis Dammerman, more feared in some ways than all of them, including Welch, had a zero tolerance for fools, and for poorly prepared presentations.

"The thing that drives me crazy," he told me once, "is when they put up some broad generalization and then they don't give me any facts." He was apparently driven to angry, volcanic eruptions by a series of NBC presentations in the latter '90s that he sat through at 30 Rock.

You can imagine the wild enthusiasm with which GE's initiatives were greeted at NBC, which never really became comfortable with being part of GE, or assimilated into the GE culture. Despite this "the talent"—people like Brian Williams, the CNBC crowd, and Jerry Seinfeld—were becoming *very* comfortable with a life of owning stock options on a GE that kept soaring and splitting over a heady 15-year run.

Jack supposedly backed a dump-truck load of options up to Jerry Seinfeld's door in order to get him to stay one more year; and Seinfeld, to his credit, simply declined to take a great, but maturing, show into mediocrity.

So some NBC talent was comfortable—even thrilled—to be a part of GE.

Brian Williams told a couple of us, in Washington, that he would point to his deck, or some other addition to his house, and say to his children, "Mr. Welch built that."

But among the administrators, "creative" people, NBC news, and other functions, there were a fair number of people who felt they had become the unfortunate step-dependents of a crabby, boring stepmother who would have done better sticking to her knitting—making light bulbs and rust-belt crap like transformers—rather than trying to "manage" gifted and creative geniuses like themselves.

But NBC generally played the GE game—at least in part—because former GE housewares CEO, Bob Wright was NBC president. And Welch did cut them a little slack, being the groupie and starstruck Irish kid he was, and has always remained.

Dennis Dammerman did *not* cut them slack, and descended on NBC for a review of their execution of one of GE's initiatives in the '90s—a review that was described, the next day, in Fairfield, as "a strafing run."

The NBC presenters had apparently decided to try to finesse Dennis with a cloud of smoke and generalizations, exaggerating what—if any— effort NBC had put into the initiative being reviewed. And Dennis had immediately blown it all away. He then blew away the presenters—one of whom began crying under the onslaught.

It was not a glorious day; but from that day forward "blowing smoke" at the "suits" from Fairfield was considered a "non-starter," and was not, as I understand, ever done again.

Never, as the leader of an organization or a business or a component, walk out of a meeting room knowing you have been dissembled, or had "smoke blown up your ass." Walk out of any pitch, in your first days on the job, if you know it's a lie. Violently counsel anyone you believe has tried to trick you. Ream, even more violently, their bosses. The organization will resonate like a hive after your early "strafing run."

After this, everything becomes simple: public humiliation and hanging of anyone who ever delivers a presentation—or orders it to be delivered— that is not 100 percent honest. Hang them from whatever limb they inhabit, no matter how high in the tree.

Total candor does not have a lengthy learning curve. Instill it as your first management principle. You can instill the more nuanced things further down the line.

Peeing on the Kidder Body

Welch could be devastating when he saw what he called—and still calls—"candor" being violated.

In the late fall of '86, he asked me to meet him at some hotel in New York state—on a rainy, cold and miserable Saturday morning. The occasion was a meeting of 150 or so of the top people from Kidder Peabody, the crook-ridden Wall Street snake pit Welch had just, mistakenly, bought.

My job, besides giving him some "bullets" a week or so earlier, was to make sure the "setup" was fine for his remarks, and to provide a friendly GE face for him as he walked into a crowd that, while not hostile, was decidedly cool and possessed of a wait-and-see attitude.

"Superstar" Welch had just about arrived. He was fresh off a string of hits—notably RCA, with its jewel, NBC. As he volunteered in his first book, it was hubris and overconfidence that drove him toward the acquisition of Kidder Peabody—one that climaxed with the revelation of Joe Jett's perfidy; and Jack's subsequent puking in the bathroom of his house, as he contemplated the $350 million charge against earnings that loomed as GE prepared to go out with its quarterly earnings report.

Jack blew in from the cold, miserable day, entered the room, still with his overcoat on, and asked me briefly about "what had been said so far," before he mounted the small podium to talk. For the first eight or ten minutes or so I began to get a knot in my stomach because he seemed to be "going through the motions." He was not animated. He wasn't Jack. From the back of the hall, I could see the Kidder people—mostly assholes—kind of smirking at each other as if to say, "Is this the big-deal guy we've been hearing about?"

About seven minutes into the pitch he began talking about integrity and candor, and how both had to be the basis of *everything* we did. He continued with, "This thing could be *so great*, if honesty and candor are its basis." That set him off. The voice got louder and higher-pitched. The crowd actually leaned forward! The smirking stopped. People stood up and asked him questions, or took shots at him. He fired back, laughing and enjoying it.

At one point, the senior Kidder guy in the room stood up and delivered a mini-speech that even I could tell was bullshit—denying one of Jack's observations on his firm. My assessment was reflected, amazingly, in the faces and murmurs of the Kidder people.

Welch listened, smiled ruefully, and then said to the crowd, "It looks like we've got a long way to go to get to 'candor' in this place." The place erupted in nervous laughter. By the time he finished and left the podium, he had stolen the leadership, the hearts, and minds away from their now-wounded boss.

Terminally wounded.

I said to him after we left the room, "You were great; you blew them away. But what happened for the first few minutes? You *sucked.*" "I know, I know," he said sheepishly. "I just came in from outside and I was cold."

The subject of "candor" had warmed him up.

A Shout from the Bathroom

The culture of criticism grew at GE in the '80s and all through the '90s. You could no longer get away with a stupid, poorly prepared presentation at corporate without a distinct chance of being roughed up, or worse.

Jim Rogers, CEO of one of our businesses at the time, kept questioning a presenter as to what was "the point" of the data he was spewing, orally and visually, all over the meeting room. In response, the man would cough up even more data, until, in frustration, Rogers left his seat, grabbed the presenter firmly by the elbow, led him over to the screen, and demanded to know "*Exactly* what is the point of all of this?"

A friend of mine from another company sagely pointed out what this perpetrator/victim was trying to do at this GE "blow and go." My friend's company calls it a "show up and throw up," in which the presenter fires into the air, and up on the screen, everything he knows or has done, on any vaguely related topic, regardless of his audience having any interest in, or use for, the huge dump he is taking in front of the room.

The intended effect is to show how smart he is.

That is no longer the *actual* effect at GE.

Welch's critiques were angry and loud, dismissive (death), or sometimes hilarious.

On a few occasions, when we had been working all morning on a speech in his conference room, he would get hungry, as lunchtime neared, and invite me across the hall to the officers dining room, where he held court for a half hour or so while eating and badgering the waitresses for being slow.

The officers all sat on both sides of a long, King Arthur–style table.

One of the few days I ate with him and the officers, he had brought with him a copy of a letter he had been sent that was written by one of our very senior business leaders that intended to explain some GE corporate initiative to his 20- or 30,000 people.

The letter was not a success. It made *no sense*, and Jack read passages of it aloud, as we tried to eat, with inflections that emphasized the absurdities in what the man had written.

We were all laughing too hard to eat—soup especially. Finally he stopped laughing long enough to render his final criticism of the letter. "It's like something he yelled out the bathroom door to his secretary while he was sitting on the can." Laughter erupted around the table. "That's it exactly. *This is a shout from the bathroom.*"

I asked one of my officer friends who was sitting next to me, "How do you people eat with this going on?" He said, "He's usually only in here for a few minutes, or some days not at all."

Jack traveled a lot. But as my friend, Chuck Welch—not related to Jack— a GE manager, often observed, "When Jack was in Fairfield, everyone *knew* he was here." There was an aura about the place. The sounds were different. There would be a lot of scurrying among upper and middle managers, and occasional runs up and down the flight of stairs from the third floor by Welch. Secretaries fluttered.

Managers, watching the Tasmanian Devil rocketing by their offices, whispered on their phones, "I need to cancel my tee time."

I returned to my office one day from the gym, and Linda, my secretary, was clearly agitated about something. "Bill, Mr. Welch was down here looking for you. I told him that you were in the gym. He went into your office. He was in there a little while, and I think he 'did something.'"

I went to my office and investigated. Monday was the after-work, nine-hole GE golf league; and my loud and mismatched golf attire was laid out on one of the chairs in my office. On top of the clothes was a note written, on my stationery which had been taken from my desk. The Flair-pen scrawl was unmistakable. The note read, "This is a fag outfit. Do not wear outside. J"

On another day he flung himself through the doorway into my office and said, "Come with me!" Grabbing me by the arm he pulled me outside my door, into the hallway, and approximately 10 feet, to the next office, occupied by my speechwriter friend.

"Look at that!" Jack shrieked. "What kind of *mind* would produce something like that?"

My neighbor, a liberal, hyper-political, Oxford intellectual, and a Fritz Mondale speechwriter, went through the papers every day "clipping" and filing, sloppily, in folders, all over his office. Old newsprint stinks.

In addition, he would lean back in his chair, roll up pieces of whatever paper was handy, pop them in his mouth to classic spitball dimensions, and fire them at his waste basket, hitting roughly seventy percent. The collateral damage to his office environment was horrific.

I had no explanation for my friend's behavior, and besides, like Welch by now, I was laughing too hard to express an explanation even if I had one.

On one of his next visits to our floor, in search of some prey or other—I think it was probably me—I heard Jack push in my neighbor's glass door and ask, "Are you still here? (on the GE payroll) What are you doing?"

"Just trying to make a contribution, Jack."

"Yeah, well, you came for lunch and stayed for dinner," another '50s-era Irish cliché he wielded on occasion.

He really made the poor guy's day.

On another truly bizarre visit to our floor, he announced loudly: "I need to talk to some black people about this OJ thing," referring to the trial, upon which he was fixated.

He immediately accosted Betti Teel, Joyce's secretary, and said, "Betti, you're black; do you think he's guilty?"

Betti, who was apparently unaware she was black, expounded on her bizarre theory: it was actually another football pro who was the killer. Welch listened, fascinated, and moved on to playfully harass anyone else in his path, on his way down to my office to torment me.

The OJ fixation reached a climax when the jury went out the morning of our corporate officers meeting, and Welch counted the show of hands on what his officers thought the verdict would be.

After the verdict came in a few hours later, he got bored with the subject and moved on.

I once accompanied Jack around from breakout to breakout session at a big GE meeting whose subject and location I've long since forgotten. He and I entered and stood in the back of a fairly small room at one session, and saw the presenter flinch momentarily, and then continue. It was someone Welch liked, I could tell; but after two or three minutes with his new audience member, "Ed" threw-up an early PowerPoint chart—and it was a cluttered mess—an abortion. A horror.

That was Jack's cue. The shout from the back of the room was, "Nice 'Power Systems chart,' Ed. How long did it take to type that one up? What's it say? We can't read it back here. Ha, ha."

"Ed" and the "breakout group" of 60 or so laughed, and there was some kidding back and forth; and we left; but "Ed" had to know, as he closed his eyes that night, that he did not advance the career ball for himself that day—nothing serious, mind you, but no advance.

"Ed" needed to call in his communications person the next morning and tell him or her, "If you *ever* give me an unreadable piece of crap like that again and get me laughed at by the CEO and by my colleagues, don't bother showing up the next day."

And "Ed" would need to resolve, himself, never to throw-up an idiotic chart, regardless of the source.

The Wright Stuff

In 1986 Jack named Bob Wright, an old plastics veteran and lawyer (and high school classmate of mine, although I don't recall that being a factor in his promotion) to the presidency of NBC. Bob had worked at plastics, housewares, and GE Capital, as well as an outside stint at Cox Cable. The senior NBC establishment—namely Grant Tinker and Larry Grossman—wanted an NBC insider rather than a toaster-and-can-opener salesman to run the network.

Wright faced stolid, sullen opposition at NBC, with jokes and whispered ridicule about a GE "suit" and vacuum cleaner pimp being sent into New York to run something no corporate type could *possibly* understand. The NBC view was that network news was something sacred; and that only a corporate stiff could object to its losing tens of millions every year.

Grant Tinker wrote a book about his life in television that expressed horror at the GE takeover at NBC; and predicted disaster for the network, if GE management was allowed to pollute the hallowed culture at 30 Rock.

Bob Wright, after his selection by Jack, was in for intense grilling at press conferences and interviews. Every communication he would make to employees would be picked over, leaked, and ridiculed.

Welch had Joyce Hergenhan, his VP of PR, bring in an expensive pro, the late Jack Hilton, to do a "murder board" and prep session to get Bob ready.

Hilton was good.

Wright did generally well, as Joyce and Jack and I watched him and Hilton in the TV studio in the Fairfield basement.

He was loose—a little too loose in my view—but it was better that he leaned in that direction than into the "stiff" zone, which would reinforce all the stereotypes the showbiz types held about their new owners.

Hilton threw him some excellent curves, many of which revolved around the inability of an industrial outsider to manage "artists." Bob would parry them, often with some form of self-deprecating criticism—but then he'd go just a little too far. Welch would jump in and say something like, "Don't *say* things like that. What you have to focus on is this…" all the while assuring Bob that he was doing "a great, terrific job."

We did this for an hour or two, and finally closed with more enthusiastic pumping-up of the new NBC President by Jack; but as soon as Wright was out of earshot, Welch, genuinely concerned, said to Joyce and me, "He scares me. He thinks out loud too much."

Wright did and does, indeed, think out loud too much, turning loose his witty and often funny tongue prematurely in the process of engaging a first-rate brain; and he paid for it with satirized and snotty material sent, anonymously, to the press by the NBC people who hated being owned by GE.

But he, and GE, wound up succeeding at NBC beyond anyone's expectations—taking the network to new ratings and earnings levels, and running it with GE-quality management and financial controls. He did so well, that in the latter '90s *Fortune* magazine ran a cover story entitled, *How GE Saved NBC*.

Not being one to forget bogus maledictions from amiable egomaniacs like Tinker, especially about GE, I nagged Welch into sending the *Fortune* story to Tinker with a note suggesting, with mild sarcasm, that he might want to add an afterword to his book that had argued that GE ownership would ruin NBC. Welch did so, finally, and got a cordial reply back from Tinker, which he sent down to me with a note remarking on how Grant had completely missed the point.

Diversity Is Our...er...Strength

The diversity of GE, especially with the shocking growth of GE Capital, was not a problem for Jack, but he began to see our big annual meeting at Boca as an anachronism; with the 500 of us sitting there, from every conceivable business, and from the four corners of the earth, as an exercise akin to the UN General Assembly attempting a session without simultaneous translation.

For sure, we had gotten better, much better, than the absurd days of speechwriter "visions" and pompous predictions of the glories of the future.

The "visions" were long gone, but the self-absorption was still there, and if someone from locomotives delivered 15 minutes on how his new model was going to be technically superior to GM's, and if in doing so someone from major appliances picked up a couple of ideas on how to improve his next generation dishwasher—well, fine. To be honest, though, that was fairly rare. These were show-and-tell sessions, *honest* shows-and-tells, with Welch sitting there in the front row; but they were not as useful as they could be, and one day *would* be.

So one day in 1986, Joyce Hergenhan, my boss, walked in my office and said, "Jack thinks it's time to get rid of Boca. He doesn't think it's useful anymore, and he wants you to write a letter from him to all the attendees telling them why."

So I did, saying the things I knew were his views: that Boca was "becoming more of a habit than a necessity"; that we had grown in different directions, and that our problems were so different that it really was impossible to find "least-common-denominator solutions to them," and so on.

Which was all true.

I thought, however, that *he was making a huge mistake*, and I wrote *him* a letter arguing how important it was to have "the family" get together once a year to hear one another, network, and talk business on the golf course and at the cocktail hours. My biggest point was that "ending Boca would send everyone a message about GE—that we were, despite passionate denials, a conglomerate—the "C-word." That we were railing against in the annual report and elsewhere. Distancing ourselves from the conglomerate label was by no means mere vanity. Conglomerates typically traded at far lower earnings multiples in the market, depressing the stock price.

After a few suggestions on how we could improve the meeting, I closed with "I guess I just instinctively feel that the team, the family, needs to get together once a year, hear the boss, renew old ties, and make new ones. I would suggest you get a few opinions you respect before canceling our meeting."

I guess he did, or maybe not, get other opinions, but he told me later that he loved *both* letters—the one rationalizing *killing* the meeting, and the one making the case for *saving* it. Talk about having a wideband decision-processing capacity.

He decided to keep Boca; and we did, with an iron resolve, make it better and more useful to the 400 or so veterans, and the 150 or so "rookies" who arrived starry-eyed each year, seeing it as a rite of passage into the senior management ranks of the world's greatest company.

Every company of more than 500 employees needs "a Boca," but it must be a thrilling, inspiring, and useful event run from inception to execution by the CEO. He or she must write the agenda, or at least cull it from a menu furnished by his or her smartest people. The CEO must be omnipresent at the meeting, welcoming, intense with a sense of urgency—and sober. I've been to, and heard of, meetings of the Boca-type at companies facing real challenges—even in trouble—where the CEO is a passive spectator and delivers an obviously scripted "wrap-up" of things that need to be done, reads some word charts, and throws up some "targets" the CFO has given him for the coming year. There are no insights on how to achieve them.

He then stumbles around the cocktail reception and dinner, slurring. Don't have a meeting if you think this is an acceptable way to conduct it.

A male CEO may get away with two or three performances of the type I've just described.

One is probably lethal for a female.

Welch's management attention to communications and his fostering of a climate intolerant of what he used to call "canned speeches" played a big part in improving things, but little would have happened had he been a "reader," or a bore, himself, at the meetings at which he spoke.

At the October corporate officers meeting, held at the beautiful Frank Lloyd Wright Arizona Biltmore, Welch was in his rarest form during the mid-to-latter '80s. The remnants of the *ancien régime*: "hacks," "sluggos," and twenty other descriptive, often funny and often unfair and mean sobriquets, had been cleansed and sent to "the beach"; and in the smallish room were 130 or so of Jack's boys—and one "girl"—my boss, Joyce.

As usual, I was perched in the back of the room, in a "schoolroom" setting with tables in front of everyone, so notes could be taken. I sat next to Helga, Jack's secretary. We two were the only non-officers in the room. One year I leaned over and whispered to her as the meeting was about to start, "Did you know, Helga, there are actually some people in this room who make more money than I do?"

Helga was quiet, almost shy, and despite her important job, modest and self-effacing; but she leaned over and addressed me very seriously, "Bill, *I* make more money than you do."

And she did.

I would sit in back and see if Jack would use any of the ten or fifteen pages of bullets I had given him. Occasionally, I would hear a few of my thoughts, or a complete phrase or two, maybe a sentence; sometimes a short paragraph of mine jump out of his pitch; but it was almost all his, done from neatly handwritten notes that represented hours of work on his own. The points he made, he made with phrasing perfectly suited to his high-pitched voice and the occasional stutter. *Reading* something that I, or even he, had written would have been awful—an embarrassment—so he almost never did it, except for major "outside" speeches, or presentations such as the speech at the shareowners meeting.

And in cases like that we wrote them together over a couple of weeks; and together we made them "his."

No CEO or business should be without "help," especially if he or she speaks publicly on a frequent basis. But when speaking to one's own management or employees, it is, in my view, an abdication of leadership to read something written by someone else. Your people need to hear what is in your heart or spleen: your anger, your joy, your pleading if necessary—not some crafted rhetoric from a creature like me.

If you speak frequently to your people—as you should—a few 3x5 cards of "points" that reflect your passions can be kept in your jacket pocket or purse holster, and modified for the occasion as you see fit. Someone can help you with the modifications. The body of the talk must be all "you" and, most importantly, it must be known to be all "you."

Welch, in the relatively close confines of the officers meeting, would hold the room spellbound with a mixture of inspiration, pathos, menace, and humor. Everything he said was taken personally by everyone in the room.

Back in the early '80s—before options were given to "little people," as part of the "options-for-assholes program," as I called it—management awards were one of Jack's hot buttons. He had given his officers reserves of cash to hand out, on the spot, to heroes, and even mini-heroes, to get some excitement and energy pumping through this sclerotic, dusty old company. But these cheapskates were treating the money as if it were theirs *personally*—grudgingly doling out pittances only when they had to. Old GE thinking.

This drove Welch nuts, and he flamed them from the stage on the subject; and then downshifted emotional gears to an almost tender, intensely personal plea, "What's the matter, guys? We're all fat cats now, but don't you remember when three grand or even one thousand was a big deal—something you'd call home and tell your wife about? Don't you remember? There are good people doing great things in your businesses, and they're being stiffed! Open up and start giving out this money. Give out those awards to your good people. Do it."

They did.

The emotional atmosphere in the room was as intense as in the very early stages of a thunderstorm, with the ominous anvil cloud formation rising in the sky.

I recall watching a vice president, a "player," about three rows in front of me and Helga, pick up a pitcher and begin to pour water into the glass he held—when the ice shifted slightly, and started clinking. I could see, even from behind and off to the side, a panicky look come over his face, as he quietly set down the empty glass and the pitcher.

The dry glass could wait for a drop in the emotional intensity coming from the lectern that, at that moment, was way too intense.

"Well," you might say, "how difficult is it to transfix 130 people, most of whom you have hired, and all of whom you effectively "own?" *Of course* you would hang on his every word. He was in the process of making you a millionaire in an era when being a millionaire was still a big deal. How about putting him up in front of a cynical audience over whom he has no control, an audience armed to the man (or woman) with extremely sensitive and finely calibrated "bullshit detectors"; an audience whose "reviews" mean the gain or loss of billions—literally—in stock value?

Let's put him up in front of the financial analysts and portfolio managers who exert enormous control over the price of stock and see if this vaunted "wild man" can intimidate this audience into fearing the clinking of ice in its water pitchers.

You can "will" better communications in your organization:
1. *by refusing to tolerate bad presentations, made to you or to others;*
2. *by defining the characteristics of "good" and "bad" ones;*
3. *by* never making a "bad one" yourself.

Part VI

Pop Fly at The Pierre

Welch's debutante ball presentation as CEO took place at the Hotel Pierre, in New York City, on December 8, 1981.

His reputation as a radical, iconoclast, and bomb thrower had preceded him, and the analysts were genuinely anxious to see what this guy had to say and to hear his plan for building a fire under this Edisonian artifact whose performance was reliable, if not interesting, and whose stock had been snoozing peacefully for decades.

Welch's energy and voltage level were apparent to all present. The difference between him and his aristocratic predecessor was noted. Still, the presentation was not a triumph or even, really, a success. It was not a disaster—more like a mild disappointment.

The crowd of analysts was hoping to hear, that day, the "Vision," the "Plan"—the bold new course for GE that would send them racing for the phone booths like *Daily Planet* reporters in the Superman comics, with "buy" or "strong buy" or even "bail out" recommendations.

They actually got the "Plan," and didn't know it; and I suspect that Welch himself only dimly grasped it.

He started out by refusing "to withdraw from my pocket a sealed envelope containing the grand strategy of the General Electric Company." This, in retrospect, smacks of arrogance. It was more like *diffidence*, I suspect. But it would probably have evinced from me, thinking in retrospect, a response like "Okay, son, why don't you think about this 'plan' for a year or so, and let us know when you're ready to make a presentation to us."

What he *did* announce for GE was the *intention*—not just the desire—to keep within the company only those businesses that were, or could become, "number one or number two in their marketplaces."

Those that could not make that cut were to be "fixed, closed, or sold."

Financial services businesses, with a whole different set of market dynamics, were not subject to this triage.

This plan was dismissed out of hand as a wish or a slogan; and not a very good one of either.

The analysts knew GE's businesses. Besides the "number-ones-or-twos"—power systems, jet engines, locomotives, medical, and lighting—we had, literally, hundreds of other businesses, from toasters, potato peelers, and transistor radios, to Brazilian iron ore pellets, air conditioners, and odd-sized transformers. Many of them dated to Edison's time. None of these were "number one or two," and never would be; and yet most produced earnings, at least intermittently.

And this guy is claiming he's going to get out of these businesses? Get rid of them? C'mon.

The analysts didn't buy that part of the pitch, and nearly gagged on the rest, which consisted of the "values" that were to become "second nature" in the new GE. There was "reality"—seeing things the way they *are* rather than the way one *wishes* they were.

Then there was "excellence": "all of us stretching beyond our limits to be, in some cases, better than we ever thought we could be"; and what he somewhat inelegantly (I wasn't writing for him yet) called, "the human resource element—people working in an atmosphere where they feel assured in knowing that only the limits of their creativity and drive, their own standards of personal excellence, will be the ceiling on how far and how fast they move."

No one was particularly impressed with any of this and many deemed it rhetoric more appropriate to an employee meeting rather than to analysts, people who dealt with sales and earning targets, and more tangible strategic directions. "Number one or number two" was "too simple and not credible," and the "human resources" stuff was a yawn.

Welch's energy and fire and youth impressed the crowd, but not enough to raise GE's anemic 7.9 "multiple," which was nearly a full point discounted to the S&P 500.

What did he do wrong that we can learn from? Nothing, really. With 20/20 hindsight, I would have taken a pass on that pitch after less than eight months as CEO, and waited until another year, at minimum. Then I would have offered at least preliminary evidence of movement in the direction of the "Plan."

I remember, from the Pentagon, hearing about a new general arriving in the European Theater during World War II. When asked for a statement by the press, he said, "I'm glad to be here. When I've done more, I'll talk more."

Welch quickly began to "do more" and to talk more; and he immediately gravitated toward an approach of dealing with analysts that I believe deserves shameless copying by CEOs, CFOs, and other representatives of publicly held companies.

Jack told the GE investor relations people early in the game, "If you don't have credibility with these people you have nothing." As the '80s wore on, his presentations—particularly to the Electrical Products Group in Florida—were formulaic, but incredibly well received, and built on a common theme: "This is what I told you last year" (and he would slap one of last year's charts on his projector) and then, "This is what we did." In other words, this is what we promised; and this is what we delivered.

The main part of the presentation came next.

"This is what we're going to do this year," followed by this year's plan and promises.

On some charts all three parts were arrayed in succinct, readable, columns on one chart; "spun," and then the first two columns were crossed out and the focus put on the third column: "What we're telling you this year."

If one of last year's numbers or promises had not quite been met, that was pointed out clearly, reasons given; and then he would move on.

Actually, citing a "miss" or two enhances credibility, even—incredibly enough—if the "miss" has to be manufactured.

Think about this!

In any presentation, to any audience, you must "season" a success story—even a triumphant success story—with some commentary on "where we came up short" or "where we could have done better" or "if we had to do it over, we might have taken a slightly different approach." These are enormous credibility-enhancers. An unalloyed "success story" sounds like a "blow and go," and causes any audience to switch on its BS detectors.

Nearly 10 years later, Welch got his vindication at an analysts gathering at Long Boat Key, Florida. It was the apotheosis of the "this-is-what-we-told-you-and-this-is-what-we-did" approach. Welch, an inveterate score-keeper, had always resented the lukewarm-to-ho-hum reviews of his Hotel Pierre pitch to the analysts, and decided he wanted the last word on the subject, just as he had, with his sarcastic note to Grant Tinker. Subtly, but clearly, criticizing the critics is not ordinarily a profitable approach, particularly to people who "set" your stock price; but that is *exactly* what he did. Strolling into the meeting room that year, he threw a chart up on the overhead titled "December 1981—Hotel Pierre." Under this title, he listed three of what he considered to be his most important and prescient quotes from the Pierre pitch:

- *"In this slower growth environment of the '80s, the winners will be those who insist upon being number one or number two in every business they are in."*
- *"The managements and companies in the '80s that hang on to losers for whatever reason won't be around in 1990."*
- *"We believe this central idea—being number one or number two— will give us a set of businesses that will be unique in the world business equation at the end of this decade."*

He then—not exactly modestly—laid out his moves during the '80s that were consistent with the Pierre predictions.

- *In 1980, two-thirds of GE's revenues came from slow-growth core manufacturing and non-strategic businesses like natural resources. Ten years later, two-thirds came from high-growth technology and services.*
- *Whether guided by the ghost of von Moltke or some internal compass; or sheer force of will, Welch had managed to rack up 40 consecutive quarters of earnings growth, and had accelerated from high single-digit increases to consistent double-digits as the decade progressed.*
- *He had sold businesses that made up 25 percent of his 1980 sales, dumping, among others, the sacred cows of consumer electronics, housewares, air conditioning, and other things the 1980 analysts simply could not believe he would sell. He had doubled 1980 revenues, and drove operating margins to historic highs.*
- *He "alluded" to, but did not name, the companies that "hung on to losers for whatever reason"; and were not around as the new decade began. He would never criticize or ridicule another company, even*

if it were not a competitor. And you shouldn't either. It's "poor form," as the Brits say, and analysts react negatively to it.

In short, Welch rolled up his 1981 Pierre speech into a "Q-tip format"; and stuck it in the ears of his former doubters. And they loved it! Having the last word on the Pierre speech was not just an ego trip, although there was a fair amount of ego involved. This early part of his pitch tied into the important part, introduced *explicitly* as, "That's what I told you in 1980 and this is what we did. Now I'm going to tell you what we're *going to do* in the '90s."

The stock roared along. He had, in a decade, turned a hard bitten, cynical bunch of New York analysts into a bunch of groupies who would, as the '90s neared, pump the stock higher every year *in anticipation of his Florida EPG pitch*, without having an inkling of what it would contain.

Welch spoke to these analysts *on his terms*, and he made the rules. Even in the early '80s he would demand the *last* slot on the program, and told his people he would not appear if he didn't get it. He *always* got it, and delivered a "stem-winder" to end the meeting, making the analysts forget many of the previous talks from Westinghouse, Motorola, Siemens, and others; and exited the room to head for lunch—like Harry Truman on a walk—with an entourage of analysts backslapping and peppering him with further questions.

His performance at the meeting was designed not to make the presenters from other companies look bad—just not in the same league as GE.

One review I took off the Dow ticker in '92 had the following quotes—which should be read by any CEO—any leader—who doesn't think presentations are "that big a deal":

- *"Shares of Westinghouse Electric are down again today… following what one analyst called a 'lackluster' presentation by the company's president at a Florida analyst meeting."*
- *"At least two analysts cut their rating on the company's stock."*
- *"UBS Securities, Inc. analyst tells Dow Jones he reduced his rating on Westinghouse to 'Hold-Sell' from 'Buy' yesterday morning after ten years of recommending the stock."*
- *According to the same analyst, the "Westinghouse presentation was 'lackluster' compared to General Electric Company's and Emerson's, which were given on Wednesday. People came away somewhat concerned about the direction of the company under the new management."*

Not to speak ill of dead companies, but poor Westinghouse. Granted, they did not have the performance numbers that Jack had, but they could have done a much better job presenting what they *did* have.

The point here, and the point of this whole book, is not just that you must have a good "story"—and "good data"—but that you *can* learn, and *must* learn, how to put the best possible face on whatever you *do* have, by presenting well. The Westinghouse president came back from Florida with people questioning his leadership and management ability because he did a lousy job making a presentation! That may not be fair, but that's the way the world works.

Welch understood that; some of the others did not, and we feasted on the carcasses of their market value.

Welch would show up in Florida by himself, and be met by his investor relations manager at the airport. The IR people would have sat in on every pitch that they were allowed in; and the interrogation in the limo would begin: "How did Emerson do? How about Maytag? What about Whirlpool? What did they get asked? What did so-and-so (an analyst) ask? How did they handle that? What's the 'mood?' What do you think they'll focus on? Have you heard any 'concerns' about this-or-that GE issue?"

So, by the time our boy walked in from the Florida sun and personally turned on the "overhead projector," he was pumped and ready, and so was the crowd. The stock price rumbled skyward and one of the most powerful analysts (I believe it was "Jennifer" who had a barely pronounceable—and totally un-spellable—Polish last name, and great legs) began telling the media that GE was a "get rich slow" stock.

And that was fine with us.

In 1980 we had a total market value of $12 billion, which ranked us 11th among American companies. At the end of a decade of Welch analyst pitches, and, obviously, the business performance that they were based upon, we had a value of $58 billion, and were ranked *second* in the U.S. in "market cap."

The $46 billion increase during the '80s was the largest of any company in America.

How much of this was a result of "the sizzle of presentation" as opposed to "the steak" of performance? I don't know. But I do know that he could move the stock, almost at will, because he could present better than any business leader I have ever seen.

I'll tell you exactly what I mean. Much of that increase in GE market value took place in the latter part of the '80s. During the first several years of Welch's tenure he made several huge moves—selling the enormous Utah International Coal business, moving into Silicon Valley in semiconductors, robots, and computer-aided design. He reduced head count by more than 100,000, and began kindling a constructive—and destructive—hyperactivity that was waking up our old company and drawing favorable press and analyst commentary.

But, for the first five years, the stock just sat there and did nothing.

I got my first stock options in '84, and, after my boss, Joyce, explained to me what options were and how they worked, she added that they had "performance units" attached to them that would reward you based on the company's earnings performance—even if the stock price never lifted the options "above water." The "performance units" were a carryover from the '70s, when management morale was somewhat depressed, because the stock-price-based-only option certificates were more useful as toilet paper than they were for wealth accumulation.

The first option grant I got had the cushion and crutch of the aforementioned performance units. After that none did. We didn't need them. The stock had "lifted off," and ignition had come, *in large part from a business presentation that Jack made to the analysts in 1984—the most important, and effective in my view, of his entire career.*

Learn from this...

Welch believed, after three years of solid numbers and decisive actions, that the analysts were "not doing their jobs"—e.g., bestowing upon GE a "buy," or—better—a "strong buy," recommendation. He was increasingly impatient, and even cross with them, as the May analyst meeting approached.

He summoned his investor relations people (all two or three of them), sat them down, and told them that, within two weeks that he wanted to know every single objection each analyst in that room would have to putting a "strong buy" on GE.

When the allotted time had elapsed the IR people returned and laid out the data—the rap on every analyst and portfolio manager, and their views of GE. Welch then took Flair pen in hand and doodled a chart.

Black Clouds Lift the Stock

The chart was a masterpiece: a *tour de force* in the planning of an aggressive, audience-centered presentation. It was a data-driven, yet emotionally charged appeal to what turned out to be a spellbound audience, to change their errant ways and do the right thing: *hump this stock!*

He walked into the room that day, in his catbird time slot, with a Welch scowl on his face. Some of the audience members looked at each other as if to say, "What's his problem?"

Silence. The lights went down a bit, and he put up the chart.

There were six simply drawn "black clouds" at the top of the chart with accusatory labels on each.

He began: "*These* are the black clouds *you* have put over GE stock." He barked, piling on the guilt like a Jewish mother, the accusations on each "black cloud."

"*You* don't think we have a consistent strategy."

"*You* think we are too much into financial services and defense."

"*You're* not impressed with our potential top-line growth."

"*You* don't think we have an acquisition strategy."

"*You* think we're a 'GNP company'"; and

"*You* don't think the sum of our company businesses is greater than their parts."

Fair enough. That's what the investor relations people reported the analysts thought—and that's what they *did* think—many of them.

But underneath the black clouds were six bullets—each addressing the black clouds. And the high, urgent, menacing voice continued...

"When I get through with you this morning, you will *know* that:
- *We have a clear consistent strategy*
- *We are an array of strong number-one market position businesses*
- *Our earnings growth is not GNP, but* one-point-five-to-twice GNP!!!
- *We produce terrific returns*
- *We have more financial strength than anyone*
- *And we outperform* every one of our peers."

And then he began a frontal assault on the first "cloud," which he shook and shredded like my golden retriever attacking one of his stuffed animals.

Then on to the case for GE having strong market-position business; then top-line growth; then acquisition strategy; and then on down the line, blowing each cloud away with hard data.

Jack exited the room with his chastened entourage of analysts in tow, on their way to lunch. The way Wall Street looked at GE had been abruptly changed; and the stock embarked on a 15-year growth spurt that took us through five splits.

The reviews were awesome, and those of us who were not there—he wanted few, if any, GE people in the room—asked some of the analysts, "What the hell went on in there? Did he transfigure himself? Speak in tongues? Fly around the room?"

And they answered, "No. He just knew *every* attitude every one of us had developed toward GE over the years, and he basically stuck them in our ears. We hardly had any questions when he was through."

Jeff Immelt faced the EPG audience a year or so ago, and I, like a retired crank, sent him a letter and a copy of Jack's old "black cloud chart," and suggested he smack these people who are not "paying" GE for generally outstanding performance.

And Jeff used it in his opening, filling his black clouds with the prevailing analyst views that affect our stock today.

- *Capital allocation*
- *Too much cheerleading*
- *Too big to grow*
- *Too much volatility*
- *Quality of earnings*

Jeff's pitch got great reviews!

The Chairman and the Strawman

In 1996 Jack and I sat down to "noodle" the 1995 annual report letter. He said, right away, "Write this down. The hottest trend in 1995 was the rush toward breaking up multi-business companies and 'spinning off' their components. The obvious question to General Electric, as the world's largest multi-business company, is, 'When are *you* going to do it?' The short answer is that we're not. Breaking up is the right answer for some big companies. For us it is the wrong answer. 'Why' is the subject of our letter to you this year."

I asked him, "Who says we should be broken up? I haven't heard anyone say that?"

"No, no, don't you see? It's a 'set-up' to takeoff from so we can make the case for the way the company is and where we're going."

"So it's a 'strawman'?"

Impatient noise. I'm not 100 percent sure he knew what a strawman was; but he had the theory of the case mastered for attacking strawmen. What followed was essentially a restatement of his greatest strategic and managerial hits of the previous 15 years. Stock growth, top-line, inventory turns, acquisitions, dispositions, and on and on.

I chimed in again at the end of our first draft with, "We are a company intent on getting *bigger*, not smaller—a company whose only answer to the trendy question—'What do you intend to spin off'—is *cash*—and lots of it."

He and I, and Vice Chairman Paolo Fresco sat down to review the letter before it was sent to the printer, and Jack toyed with taking out my line about "spinning-off" cash. "Paolo, is this a little too braggy? Should we take this out?" He always debated taking *my* stuff out, never his. I started becoming angry and whined that it was the "best line in the whole letter." He said, "See Paolo, he gets snippy." He laughed and said "Okay, we'll leave it in." The line made up the huge business page headline in *USA Today* a week later. The stock kicked into overdrive. I went home and told Beth, "I moved the stock." I did, or maybe I at least helped move it.

And Welch made me *feel* like I really did, with notes and phone calls telling me about the reviews we were getting.

Welch resisted, well into the latter '90s, going to PowerPoint charts—until making the case for "e-business" made using his cherished overhead transparencies absurd. In the earlier years, as he slapped down a transparency on this or that subject, he sent a message to his audience that said, "This is *mine*. This is *my* chart, *my* thinking, *my* argument. *I* made it. *I* drew it. *I'm* putting it on the machine and *I* want you to look at it. *I* can defend it. Tell me what your problem with my case is and let's settle it now, rather than in some 'analyst report' or business news story day after tomorrow."

I only restate the obvious: If you have a crappy company with lousy people and no future, you should probably consider dumping it for whatever you can get and moving to Florida. But if you really have something with a future, get yourself a lectern, stand up at it, and *make your case*.

One big change that Welch made in his communications with the analyst community was that he held their behavior to the same standards, as an audience, as the standards he applied to his subordinates presenting to him; namely, that you cannot get away with throwing out some cliché, bromide, or generality without having the data to back it up. Doing so *as an employee* to Welch (or Bossidy or Dammerman or many others) would produce a torrent of abuse that would engulf you.

Welch would not exactly humiliate an analyst who surfaced some stupid generalization about GE businesses or markets; but after Jack's superficially good-humored refutation of what the analyst said; and the exposure of the lack of facts it bespoke, the analysts would never, without more homework, try it again.

Years back, Jack used to hold a small, invitation-only dinner in New York for a rotating list of analysts. At one of the dinners, during a period when the stock wasn't splitting fast enough for his taste, he again began chewing on them to raise their ratings. He implied that *not* to do so was inconsistent with the data, and potentially embarrassing for their careers if they "missed the boat" for their clients; haranguing them further that it was unjust, immoral, dumb…. They loved this type of over-the-top tirade because very few CEOs ever did it.

And he had the numbers to back it up.

During one of his dinner sermonettes, one of the analysts interrupted with, "Jack, what do you want? You're getting the average multiple for your kind of company…" He didn't get any further. Welch staged a histrionic assault on the blasphemer. "*Average*? If we're getting an *average* multiple it must mean that it is a fair multiple for an *average* company. 'Average' means, then, that there are some companies not as good as GE, and some that are better. Let's find out which ones are better…" He then literally went around the room and interrogated *each* of them by their names, which he knew: "Nick (or Jennifer or Claudia), name *one* company in our type of business anywhere, that's better than GE."

I was told he even began prompting the flustered, laughing analysts with suggestions for their consideration: "How about Siemens? Emerson? Allied Signal? ITT?" While Jack did not denigrate any of these companies, no one in the room had a candidate for a "better" company than GE; and the stock soared skyward over the next few days.

Bravado masterpieces were demanded of his business leaders, the CEOs of the various large GE businesses, who presented to the analysts many times during the year, on the power sector, aircraft engines, plastics, medical, and others.

And Jack, like a magpie, would hover around the presentation teams, coach them, direct them, and demand high levels of performance—gauged by stock price movement—from them all.

If you are a big shot, do not let staff write your presentations or your annual report letter for you. You need to sit and mine your soul and pour bile and passion all over a piece of paper on what these people really need to know about you and your company before you bring in people to back up what you say with rock solid data; and better phrasing, if you are not that good with words. If you are any good at what you do—and you must be if you have reached this position—you must have a feel for changing the minds of others and bringing them into the fold of your thinking. The first draft, even if crude, must be yours.

Don't Screw This Up

I worked with several of the analyst presentation teams, in high-tension prep sessions, advising on areas within my expertise, which was limited. The investor relations people, who were brilliant without exception, spun the technical and business stuff.

It was the early '90s. Ten or twelve of us are sweating through the final cut of an investor pitch we have to do in the *Saturday Night Live* studio at 30 Rock in about two hours. Jack was not on the program because it was on one large, but limited, segment of the company.

The board room door opens about a foot. Irish face inserted. Silence. Then—"Listen to me. Don't screw this up. You're talking to your wives or to guys at the bar. The minute you get too detailed—too 'grunty'—it's over. This is not some exam you have to pass on your business. Stay at 50,000 feet."

"And remember, each point on the stock is worth $1.8 billion in market cap for the Company.

"I want *two* points. Have fun…"

I think we got 1.5 points. Not bad!

A more modest version of the "attack the audience" approach occurred in 1992, as Welch and I prepared his testimony for the Dingell Committee hearing related to a horrible scandal that had come to light several months before.

The facts have been recounted before—in Jack's first book and elsewhere—but the scandal involved a crook who worked at our aircraft engine business. This guy fancied being called "Mr. Israel," and conspired with another crook—an Israeli air-force general—to steal millions of dollars of U.S. military aid to Israel, and divert it to a joint Swiss bank account. This crook was the only GE employee who was involved in the theft, but 21 GE employees were fired, demoted, or disciplined for not having detected the scheme. GE got a big black eye, including a brief suspension of our eligibility to deal with the government.

Welch was distraught that the whole company had been dragged down and through the mud by the greed of one dirty employee.

He railed on about this crooked bastard, and how it made us all "look like shit." Once, on the plane, I said, in jest, "Jack, the solution is simple. Just send an Irishman over there (to Israel) next time, and he won't form relationships with anyone."

He looked at me for a moment and then moved on.

Welch was summoned to testify before John Dingell, who was widely reputed to be a "nasty son of a bitch" if he didn't like you or thought you were a crook or dissembler. My kind of guy.

We began to put together Jack's speech to Dingell's subcommittee two weeks in advance, when Jack seized on the "hook" he needed—something that would allow him to go into the attack mode without making an insane assault on the prosecutors, the government, or the committee.

Sounds like a job for "*Strawman*"!

And Strawman showed his face in the scribblings of a few obscure pundits who had vacuously suggested that the GE engine scandal was a direct result of "hyper-competitiveness," "demands for performance," and so on. Of course, it was nothing of the kind. The GE crook and the general hadn't stolen millions because they were being "pressured" to be "competitive." They stole because they were thieves.

We made this point before launching into a blistering assault on those unnamed people who thought we needed to become *less* competitive to avoid integrity violations and corruption.

We really got into it, as Welch ran around his conference room, and I yelled out phrases that tracked with the assault. The Summer Olympics were being staged that year and I threw in stuff like, "Should athletes be less competitive so as to avoid the accusation of substance abuse? Should they run slower and jump lower to avoid being accused of cheating?"

There were shouts of enthusiasm and approval. He could turn anything into a party.

Jack said, in his final version, "We see no conflict between taking on the world's best companies every day, all over the globe, giving 110 percent and more—to compete and win and grow—while at the same time maintaining an instinctive, unbendable commitment to absolute integrity in everything we do."

I was given greater freedom to advise on the approach to this hearing because I some had "credibility": seven years of advising and supporting witnesses in front of often hostile and rude Congressional committees.

The original plan was to have Jack, our Executive VP Frank Doyle, and their wives, pull up in a limo in front of one of the Congressional office buildings and enter through the press and photographers.

I told Frank and Jack I thought this was a horrible idea. I painted a scenario of the limo pulling up, the two pairs of female legs extending from the seats to the pavement, and then the two middle-aged moguls, robber barons, crooks caught red-handed strolling arrogantly through the camera flashes and TV lights into the hearing room.

I told them that bringing your wife to a hearing at which you are to testify is considered so amateurish and *gauche* in Washington that it is almost never done—particularly if she is not there as a contributor, but merely as a "date."

Both Frank and Jack listened to me, as they occasionally did; and decided that the wives would be dropped off early and should come in by another entrance, to sit with me and the one or two other GE people in the hearing room.

It went very well. Welch blasted "straw" all over the walls of the hearing room with a spectacular "read" of the speech; and the committee, including Dingell, was pleasant and complimentary toward GE.

Several members of the press, after salivating over a potential bloodbath, walked out the door scratching their heads, wondering aloud, "What the hell happened there?"

"What had happened" was that we paid $69 million in fines a week before Jack testified, had lobbied the hell out of the relevant Congressional staff members, and had made the case that two scumbags, neither of whom were named Welch or Doyle, stole money.

The 300,000 people of GE were innocent.

We reprinted the speech and sent it to employees, reporters, and financial analysts.

I can't prove it, but I think it moved the stock!

The "strawman technique" is extremely useful for dealing with outside audiences, but you should never use it with employees because there will be a stink of dishonesty about it—especially if you attack a strawman position that your colleagues will know is bogus.

They'll say, "Nobody believes we should do that. Who said that? That's bullshit."

Don't Care About It? Don't Do It!

I got a call in 2001, with the high-pitched benevolent voice on the line, as opposed to the scary, shouting voice-of-doom I've had to brace myself for on a few other occasions. "Bill, I'm putting you in the book!"

"Great, Jack, thanks." For some reason I hadn't thought about whether I would be in Jack's book or not. I'm not sure it mattered that much to me. I had never been a big player in the company, and besides, "ghosts" like me are paid very well to be unmentioned in memoirs.

So I showed up in the book. I was mentioned not in the body, but in the "back of the bus." My name appeared in the acknowledgments section; but what he said was a source of pride to me, and always will be—and there is an insight in it that you need to embrace in your presentations and communications.

He said: "I'm especially grateful to Bill Lane, a guy who worked with me on the annual report letters every year. Bill took them as seriously as I did."

That probably sounds fairly innocuous to you, and it should.

It was not: "Bill changed the course of GE communications forever," or something like that—because I didn't. What it *did* say was what kept me employed for 23 years working next to the third rail: I deeply, fanatically *cared* about everything I did for GE: annual reports, meetings, letters, speeches, whatever.

And he used to tell people, approvingly, that I was crazier and more radical than he was on every issue. And nastier. Ten or twelve years ago some friends from Australia, and my wife and I, were in Manhattan on a snowy day, watching a football game for a few moments through a store window, when a defensive player, rushing to make a tackle, injured his neck. It was one of those injuries where the players all kneel down and start praying that it's not "quad city," as they wheel him off.

Prognosis guarded.

Next day. Up to see Jack and Paolo.

Welch says, "Wasn't that awful that guy getting hurt like that? He may be paralyzed. Awful."

I said, curtly, "He was trying to 'spear' the guy (with his helmet). It was a dirty play. He deserved it."

Welch, running around the room, "Paolo, do you hear that? I spent the whole afternoon *dying* for this guy and praying that he's not paralyzed, and this prick says he deserved it! Unbelievable. All the time I'm worrying for this guy I don't know, and Bill thinks he *deserved* it. What a prick!"

And then laughing, helplessly, we all went back to work. The player recovered.

Welch used to use Paolo as a vehicle to break my shoes or just torment me.

I was summoned to his little conference room—I had been "on call" for an hour or so. I asked Rosanne what he could possibly be doing that was more important than meeting with me. "Is he 'tycooning' again?" That was a word I made up.

"Yes," Rosanne said, in her quiet, deadpan voice, "There has been some 'tycooning' going on, but now he's with Paolo, and I'll call you in a few minutes when he's ready."

I breeze into the room. Subject: annual report letter. "Hi Jack." "Hi." "Hi Paolo." "Hi *Beel.*"(Paolo's Italian pronunciation of "Bill")

"Paolo, let's see if Bill knows this. Bill, what does 'sanguine' mean?"

Hanging curve ball, so I crank it out of the park, or so I thought. "It comes from a Latin word that means 'blood.'" Welch nods. "It means you feel good about the way something is going to turn out. That you're optimistic."

Welch looks disappointed. "No, that's not it, but you got the 'blood' part right."

"What do you mean that's not it? That's what it means!! What do *you* mean?"

"C'mon Bill. Paolo has some ideas on the letter that we need to think about…"

Late into the day, and then at night at home. "He's wrong. And he thinks I was bullshitting. That's the gist of what that word means."

Multiple dictionary look-ups. Notes to Welch. Injections into conversations with him. No interest. Pure employee abuse.

Only speak on things you care about—really care about.

The 110 Percent Solution and Jack's Perks

I learned early the consequences of giving only 90 percent to Welch.

Welch, in the early '80s, auditioned several of us for the job as his writer. One by one we failed and were shunted back to the stable of speechwriters for one reason or another. My first failure was due, in part, to a perception on his part that I "did not care enough."

I was told to write a speech for Welch for some venue, and I did so. My manager reviewed it, found it had merit, and sent it up to Jack.

Days later we were summoned to his office, and we were told by Welch that this speech was "not bad," but had to have its direction changed in this-way-and-that. "Too much of this stuff. More on this, etc. Today's Monday. Let's do another pass on Thursday. Thanks. See you then."

So I went back down and pounded away at the changes he wanted for maybe four or five hours, including rewrites. Then I did other things, of which I had plenty; a couple of other upcoming speeches for my factory automation czar; something for Larry Bossidy, and others.

My manager reviewed what I had done for Welch, "blessed it," and sent it up again.

Thursday, he and I went up to Welch's conference room, and a while later Jack entered, finishing reading the draft as he entered the room, a habit I later came to hate, and often pleaded with Rosanne not to let him do.

He sat down—scowl-faced—at the opposite end of the table, picked up my speech with thumb and forefinger—like it was a turd—and said, "This isn't three days' work."

My manager went into controlled cardiac arrest, and began to defend all the improvements I had made to the draft. I probably smirked a bit because, after years of dealing with generals, senators, and big shots, I wasn't particularly interested in swooning before some guy who was being widely described by the older managers as a psycho. I had already decided, with my new wife, to leave GE and bum around the world for a year or two if my bonus was not at some number at which we had arrived.

In any case, "the number"—that I think was *15 grand*—was *not* met; but Beth had a teary announcement for me just days before I planned to burn my bridges; and we began to await the birth of Billy.

At WKL III's arrival, which was greeted by a bunch of flowers and a note from Jack promising to "buy him a beer" when he hit 18—the drinking age at the time. I had become "Jack's speechwriter" after connecting with him on a speech on tax and trade policy, after I was able to pick up his rhythm and *modus operandi*, instead of just trying to inject all the off-the-wall Lane stuff into it.

And I never—ever—would hand him something that was not the very best I could do.

Welch was named, back in the '80s, one of the "world's toughest bosses"—along with, amongst other people—Henry Kissinger, former Secretary of State to Richard Nixon. Kissinger, as the story went, would summon some policy wonk who had written a "position paper" for him, hold it up, and say, "Is this the best you can do?" The guy would say, "Let me give it another pass," then return in a few days and have the paper waved at him with the same question.

After two or three of these encounters, resolving each time to do better, the deflated, defeated wonk would say, "Yes, sir, it's the best I can do."

And Kissinger, according to the story, would say, "Alright, now I'll read it."

What an endearing trait in a boss! Kissinger had an arrogance and egomania that reportedly led Carolyn—Jack's first wife—to remark that the best thing about being divorced from Jack was that she "didn't have to have dinner with Henry Kissinger again."

Welch would never do something as arrogant and enraging as that. He was usually fair, and had an awareness of the possible consequences of being unfair. He asked me once, a little nervously, as I brought him down to the "departure" ceremony of someone whose department he had just blown up, "Is he going to throw rocks at me?"

"No," I said. "He understands. And he got a good deal." He *had* gotten a "good deal." And no rocks were thrown.

He only wanted fanatics, nuts, and true-believers near him—people that were willing to give everything they had in their beings to produce excellence.

He would tune out, and write-off, people who made presentations that had an air of "going through the motions" or "reporting" rather than passionately advocating some course or other. He loved the latter even if he disagreed with the course being suggested.

I would often hear reviews the next day on pitches made to him and he would chuckle and say things like, "Wasn't that Irish kid great; or the Indian guy; or that black kid? What a fanatic. They've really taken (Six Sigma or e-business or whatever) to another level. These guys are great." And when the S-IIs—the reviews on people—were held, that Irish or black kid or woman or Indian would be on Jack's agenda. Working from his "reminders" or "ticklers" he had Rosanne save for him over the year, he would ask, "Are you moving him fast enough? Are you sure? What are you waiting for? This kid's ready."

Sometimes this swooning moved people *too* fast, and the Icarian wings came off. One gifted young manager adopted a method of cost reduction—a "best practice"—that he borrowed from another company, implemented it at his unit; and shared it at a presentation at the officers meeting. The presentation was a success and it propelled him to a GE vice presidency at the tender age of 34 or so. He wasn't ready, I believe; and, in two years or less he was "sent home." He now runs, and runs very well, a major manufacturing company.

One of his fifty-ish senior VPs seemed to be less interested as time went on and departed comfortably after suggestions to that effect were made.

Another, much younger, and a key acquisition, worried Welch that he "might not be 'into this' as much as we are."

Yet another, 38-year-old Dennis Dammerman—anointed by Welch, as CFO and youngest senior VP in GE history—never lost the fire. Dennis told me once that he was not "remotely ready for the job," and survived only because "Jack had his neck on the line" and backed him through some rough times. He never lost his edge and his fire, and many people I knew were more comfortable dealing with Jack than with Dennis. He could be tough—as the legendary case of the weeping NBC presenter during the "strafing run" would attest—but I always liked him, and he had everyone's respect—if not affection—including Jack's.

Dennis was about my age, and part of the fiery new team Welch brought in. That team and its hyperactivity and passion mixed for six or seven years with the old GE—the comfortable GE—that I had become a part of when I joined the company.

I was told stuff like, "you never go to a business location or a factory without wearing a suit and tie," in order to distinguish yourself from the peasant workers who actually made things. We were managers—even though, for much of my career I didn't actually manage anything except a pen, and made attempts at managing a maniac's communications. I thought that "suit thing" was odd, Edisonian, Dickensian, and funny, but I did what I was told.

As a speechwriter I was a denizen of the corporate public relations world, a world viewed by Welch as largely a sinecure for old GE guys straining toward the finish line. It was bereft, in his view, of most of the passions that drove him and his boys—many of whom were from the plastics business.

The old PR crowd was transplanted to Connecticut when Reg Jones moved the main corporate offices from 570 Lexington Avenue in Manhattan in the early '70s. Welch later said that move, "away from where the action was," would not have been made had he been CEO at the time.

Within a few years, a beautiful suite of offices in the RCA—now GE—building, and a couple of helicopters, moved the GE cockpit back to New York, whenever necessary, in less than an hour.

A minor insight into "the old GE" is the fact that Reg Jones, while Jack's biggest supporter and fan, was only heard to grumble about the "extravagance" of the helicopters. Welch found this amusing, but chided Reg "for setting a bad precedent" by not using the GE Corporate Air, and the other perks afforded a retired Chairman of GE.

Welch, even then looking down the foggy road toward some day "on the beach," did not want himself to be the one to start a trend of former GE CEOs pigging out at shareowner expense.

Of course that is exactly what he seemed to do when all the perks surfaced in an ugly divorce battle. Welch's "consulting agreement" was put before the shareowners well ahead of his retirement; and it entitled him to the same perks and privileges he had as an active GE Chairman. Clear enough. But it did not (as it *needed* not) list every little item such as the "toiletries" or "groceries" that later became catnip for the business media.

He eventually, voluntarily, gave them up; or, more accurately, agreed to pay for them. He called me up and sent me a draft article he had written for the *Wall Street Journal* explaining his perk-surrender; asked what I thought of it, and what I would add.

I rewrote it, and he used *none* of the points I made—but I made two points with him on the phone:

1. "Jack, you are not the center of the universe; and in a few days—maybe tomorrow—no one will give a damn about the free groceries you got at Trump Tower or Knicks tickets or the other stuff. Why throw away things to which you are legally entitled?"

2. There are probably fewer than a hundred shareowners who rode this horse—GE stock—for twenty, ten, five, or even *two years* of the Welch era, who would begrudge him tickets to the Red Sox or Knicks, or some shampoo or conditioner (that he used very sparingly) in the GE digs in Manhattan. He made, probably, several hundred thousand—maybe a million of us—*millionaires*, and we did not begrudge him his airplane rides and shampoo.

But his answer was, "Yeah, but it's hurtin' the company," and, as was his wont, he would ask for advice, listen to it carefully and then do exactly what he wanted to do.

Stalinist liquidations of thousands of experienced managers and bureaucrats were never in the picture. He was seldom cruel, although he was sorely impatient with them. Most of the ones he knew simply didn't "care as much as he did."

But the phrase, "soft landings—give them soft landings," was in nearly every pitch he made to his leaders.

Even the guy who allegedly threatened to blow himself and his wife away in the Fairfield lobby, apparently walked away happy—or at least I *surmise* that, since I never saw any mess on the Motherwell painting.

Actually, it would be hard to tell…

Life in the old GE, as I entered it, particularly in PR management, consisted of arriving at 8:15 or so, writing speeches or memos, reviewing other people's writing, listening to presentations from vendors, managing meetings and the like, sometimes on the road at company functions, long into the night.

There was also a fair amount of booze.

I was invited up to Fairfield, Connecticut for an interview with GE in the spring of 1980. Somebody was going to pay my $50 round-trip Eastern Airlines shuttle from Washington to New York, pay for a rental car to drive the hour to Fairfield, put me up in a motel in wealthy Westport, take me out to lunch, and have attractive female secretaries show me around the spectacular campus and offices.

Okay, I could do that. Although as warm and rich and lovely as Westport and Connecticut in general were in those summer days, I was well aware that if I took this job—not yet offered to me—damp, drizzly Novembers and depressing Februarys would be in my future, away from my beloved Washington, the cherry blossoms at the Tidal Basin in the spring, the parties, and the girls.

My interviews, with two or three levels of PR managers simultaneously, were done at lunchtime, with tours done in the morning. The lunches were all "off campus," at a restaurant in Westport, a golf course facility in Fairfield, and one other place—I forget. And, if I forget, it was because, I, like my interviewers, had a couple of "see throughs" with lunch—gin or vodka.

The gin and the warmth and humor of these men, who were 20 to 25 years my senior, won me over; and the fierce loyalty to, and love they exuded for GE, won me over as well. But it was my "what-the-hell" instinct that tore me from the Pentagon and up to a place I thought I would hate—Connecticut.

My son Billy, now an ROTC cadet at Georgetown, returned one summer from Airborne School at Fort Benning, Georgia, and he and I discussed what I call the "leap of faith" of a night jump: exiting a "perfectly good airplane," twelve hundred feet above the ground, into an inky void, while trusting in God and the United States Army to assure at least a chance of a favorable outcome.

So I decided to jump from my perfectly good Washington airplane. I drove from GE back to La Guardia with a pleasant gin buzz, and decided that I would accept the job if it were offered to me.

Offer they did; something like $40,000—about $5,000 more than I was getting at the Pentagon. Within a few years I had a secretary who was pulling more than that. But, then again, I too, was pulling quite a bit more.

But my first days on the job proved interesting—and then scary. I was seated in my cool new office with not really much in the way of work to do yet. People stopped in and introduced themselves, and welcomed me "to the company" in a very friendly, classy GE way.

I thought it might be time to buy a car, once again envisioning the coming Connecticut winter and dreading the prospect of riding my motorcycle to work in my suit jacket, with the wind whipping the fabric out of my cheap tie.

Wanna Drink Lunch with Us?

"Bill, how about lunch?" Four or five of my new colleagues had stopped at my door, obviously on the way out.

"Sure."

Down to the indoor parking, and into a huge '70s four-door sedan, for the four or five minute ride to the golf course. The table was ready when we entered, and there was scurrying at the bar. Three minutes later the drinks were delivered with smart bomb precision: vodka martini, straight up, rocks on the side (better yield). "No fruit."

"And what would you like?" asked the cute waitress after greeting my mates by "Mr." and their last names. "I'll have the same, uh—gin."

I had two of those, as did the boys, with a white wine to accompany the token food—a little sandwich of some kind. The conversation was delightful, full of wit and irony. There were literary allusions, as well as talk about company politics. There was much laughter. It lasted probably an hour and a half. There was a nostalgic reference to a Chinese restaurant in New York, near "570 Lex"—the old GE headquarters—and I asked, naively, how good the food was, since I might be going into Manhattan for dinner with a date the next weekend. They gave me a quizzical look and then gently explained that it was the *martinis* they were reminiscing about, and that the food was, "okay."

We got back into the gigantic sedan, and I asked if it had "thrusters," like a cruise ship, to push it away from the curb. This passed for a witticism, and we cruised back to GE. Everyone said a warm "see you later" at the elevator, and then it was back to my office, where I sat with a "no-TV-input"–style buzz until "quitting time," when I went home on the bike, had a few beers, and crashed in my ridiculously expensive $600-a-month condo.

Day One ended, and Bill rested.

Day Two dawned, and Bill did the same thing. "Hi, Bill. Coming with us?" "Sure." I returned to the office, still laughing at how smart and cultured, gentlemanly, and incisive these guys were. I looked out the window with the buzz working until the day mercifully ended. Secretaries began looking at me with the knowing "fish eye," as I walked around getting boring annual reports, and making believe I would read them while I breathed Beefeater fumes on everyone in my path.

If you get the picture, I will skip to about Day Four of this odyssey.

As Day Four dawned, I began to wonder if "this is where I want to be."

How does this company get anything done if everyone is walking around all afternoon shit-faced?

I'd observed my "lunch" colleagues during the afternoon and they *seemed* like they were getting things done. They were tapping away on the IBM Selectrics; slides were being projected onto office walls as they reviewed them with vendors; and clips from the papers were being copied for the "clip report," with seeming efficiency.

One of my younger colleagues did emerge from the copy room one day as one of the "lunch team" was Xeroxing away and said, with his thumb pointed over his shoulder, "If you go in there don't light any matches. The whole place could go up."

After a few days of observation, and a conversation with two other speechwriters, it finally became apparent that the whole company *didn't* go out to drink lunch at corporate.

Only these guys did.

One of the other writers, in about his third year at GE, told me that he too had been initiated into the lunch routine in his first days in Fairfield. He's not much of a drinker, but went along on a few of the excursions despite being told that his companions were the subject of active disapproval by the VP, Public Relations, who was the *uber* boss of all of them. The VP had *strongly* suggested in the past that they modify their "dining" habits.

My friend related to me how one day the pack of four or five had dragooned him as they passed his office on the way to the elevator, on the way to the parking garage—and "Martiniville."

The pack, in a hurry, moved out several paces in front of my friend, and rounded a corner out of his sight, only to spot the dreaded VP emerging from the elevator.

My friend described what happened next.

If you have seen the Blue Angels or the Air Force Thunderbirds at air shows, there is one exciting exhibition where they fly straight up thousands of feet into the sky in formation, and then suddenly split and peel off in different directions.

The VP's emergence from the elevator produced a similar effect on the pack. They scattered, as if on command, one heading for the men's room, another turned on his heel and headed back to the office, another just wandered vaguely but purposefully *in any other direction than the elevator*, and where the scowling VP knew they were going. They left my friend, a brand new employee, standing alone in the glare of his new master's disapproval.

He never again joined the pack, which incidentally regrouped in the garage after the Blue Angels maneuver and continued on their mission.

The next time I got the noon-ish friendly wave and beckon at my door, I said, "I have to pass. I've got a—uh—speech I've got to get going on."

"Okay, Bill, see yah later."

I never went out "with the pack" to lunch again, but, as a bachelor, I had little to do on a weekday afternoon, and occasionally accompanied them at quittin' time to another local watering hole—the Hi Ho—for two *more* Martinis, prepared in exactly the same fashion as the lunchtime variety.

It was at the Hi Ho, after "see-through" number two was almost finished, where one of the team, after reflecting on what was viewed as Welch's "increasingly crazy" pronouncements ("number one or number two in every business", or "fix, close, or sell", or "a company 'better than the best'"), said, "I'll give him two years—then it's Bellevue." The speaker—my boss, and a great man he was—uttered this more in sorrow than anger, as he lowered his eyes and addressed his dwindling second martini.

I laughed at the absurdity and eloquence of that pronouncement, and nine years later, when Rosanne—Jack's Executive Assistant—had a little surprise reception for Jack's 10th anniversary as CEO, I made an overhead of the quote and flashed it on the wall when he walked in. He loved it, thought it was hilarious, and has referred to it ever since.

By '85 it became obvious that Welch was not headed for "Bellevue"; and the old school he had inherited, which had "run out of gas," was *not* going to outlast him. Many had been "sent home," sometimes in bunches.

One morning, in the summer of 1986, Vice Chairman Larry Bossidy boarded an "air-GE" flight at Westchester County Airport, for what, in company legend, is known as either the "Midwest Murder Tour," or the "Midwest Massacre."

The first stop, Nela Park, Cleveland, is home to the GE lighting business and the headquarters of a GE senior VP. Welch described him using an epithet I cannot repeat as long as my mother and children are still alive.

That morning, after landing, Larry was chauffeured from the airport to the lighting business. As the legend goes, Larry told the driver, "You can keep the engine running. This won't take long."

Bang. Senior VP slumped over his desk, bleeding all over his "package." Larry was out the door, into the limo, back to the airport, jet engines whining back to life as he pulled up. He then headed to Columbus, Ohio, and another big GE business, where a senior VP and former Welch golf partner was on the throne.

Then, within minutes, the senior VP was lying *next* to the throne in a pool of appreciating stock options.

Wheels went up again, on the Gulf stream, and he headed to fabulous Ft. Wayne, Indiana.

Whether the unit had been "tipped off" about the impending arrival of the deputy grim reaper or not, was unclear; but their HR manager met Larry at the airport and brought him to the plant.

They arrived at the unit's headquarters so Larry could visit the senior VP. (This is the VP who gave the presentation at Boca that I thought was great, but Larry thought was "for low IQs.")

Blam! The author of one of my favorite presentations staggers away from his desk and slumps facedown into a huge pile of cash, options, pension, supplemental pension, and free appliances.

Then Larry left. One can only imagine the late VP's secretary screaming, "Oh my God. Call human resources. Call legal! Call his accountant. Call the security people to scrape the parking sticker off his windshield!"

Larry got back in the car with the whey-faced HR manager for the ride back to the airport. I can only imagine how much the fun this trip was.

Larry edges his linebacker frame out the door, and turns to address the HR guy—over the increasing whine of the jets: "You are also removed."

Bang!

Leave the package. Take the cannoli.

And back to Connecticut in time for dinner.

The Firing Squad

I don't think Larry enjoyed firing people, despite my fanciful dramatization of his Midwest massacre, but he did not hesitate to do what had to be done. Welch, despite his reputation—and despite his confrontational and combative nature—*hated* to do it, in person, most of all.

We did have one holdover VP from the Jones era in the early '80s who, I believe, actually *did* relish firing people. But he was "a prick," and Welch had him "shot" before he could fire too many more.

I had to see Jack on one occasion, a few days after firing a speechwriter whom I had only hired a few months before. I had decided to hire a female speechwriter; the second in GE history. This was a primitive but sincere attempt to "diversify" my speechwriter stable.

Welch had perhaps influenced me in this, as he sought a replacement for his vice president of public relations. He announced to his HR people, "I want a woman" (an exact quote, but one that should never be taken out of its context); and, shortly after, hired Joyce Hergenhan from Consolidated Edison in New York—who was also, coincidentally, probably the best in the business.

We used to kid Joyce, to whom we now reported, that her primary responsibility at "Con Ed" was to issue press releases that began with, "We regret the explosion this morning on First Avenue that fired the manhole cover onto York Avenue and through the window of the hospital orphanage into the pediatric burn unit. The power outage that shut down all the respirators at Sloan-Kettering is in the process of being rectified and the union is cooperating—after intense negotiations—with this effort."

So I found a woman in the Midwest—a speechwriter and former reporter—with a pile of clips and speeches that I read assiduously and enjoyed. She was moderately attractive, well-spoken, and promised to interact well with the executives for whom my people wrote speeches.

So I hired her, brought her to Connecticut, and had a nice office awaiting her with her nameplate already on the door. I told her that her job for the next month was to relax, get comfortable, and learn all she could about the World's Greatest Company. I would then start her out with a speech for one of the company's less off-the-wall vice presidents.

The month or so went by, and I began to align her with a VP who had to make a speech to some friendly outside audience—a chamber of commerce or something. I kicked some ideas around with her—or rather I gave her some ideas. She seemed a little passive—not a healthy trait for a speech-writer—but she understood the material I gave her, and set out to write her first GE speech. I told her to take her time, a couple of weeks, and give me her best effort. I would give her my reaction and possibly some suggestions, and then she could send it to the VP and make him one of her "clients" from that point on.

Over the next two weeks I left work a couple of evenings, and saw her, door closed, working away. The few inquiries I made as to "how is it com-ing?" elicited vague, but generally positive, reports.

I couldn't wait to see this speech. I had some personal credibility riding on her success; but more than that, I really liked her and hoped that she'd "knock it out of the park."

Toward the end of week two, at the multi-hour period known as "close of business," she knocked on my glass door, came in, and handed me the speech. I asked her, "How is it?" She said, "I think it's okay. I don't know."

"I'm sure it's great." I folded it up in squares, stuffed it in my back pocket, left the office on the motorcycle, and headed down the Merritt Parkway to a bar named Connelly's near the bachelor pad I still occupied. I strolled in, sat at the bar, ordered a beer, fired up a Marlboro Light 100, unfolded the speech, and, aglow with genuine anticipation, began to read.

By the end of page two all the 'glow' had gone, and, without even look-ing at my face in the bar mirror, I could tell I'd gone pale. My face was cold.

It was *horrible. God-awful.* Written as though it were an assignment in an English-as-a-second-language class. Riddled with clichés, and worse, clichés used in the wrong sense, the way an Eastern European or French Canadian might try and affect American colloquial speech.

The speech was a blur by the time I finished my beer, as I wondered, "What am I going to do?" An editor can be like a surgeon, who, opening up a patient and seeing the malignant mess inside, just sews him back up. Nothing can be done.

But I went in the next morning, sat down with her, and disingenuously said, "Not a bad start." And then I gave her maybe an hour of very specific guidance: phrases, sentences, whole paragraphs. Everything gentle and posi-tively couched. And then I finished, again, with something like, "Not a bad first draft; I just think we need to take it in a little different direction and make it sound like something a GE VP would say to this type of audience."

Another week or two went by, and she, with a sort of resigned smile on her face said that she "had done everything I had told her, and hoped that this was better."

It was *worse*. She had butchered everything I had given her into as ham-fisted and incoherent piece of trash as I had ever seen in my career—including at the Pentagon. The thing was a rotten-vegetable-magnet no matter how "friendly" the audience and even the most tone-deaf GE engineering VP would have called for my execution if I ever gave him something like this.

"Well, what do you think?" she asked hopefully, poking her head in my door. "I haven't really had a chance to look at it yet," I lied, and then went down the hall to talk to Joyce.

"Joyce, she's horrible. She can't write. I don't know where all those samples came from or who edited them, but she's hopeless. I have to get rid of her."

"Then you do what you have to."

Joyce was a fairly tough customer, despite the fact that she had recently had tears run down her face while letting go the woman who ran a small public opinion polling component attached to corporate PR, which was being abolished, as "suggested" by Welch.

The polling component was a bureaucratic artifact, and *should* have been eliminated, but included in the shutting down was a very nice, handicapped black man, who walked with a cane and was in his sixties.

Wonderful "optics." Blasting him, in a company with a miniscule female and minority population among managers, was embarrassing. And here we were "outplacing a threefer": old, black, and handicapped. I never found out why he limped, but it was probably from having his leg blown off on Iwo Jima.

But now I had my own problems, like whacking this poor woman whose life I had disrupted and now had to devalue further by letting her go.

And, in a way, it was my fault.

No. It was my fault.

Never hire a writer, particularly a speechwriter, on the basis of a résumé and samples, no matter how good he or she may seem. Bring him or her to your organization, set him or her up with a "real" client, and have

the candidate write a real speech after talking with the client, and then see what you've got. Hiring a writer on the basis of résumés and samples is an incredibly widespread practice and a frequent cause of embarrassment, disaster, and unhappiness for everyone concerned.

And a further observation of mine, not Jack's: If you are looking for a writer for a volcanic, ferocious, and perverse client (without mentioning names), do not hire a quiet, passive male—nor any female.

Peggy Noonan is one of the greats—but she had, in Ronald Reagan (for whom my daughter, Regan, is named) a gentle, amicable, wonderful old man. Peggy Noonan would not have lasted three months with a Tasmanian Devil named Jack Welch.

So I went off to begin procrastinating before firing my first human being, aside from the Army. Joyce went up to see Welch on some matter or other later in the day.

While they were talking, Jack veered off. "How's the new speechwriter doing?"

Understand that this was a $50,000 new employee in a headquarters of 600 to 700 people, in a global company of 350,000-plus; where the CEO maintains little databases in his brain that produce questions such as "How's the new speechwriter doing?"

Not a "deep dive." Simply, effortlessly being "on top" of things.

Joyce, cringing before a possible volcanic eruption said, "Jack, Bill's letting her go. He says she's not that good."

Welch's view was as perverse (and logical) as I came to expect: "Good for him! That's *exactly* how we should separate people we don't want. Do it right away, rather than wait till the guy is in his fifties and can't get another job." And he went on about how "cowardly" managers keep avoiding making the painful decision to go in some guy's office, shut the door, and say, "You got a minute?" and then "send him home." They pass that rotten job on to some future manager, who has to do it when the victim is now unemployable anywhere else.

And so I went in and closed the door, and said to my speechwriter, as gently as I could, "This isn't working out." I told her that her writing style was not compatible with GE executives, and that she should begin looking for something else, using her GE office and facilities as a base. She looked surprised for a moment, and then quietly resigned.

I told her I was sorry.

I was *very* sorry.

I had to see Welch shortly after, and he praised me, once again, for "doing it right."

"Yeah," I said, "but I don't *like* doing it. I *hate* it."

He became very animated and loud—even angry. "You think *I* like it? I do it every day."

And I believed he really *did* hate it, despite his reputation.

Part VII

Why Gary Wendt

The dismissals of the '90s were usually, simply, for performance reasons—missing numbers or "not sharing GE values."

This brings us to the case of the departure of Gary Wendt—"The Smartest Man in General Electric."

Gary was CEO of what was known for a time as GE Capital; and he was a true visionary whose high batting average with deals and acquisitions made the financial services business soar to well over 40 percent of GE's net income.

After meetings with Wendt, Welch would sometimes hold his hands, palms pointed toward his head, about a foot from each of his ears, and say, "*Huge*" to describe Gary's intellect.

Welch's top two attributes in a business leader, were, first, IQ, and, second, fanaticism. A little craziness was okay, as well.

Up to a point.

In my view, Gary Wendt could have been Chairman of the General Electric Company but for two problems.

1. He was just a few years too old to achieve the 20-year reign that Jack, with the usual self-reference, would have felt was needed to achieve organizational Valhalla. That, in itself, might not have been prohibitive had it not been for issue number two.

2. Gary was nuts.

I knew Gary through running the company meetings and through working with GE Capital for 20 years. I thought he was a riot and I liked him.

Most people did *not* like him.

When he was "on the program," presenting at the officers meeting or at Boca, his presentation always missed the deadline to be sent to me for review by Jack, myself, and Gary Reiner, our Senior VP and later Chief Information Officer.

This led to a typical phone call I really didn't look forward to making.

Secretary puts me through. "Gary, where's your pitch?" Angry little noises, then a switch in tone. "Mr. Lane, have I *ever* failed you or gone overtime or done a bad job on these things?"—in mock, droll, amusing tones.

"No Gary, you haven't, but I need whatever you've got so far to show to Jack and Gary Reiner."

"I'll get you something, Mr. Lane, fear not."

"Bye, Gary."

And true to his word he did provide his pitch, in the sketchiest of detail, in time for me to "run it by" Jack and Gary Reiner.

And his presentation was *always* outstanding, typically looking at some issue such as "growth" with a provocative and quirky perspective.

He would show up for his scheduled rehearsal with me, whether at Boca or Crotonville, for the corporate officers meeting and then announce that he just wanted to flip through his slides (and later his PowerPoint charts); and did not want to rehearse.

I would argue, "If we don't 'do' it, how will we know it's not too long?"

And he would say, "Mr. Lane, have I ever gone over my time limits?" And I would say "no," because *he hadn't*—unlike Bob Wright of NBC, who also would refuse to rehearse and would swear on a stack of bibles that he would be on time; and then go eight or ten minutes over. Eight or ten minutes over does not sound like much, but it *was* in the context of me grousing about other speakers going 40 *seconds* over, and asking them to take something out of their pitches overnight. Finishing 18 holes in at least partial daylight drove the whole program.

Along with its quality, of course.

And Gary Wendt *always* would deliver, masterfully, with more people asking for copies of his pitch than anyone else's, except Jack's. Welch's reaction to his pitches was often the head-sized hand gesture I described: "Huge."

But he was also a "huge" *pain in the ass* to Welch.

He wasn't a loose cannon, doing the frenetic deal stuff that was popular during the '90s; but he was more insubordinate than anyone I have *ever* observed with Welch.

I've seen correspondence he had sent to his people with sarcastic and caustic references to "our parent"—GE—and how they were screwing up GE Capital's plan to own the world—or however he put it. Nasty and insubordinate, and utterly unconcerned that Welch sat in his office and read these memos.

I could envision a scenario where some of their interactions could have come to sucker punches, furniture breaking, and heart attacks.

I think Jack saw him as a *prima donna* pain in the ass; but brilliant, and the Babe Ruth in the GE lineup.

All of the stuff that surfaced in Gary's public divorce battle with his wife, Lorna, and the loco-weed that this presented to the media, was undoubtedly one factor in his leaving GE.

But all of that has been hashed over in other books and articles, and I have no inside knowledge of Gary's public divorce—followed by Jack's—so I'll move on.

Jack hated the muck that Gary was dragging GE through, with his anti-feminist and off-the-wall rants on TV, most of with which I agreed.

Gary's wife, Lorna, whom I may or may not have met and don't know, appeared in TV interviews in which anyone at GE, or GE Capital, could tell she had no real knowledge—except in the broadest of terms—of what Gary did for a living. She would garble much of the stuff she said as if reading from a script with which she was not particularly familiar.

She came across as a pleasant, middle-aged, *nouveau riche* society housewife who was being dumped, and who wanted more than the paltry 10 or 15 million dollars she was being offered.

And she no doubt *deserved* more than that for putting up with Gary for decades. But to portray herself as an equal creator in the enormous wealth Wendt had accumulated was just stupid.

"Do you think having to get dressed up to go to dinner in New York is hard work?" Wendt asked on TV.

Good question, but it didn't play well. Welch, according to printed reports, was furious. I never talked to him about it, but often wondered what he was thinking of as he wandered down the same dumb path of not "splitting it down the middle" in a divorce settlement. Terrible publicity followed a few years later from his fighting the same ugly, unproductive issue.

GE was arguably hurt more by Jack's divorce battle than by Gary's, although I don't think either really hurt the company perceptibly.

Wendt's divorce saw the stock continue to skyrocket—in a bull market—and Jack's problems saw the stock sag in a burgeoning bear market—the dot-com bust, 9/11, and the departure of the divorcé himself.

Jane Welch certainly merited a larger slice of the pie than Lorna Wendt. She acted much more in keeping with the role of a First Lady, accompanying Jack on his trips to the White House, India, and the homes of the rich, famous, powerful, and GE-friendly of Europe.

I found her Alabama accent hilarious, especially when they were together, her drawl contrasting with Jack's high-pitched, nasal, Salem voice. Foreigners, in the couple's travels, must have found it funny as well, or maybe just confusing.

But she is bright, urbane, friendly, attractive, and above all, was always nice to me.

At one of the last of Jack's shareowner meetings, during the warm-up coffee-and-danish reception, Jane—a real star in her own right at these things—escorted me around, introducing me to, among others, Jack's adult children, whom I had never met.

I had kind of a quizzical look on my face, I guess, and suggested that she might want to hang out with the board members—people like Roger Penske, Senator Sam Nunn, and others. But she escorted me, a nobody, around for 10 minutes or so, and made me appear to be a big deal.

I don't forget things like that. Obviously.

But back to the "huge" headache of Gary Wendt, and the day in late 1998 when Welch, obviously unwilling to leave this insubordinate time bomb to his successor, did what all felt he needed to do, and said good-bye to Gary.

The day it was announced that Wendt was leaving GE, Welch called me up on some issue or another—probably the Boca meeting coming up in a week or two.

"So, Jack, how come you fired Gary? You always told me he was the smartest man in GE." While Jack didn't use the word "fire," he did list the reasons for Gary's abrupt resignation.

"Yeah, but he didn't share our values."

"What values didn't he share?"

"A lot of them! Do you have your values card?"

"Yeah, I think so," I was fumbling frantically in my wallet to get the card out. "Got it."

"Okay, read the values. I don't have my card with me."

"Okay. 'Unyielding Integrity' is the first."

Welch, almost annoyed, "No, he has integrity."

Next, "Have a passion for excellence and hate bureaucracy."

(More annoyed) "No, he was okay on those."

"Next one is: 'open to ideas from anywhere.'"

"*No, no, he didn't listen to anybody.*" He was clearly happy now.

"Behave in a boundaryless fashion."

"*Absolutely not. Didn't play that way.*" Now he was happier.

After Jack scored a few no's on Gary's values, he tired of the values card exercise, and said goodbye; and told me to come up and see him later to work on something else.

So I did, and after he and I did whatever we had to do, sitting at the round table in Jack's conference room, he said his usual thanks, and, as I got up to go, I said—for some reason—"You know, I still don't understand why you fired the 'smartest man in GE.'"

(Loudly) "It was the way he *treated* people."

"How did he treat them? I always got along with him."

"The way he treated people who made presentations to him."

"Ah," I thought "now we're getting somewhere." "*How* did he treat presenters badly?"

"Okay. *You* be a presenter and make a presentation to me. *I'll* be Gary."

"Oh, God, why do I do stuff like this?"

So I sat down and picked up some papers I had in front of me, and began reading them aloud. Jack, sitting next to me in his chair, put a polite and attentive expression on his face as he listened for 30 seconds or so, and then picked up the *Wall Street Journal*, swiveled his chair around so his back was directly in my face, and, about a foot away, held up the *Journal* and began reading it, humming pleasantly.

Then he turned back, since I had stopped reading the "presentation," and said, "That's what he does; stuff like that, and he does even worse stuff. He eats Styrofoam cups!"

And, indeed, Gary *did* do worse stuff than that to presenters who failed to interest him.

At GE Capital, he was known to express his impatience with flatulence—real "audibles"—and often even with women at the conference table, although I don't know exactly why that would matter.

But worse than the audibles was the soul-tearing squeaking noise as he ate his Styrofoam coffee cups, or rather chewed them up and spit them back into the bottom of the cup before beginning another one—all this while you were trying to pitch a deal to him.

I took my family on a small tour of France a number of years ago and found, after a day or so, that one of Lorna Wendt's divorce lawyers, a woman who seemed intent on buying every pricey shoe and handbag in the country, was one of our tour-mates.

We introduced ourselves and I, of course, immediately started an altercation about whether or not she actually believed that Lorna Wendt's "dressing for dinner" and "making cookies" actually contributed half of the startling wealth the Wendts had rung up by settlement time.

After a rowdy conversation on the subject, we came to the view that Lorna did, in fact, probably deserve half of the dough—just living with that nut possibly reason enough—but we eventually stipulated that she certainly did not "create" or "contribute" half of it by dressing for dinner, or hiring people to run dinner parties.

Lorna's lawyer and I actually became friends once this had been settled, and moved on to a more interesting discussion of exactly how crazy Gary Wendt was. Of course, I brought up the cacophonous Styrofoam cup munching; and she confirmed it from her experiences in court, relating how some court functionary angrily asked her after Gary had left the room, "Is it supposed to be my job to clean this up?" Gary had apparently chewed an entire cardboard coffee cup (no Styrofoam available, I guess) into a disgusting sodden mass, like a mud dauber, and deposited it on the table in front of him.

The oral compulsion was clear and often emerged during business presentations. On one celebrated occasion, while listening to some poor bastard make a presentation to him on a proposal for a real estate deal, he reached over and took the one-page outline out of the man's hand, crumpled it up, and stuffed it into his own mouth!

As the man *continued to present* (!), Gary chewed the paper to a manageable size and said, in garbled diction, "I hate this pitch so much I'm going to eat it and vomit it all over the table."

I got a real kick out of observing Gary, and focused on him almost as often as on Jack, every opportunity I got. I would sit, as was my wont, at my station in the back of the famous Pit at Crotonville, during the officers meeting. Gary, typically sat a few rows ahead of me. He displayed little interest in the presentations, except for Jack's and Larry Bossidy's.

Often, as the morning wore on, he would begin sorting through his mail during the pitches; after that I observed him "doing his options"—figuring their value—which was always a pleasant activity at GE in the '90s. He would never just get up and leave the room.

Insubordination has its limits, and that would have been too far over the line. Jack would have spoken to him.

"Leaving the room," the ultimate blow-off of a failed presentation, was, however, part of his repertoire. At one of these meetings—Boca—I was in the golf cart with Gary at the GE golf outing. I was in the driver's seat as we sat through the brief golf pro presentation on the rules of the day, scoring, et cetera. Gary became impatient and said, fairly loudly, "This is bullshit; let's get going out to the hole."

This would have required me to leave by driving over a Belgian-block curb right in the golf pro's face, an act of rudeness that was beyond me.

"No, Gary. I'm not doing that. Let's just wait a minute."

"C'mon, let's go. He reached over with his foot to hit the gas. I blocked his foot with mine.

"No, wait a minute. *Just a minute.* C'mon, Gary!"—with 20 or so of the surrounding GE golfers gawking at this loud and stupid conversation taking place as the pro was trying to finish his instructions.

I was very uncomfortable, and almost at the point of caving in— which would have been a cowardly deferral to the rudeness of a nutty big shot.

To be honest, I probably *would* have driven off if Welch had been in the seat rather than Gary, but Jack would *never* have been that rude, especially when representing GE.

But at that tension-filled moment, the briefing mercifully ended, and the armada of golf carts all moved out to their assigned holes.

And we had a nice afternoon, actually.

But when Gary was on his own turf—in Stamford—his abrupt departures from presentations were the stuff of legend.

One time, there were five fairly junior presenters in his conference room pitching a deal. Gary, reasonably pleasant and attentive for 10 minutes or so, began looking like he forgot something—maybe a paper—or as if he had to make a quick call. He jumped up abruptly and exited the room. The presenters sat there waiting quietly, then chatting, then looking at their watches as time wore on—and laughing—nervously.

An *hour* went by. Then another half hour. One of them ventured courageously out of the conference room to ask the secretary where Mr. Wendt was. She gave him a strange pitying look. She hadn't known they were still in the conference room; and Gary was now approaching 40,000 feet in his Canadair Challenger, two states away, on the way to listen to a presentation that, I guess, sounded more interesting.

With Gary gone, Jack didn't have to worry about Jeff being saddled with him.

Lack of Care Packages

In sum, the '80s at GE were punctuated by gunshots removing people who seemed to Welch to be caring about what they did a little less than they used to. The irony is that the enormous wealth being accumulated by fifty-ish senior people by the surging stock left some of them looking wistfully out the window and longing for Florida: the dark downside of option-heavy compensation.

In the '90s—especially the mid-to-later '90s—there was no one who appeared to be "out of gas," "out of it," or who had "lost the edge," or were just "going through the motions."

The packages in that decade went to people who simply failed, or who simply would not fit in Jack's vision for the company's future. No one who did not appear passionate or fanatical about what he or she did ever even reached the radar screen of the senior people who could truly place them higher in the stratosphere. What I am describing is not a dramatic or theatrical passion—which is often fake, and *perceived* as fake.

What I am describing, in one sense, is a real urgency to enthusiastically proselytize views with one's colleagues.

A few—not many—of the quietest, least-animated people I have ever known in business, have delivered the best, most important, most well-received presentations I have ever seen. The power was not in arm-waving and dramatic gestures, but in the quality of the thought, the organization—the urgency and polish of the delivery—and, most important, the point of what they were telling their mates.

The "caring" about what they had to say came through no matter how muted their voices or the immobility of their expression—although those are not to be mistaken for good things.

My friend Bob Nelson, a former GE VP and Jack's financial analyst, was often assigned to speak at both the officers meeting and Boca. Jack would often say, "Put Bob on the program to talk about installed base service," or some other financial or strategic imperative.

"He's 'deadly' (referring to his professorial delivery that has the tonal variation of a leaf blower), but what he has to say is so important he's gotta be on the program."

Bob Nelson never spoke on anything he didn't care about and believe in deeply.

I've been replaying the years in my mind to see if I could remember any times when Jack spoke about things about which he didn't really care—and there were a few, but *very* few.

He would have to make a plea for contributions to the GE Political Action Committee to his officers and general managers every year. It was a chore; I could tell he didn't like it, but he had to do his job as CEO and put the arm on this highly paid crowd to contribute to this "lawful, legal" GE vehicle for greasing the politicians in Washington and the states who supported GE positions on various issues that affected our interests. So he did as he was asked and did it effectively. But it was more like a commercial interruption in the midst of the things he *really, really* cared about and wanted to talk about.

And that "caring" was never in doubt in anyone's mind—particularly at Boca. Consider some snippets from one of his early-'90s Boca "closes"— widely anticipated as his most important oral communication of the year. It was also used by him, and me, as the basis for his CEO letter in the annual report, the preparation of which began a week or so later, while he was still "pumped."

On Change

"…every one of us must totally change. Larry [Bossidy] and I get teased on it all the time. All this delegation… and empowerment you tell us to do… *you* two bullies never did when you were in our place.

"But we *did* change… thank God… and if you are the same today as you were three years ago… you're *out of it.*

"If you're not going to be a lot different this year than you were last year… *you stink.*

"Don't let anyone say, 'Good old Harry. He hasn't changed a bit in the last five years.'

"You saw what happened in the '80s to those who didn't change. They had to be let go."

On Globalization

"We'll break down geographical boundaries. We've all seen these crazy meetings where we debate and fight over who we're going to put in the important Dallas district manager's job. And then… as an afterthought… we'll say 'Well, who should we send to the Singapore job? And someone will say, 'Well… 'Harry' will go. He and Mary have always wanted to travel (laughter from the 500 managers). Their kids are all out of school now and they'd love to take a trip. And we can spare him.'

We won't *do that* anymore. We'll put our best and our brightest overseas… like we do in [jet] engines and plastics. It will be the norm for our best to go there…and to speak another language. And that geographical barrier will be *busted*…"

I doubt that there has ever been a CEO who enjoyed his job anymore than Jack Welch—or enjoyed *life* more, in many respects. He thought being the CEO of this enormous company he loved so much was the best job in the world. And it would be difficult to argue that it was not.

One day in the '80s, I sat across from him at his desk. Rosanne put a call through to him.

He listens. And then, "You know, I really appreciate your thinking of me. I'm just enjoying what I'm doing here and plan to do it for a long time to come. But I really appreciate it, and tell 'him' I said so. Thanks again." He hung up, looked at me, and said, "Why the hell would I want to be Secretary of the Navy?" I said something like, "If they can't find anyone, I'll take it."

And then we went back to work.

Jack and George Bush the First became fairly good friends and Jack, ever star struck, was thrilled to go with his wife Jane to the White House on some Friday nights and watch movies with George and Barbara.

Monday morning, gushing like a rock groupie: "We went to the White House Friday, and Barbara Bush came up and gave me the biggest kiss!" I said, "Better you than me, Jack. She's a nice lady, but I don't find her that attractive."

Dirty look.

I walked up to his third-floor conference room and sat down to wait while he talked on the phone with Ted Turner in his newly refurbished office with the doors that close with a "whoosh" at the push of a button—like *Star Trek*, or *Star Wars*, I guess. They were supposed to be soundproof, which was a joke since Welch spoke so loudly you can hear him all over the building. You could probably hear him down on the Merritt Parkway.

The door slid open; he emerged from his office. "How are you?"

"Jack, do you seriously think that door is soundproof? You're so loud I can hear everything you say on the phone"—and I repeated a snippet or two of what he said to Turner, who I believe wanted to buy NBC, or part of it.

"*Ro!* Bill says the door isn't soundproof and we need to have somebody look at it." But I could tell he didn't *really* care whether anyone heard him or not.

We sat down. I watched him trying to get himself interested in something for maybe 15 seconds—some speaking obligation he had. Then he jumps up, "Wait. You gotta see this!" He runs back in his office. The door closes. The door opens. He emerges holding a modest crystal bowl which is the trophy for the Sankaty Head (Nantucket) Golf Club Championship which he had just won the previous weekend. Crystal bowl is smudged, covered with *visible* fingerprints, has obviously been handed to people, petted, fussed and drooled over all morning. I acknowledge his achievement. He then clutches this Petri dish of germs and dirt to his chest, "I love this so freakin' much I can't stand it."

Weeks later I happened to play at my club with a guest who was the guy Jack had beaten in the club championship at Sankaty Head. He was a much better golfer than I am, obviously, and we had a nice round. I mentioned this to Welch on Monday, casually, while working on a speech with him. Galvanized. Fascinated. "Really!!! You played with him? What did he say [about me]?"

I have his total attention. Time to *torment!*

"He said you played well."

"What else did he say, *specifically?*"

"He said you beat him."

"*I know that! Tell me what he said!!! You're not feeding me.*"

"Not much. We didn't talk much about it. We talked about other stuff." A lie. We actually had talked for quite awhile about Welch, and about how well he played, shots he made, et cetera. I just didn't feel in the mood to *fuel* this gigantic ego with more nitromethane.

So, with Welch "unfed" and unsatisfied, we went back to work.

Seinfeld in Fairfield: The Yogurt Incident

I reported to the conference room. I sat there until the unsoundproof door zipped open. Jack, with a giant bowl of what looks like ice cream, zipped in. "How are you?"

"Fine."

"You see this? We've got a frozen yogurt machine across the hall [in the kitchen of the officers' dining room, about 25 feet away]. I can go over there *any time I want*, and eat as much of this as I want—*free*.

"And it's *fat* free. It's unbelievable. I would have dreamed about something like this as a kid. I can have *all I want*!!" There's yogurt all over his mouth.

The shareowners never learned of the free yogurt, since it never appeared in the proxy statement.

I think it turned out that he *couldn't* have all he wanted because he started ballooning up, and I never again saw him eating the "fat free" yogurt, at least in his office.

Welch has an addictive personality, and would have made a horrible drug addict or alcoholic—except for the iron will he would engage to brake his enthusiasms. The thought of Jack jacked up on cocaine does not even compute. I'm not sure you could tell the difference from what he was like normally.

He basically reined in what apparently was some raucous rowdiness of his Pittsfield days—none of which I have any personal knowledge of—and pretty much shut down alcohol when he got the big job because it "killed him" on the travel schedule he was signed up for as CEO. On the relatively infrequent occasions when I traveled with him to a speech and reception, I would get a beer or drink for myself and a glass of white wine for him, and fight my way through the crowd surrounding him to deliver it. He would take it gratefully, and nurse it through the evening.

The few times I saw him have a few serious drinks, and maybe have more than a little buzz, was in the period when his first marriage was ending in the mid-'80s.

Jack had been rhetorically dueling with the chairman of Sara Lee over national tax policy; and my boss, Joyce, playfully suggested to him one day, "I bet you don't have any Sara Lee products for dinner at home."

Welch said, ominously, "I don't eat at home."

Here we go.

He then, for a brief period of time, began dragging Joyce over to the pub in the spectacular GE Guest House overlooking the Merritt Parkway valley and beautiful Connecticut countryside. I got "dragged" as well, on a few occasions that I loved, and stupidly expounded on some idiotic theories on how to run the company that I'm thankful Welch had forgotten by the next day.

It may have been at one of these sessions that Joyce announced her intention to "take up golf." Jack quickly vetoed the idea with the explanation that "there's nothing more pathetic than a 40-year-old woman learning how to play golf."

So she waited until she was *60*. Armageddon!

Joyce, who was single and had the time in the evenings, would continue the "baby-sitting" at the Guest House as I drove two minutes to my own home to spew alcohol fumes all over my wife and the "Irish twins"—both under two.

The Chairman's first marriage did not last much longer. It ended in '87.

Order and Logic Out of Chaos

In preparing a presentation or a speech or an annual report letter, Welch would typically begin by extracting a pack of gum from the bowl in the middle of his conference table. One stick would go in, he'd make a whale noise or two, utter some staccato comments, and then another stick, and another, and finally the whole pack of Wrigley's would be in his mouth as he ran back and forth and around the room, throwing out bursts of rhetoric while I sat, furiously scribbling and responding to shouts of, "No, that's wrong" or "*Yeah, yeah.* Write that down! Have you got it?"

I had it, of course, because I had not one, but *two* tape recorders going.

The dual tape recorder habit was the result of a session with Larry Bossidy two years before, when we went line-by-line through a speech, to make Larry's final "word changes."

I relaxed as we went through the speech because Larry's comments were sensible and lucid, and because I had a trusty GE tape recorder going. I only wrote down a "creative" note on my own, here and there.

I returned to my office and stood by my secretary's desk. I flipped on the machine to see how good the sound was, as I got ready to listen to it and put the speech to bed.

Nothing.

The tape recorder had recorded *nothing* during the 40-minute session. I slam-dunked it onto the floor where it exploded into 50 pieces as the poor, maniac-beset secretaries once again sucked in their breath and retreated in fright.

I then barred everyone from my office and began to reconstruct Larry's changes from the freshness of my conversation with him, and it wasn't bad at all. Within four hours I had a new draft, and Larry was happy.

From then on it was *two* recorders, particularly with Welch, whose mind went in pinball-like directions while I tried to follow him, with his stuttering still a factor, a mouth full of Wrigley's spearmint, and me—probably 40 IQ points behind the man, struggling to see where he was going with the thought of the moment.

He would run a thread of argument along until he came to a lightning flash of rhetoric, and then say, modestly, "Terrific, did you get that? Play it back; let me hear it." And I would. And then he'd say, "No, no, that misses it. Try this." And off he'd go again, with me throwing in phrases or sentences, interrupting him if I knew they were better than what he had. And he'd say, "Yeah, yeah. Write that down," then toss even more gum in his maw, and continue to orbit the conference table.

After 45 minutes or an hour he would typically, wearily, say, "I'm done. Do you have enough? I'm out of gas. Let's get together Thursday. No, I'm 'out.' Maybe Friday. Yeah. Can you give me something Friday?"

The run-around-the-room-and-let-your-mind-run-free technique is not a bad one. Welch used to throw things out like this and we would sort through them—in almost real time—extracting the "ponies" from their waste. And then we'd massage them into the presentation.

It was our system, and it worked. It was easier on him than it was on me, but it was fueled by *passion*, by *caring* about every word in the speech.

In the early to mid-'80s, as I mentioned, we had a tax policy disagreement with a few other companies. Jack had a huge "outside" speech somewhere, and his point was that Japan and Europe were killing U.S. manufacturing, which needed to modernize, and we needed the investment tax credit to allow us to compete. Other, non-global competitors, like Sara Lee, wanted the International Trade Commission killed.

I was still sort of auditioning for this job (which I didn't really care that much about, at that point) and as Jack fulminated on the subject of global competitiveness—and then momentarily stalled—I jumped in with something like, "We're in a *world* war, and they've got us fighting a *civil* war."

Not Lincoln, nor even Peggy Noonan, but it captured what he was trying to say. He levitated, made a lot of noise. "*Perfect! Perfect!*" And then, being late for his feeding, he ran down to the officers' dining room and repeated, "What Bill just said," over and over to his court.

I think I got the job that day.

The way you, as CEO, or intern, or vice president, or sales manager, must begin, as you contemplate the speech or presentation you were just told you have to make, is this:

Firstly, **shun the PowerPoint.** *Avoid the computer like it was a roadkill skunk. Go into a room with no phone. Turn on a tape recorder. Stand up.*

Walk around. Yell. Sputter. Trail off. Start again. What do you know and believe that will knock this audience on its ass? What must they understand, be aware of? Make rough notes on a pad. Write down whole phrases or sentences if you absolutely love them.

All this will start to clarify within 10 or 20 minutes. Ignore the boring crap you have been told to pitch—the mind-numbing "report" or "analysis" that no one cares about.

Think, at first, only in terms of what the crowd will hear from you, and see in your face and in your passion. At this point you should put out of your mind any evil vision of a tedious word chart. Spit at the thought of turning your back to your victims and rushing through a "read" of a two hundred word chart that no one is interested in.

At this point, PowerPoint is the abortionist of the great presentation gestating within you.

Whether you are the leader or a manager among many, resist attempts by others to make you "touch all the bases" they think need to be addressed for (usually political) reasons. Only speak of things that you care about, and care a lot about. If told by your superiors to "touch on this," or "mention this," or "show this analysis or the amount of data we gathered here or there," cram as much of this crap onto one chart, zip through it in seconds, and then move quickly into the points you care about. Don't spend more than 10 seconds on that chart. Invite them to question you if they have further interest. They seldom will, and they'll be grateful for your merciful brevity in presenting it.

If you really care how well your talk will be received, you must be prepared to put the time in on it.

Doin' Time

Few people knew how much time Welch put in on preparing his presentations, speeches, and triumphant annual report letters; more time, I would wager, than any CEO in America.

His *modus operandi* on his frequent helicopter visits to Crotonville was (without my help) to jot down on a 5x7 card his thoughts on what was "hot" at the moment—such as Six Sigma, e-business, or globalization. He really never looked at the cards, but would give the class maybe 10 minutes or so of his best thinking on these subjects. He brought the Crotonville "kids" into the board room, as it were, and laid the good, bad, and ugly out on the table. A hundred of them would call home or their offices, and say, "Jack told 'me' today that he thinks deflation is going to be a big problem for pricing this year." Or, "Jack said he called Tim Russert before he talked to us, and Russert thinks the President's going to win 49 states."

This was all inside stuff; and it made the students feel as if they were really in the know, and they were.

In pounding home how much he needed the support of everyone on, say, Six Sigma; and why it was transforming the company, they would go back to their businesses "born again" in e-business or globalization, and with the knowledge that it was not just some T-shirt-and-coffee-mug slogan bull from Corporate. It was "*the future of our Company.*"

At least that's what "Jack told us a few weeks ago at Crotonville…"

Or, better still, "I asked Jack why we weren't competing in the blah-blah segment of the motors business, and he told me it was because…"

The preparation for his Crotonville visits—dozens a year—was minimal, because all he was doing was sharing with them stuff he was working on, and then learning from them.

Clear from your mind the illusion that it is "cool" or impressive to simply stand up and "wing" a presentation, or "throw up" a couple of PowerPoint word slides and bullshit your way through them.

Doing so is not "impressive" to any audience I ever saw at GE. It was insulting to the audience that you had not put the time in to prepare for them. It was enraging to Welch and Bossidy and Dammerman; and many others.

Allow your audience to see how much you value their attention and how much time you have invested in your pitch to them.

Never tell them how much work you have done on the pitch. Simply make that evident from its quality.

The preparation for "outside" presentations was a different matter.

Better Than the Best

One day he called me up to his office to work on a pitch he had agreed to do at Bechtel in California, several weeks in the future. Bechtel, an enormous global engineering and construction firm with whom GE did a lot of business, was celebrating its 100th anniversary and Steve Bechtel had asked him to be on a panel, in front of several hundred invitees. The other panel members included Charles Schwab, former Secretary of State George Shultz, and one or two other big hitters. The subject was, *"What have we learned over the past 100 years that will help us face the next 100?"*

Each speaker was to deliver an eight-minute pitch, and then the panel, run by a moderator, would kick things around.

The topic *fascinated* Welch, because among other things, it was broad enough that you could drive an intellectual truck through it. He could talk about exactly what *he* wanted to talk about; an option not often granted to you and me.

It also gave him the opportunity to take time out from the hiring and firing and hurly-burly of business, and sit and think about winning and losing; and about winners and losers, and what differentiates the breeds.

Preparing for the Bechtel pitch, we spent, over a couple of days, eight *hours* together "noodling" the pitch.

Then *I* spent another eight to twelve hours on my own replaying and refining and simplifying what I heard on the tapes. And he spent, I could tell, many hours on his own—running into the conference room, armed with scribbled scraps of paper bearing fresh thoughts to bounce off me.

All this for an *eight-minute* pitch.

After four or five days of work, the final product had been reduced to several 5x7 cards of trigger words, bullets, and rhetorical fragments. And then we rehearsed in the conference room, carrots and gum set aside for the moment. Jack emoted and soared as if he were talking to a thousand people, instead of just me and my recorder.

"Did you get that? Did you get that? Let me hear it." And I would whir back and let him hear his last minute or so, accompanied by shouts of

"Perfect, perfect." Or, "No, no. That's all wrong. Let's redo that part." Sometimes even, "What did you put *that* in there for?"

"What? *You* put that in, remember?"

"Oh, yeah. Maybe. And then, up-tempo and excitedly, "Try it this way… Yeah, *that's it; that's it!* Put it down. Did you get it? Let me hear it. Yeah! Don't change a word, not a word! Don't get 'creative' on me on that part. It's perfect."

And on and on until, "*Done.* Have Barb type it up. It's great. Don't you love it? It's so freakin' good I should write a book."

And then, *literally* hugging his note cards, he'd say, "I can't wait to get out there and do this. I can't wait. It's so good. Don't you think, Bill?"

"I love it. It's terrific, Jack." And it was.

So Jack flew out to San Francisco—probably just ahead of his plane—raced up to the lectern and knocked 'em dead. His colleagues did a good job, probably delivering customized versions of what their speechwriters gave them; but Jack soared above everyone, stunning the audience with the quality of the thought, the obvious passion that accompanied it, the flow and the logic, and the perfection of the delivery.

That Bechtel speech provoked me to observe that his passion, throughout his entire career, was always the "best on the program"—clearly, and by a large margin. And he was willing to do *whatever was necessary to be the best.* There was no such thing as getting a pitch to where it was "good enough." It had to be *the best,* or in Jack's parlance *"better than the best."*

Is this the way you feel about your presentation? That you can't wait to do it because you know it is "so good?" Or is it just another lackluster, boring pitch or report, and a race between you and your audience to see who falls asleep first?

But you don't get the "can't-wait-to-do-it" feelings without hours of mind-work, critique, rehearsal, and bouncing it off people whom you respect and who will tell you the truth.

If you care enough about the venue to do the presentation—or speech—put the time in to make it a thing of greatness. If you don't care enough, turn down the invitation.

Herb Smokes Jack;
Warren Lurks in His Nightmare

Welch would never allow himself to be upstaged. The closest I ever saw to that occurring was, ironically, on his home turf—the auditorium at GE headquarters in Fairfield.

One of the bigger stock brokerage houses had sponsored a "conversation," hooked up by satellite, to customer audiences all over the world. The "conversation" was run by an interlocutor—and a good one—sitting between Jack and the legendary Herb Kelleher of Southwest Airlines. Herb's Boeing 737s were powered by our engines, and Jack—and everyone else—loved the guy. One hundred and fifty or so GE employees filled the seats for what promised to be a fun hour or so watching these two superstars, both at the tops of their games, kick around the business issues of the day.

Kelleher is a riot, a pistol. At the time, it was reported that he kept, without apology, a bottle of Jack Daniel's or Wild Turkey for "celebrating"—a Southwest tradition—in his office desk. He was on his game that day, running around the non-smoking auditorium stage smoking and joking, and firing witty and hilarious broadsides at Jack and the moderator as the audience roared.

He was totally dominating the show.

I was sitting in the back with GE's head of HR and after watching Welch's laughter morph into a fixed smile, I nudged my seatmate and said, "Watch Jack's face. He's being upstaged. I've never seen this happen. Watch his face. He'll do something. *Watch his face!*"

And sure enough, within a minute or so Jack turned on "the Irish" and began throwing hilarious bombs at both Herb and the moderator, and even at us in the audience.

Kelleher continued to run around the stage smoking and firing salvos to which Welch responded, and then counterattacked. The crowd was laughing so hard you couldn't hear half the jabs they were throwing at each other. It was like watching two little boys competing for attention in the schoolyard—I almost expected one of them to pull his pants down to upstage the other.

The event came out to a draw, with the audience as winners; but it underlined for me, once again, Welch's absolute unwillingness to cede top dog and best-in-show honors to anyone, on any venue, anywhere.

Total egomania, of course. But what's your point?

Warren Buffett is another of Jack's pals and golf partners. Aside from being the world's most respected investor, he is also the author of the world's second most highly regarded CEO annual report letter.

One morning I got one of those day-making Jack notes—it was actually a "forward" of a note Buffett had written to Jack on a copy of the GE annual report letter. Warren had written something like "none better than this in the world"; and Jack had graciously written, "Bill—it doesn't get any better than this," and sent it down to me.

Buffett was set to introduce Welch at some huge forum somewhere. We had worked on Jack's remarks, and he was happy with them. But the looming specter—the nightmare—that was terrifying Welch was that he was going to be *introduced* by Buffett, who is notoriously mischievous and witty.

"I *know* he's going to give me a 'shot,' I just *know* it. Bill, what do you think it might be?"

"I don't know, Jack. Maybe something about golf?"

"Yeah, maybe. Probably. I've got something I can come back with on that. But what else? I *know* he's gonna do it, and I have to nail him when I get up to give the speech."

And so we went through the possibilities for the "shot" Warren would deliver, and war-gamed each one of them with appropriate retorts. And it was fun, I guess, although I was under enormous pressure to come up with, in seconds, lines that would leave Warren at the bottom of a smoking crater on stage, for the crime of daring to drop a bomb on Jack for his golf, his magazine covers, his hair, size, or whatever. We spent an hour or so working up an arsenal of retaliatory strikes.

Jack probably had people lined up in his outer office waiting their turn to be fired, and here he was, running overtime with a speechwriter, trying to construct a retort to an attack Buffett had probably not even constructed at the time.

As I recall, he dropped a prepared bomb on Buffett after Buffett "zinged" him. The crowd went wild after the zing and bomb.

Buffett is one of the many people in Welch's life that he truly enjoys. He called me once from Bill Gates' estate in Washington, and described how Buffett and he had stumbled around in their rooms in the dark trying to find how to turn on the lights that Jack vaguely described as being controlled by a PC in the center of the room. I didn't understand, but that's not important. He loves the Warren-man.

Another time he called from somewhere in Mexico and described how Gates, "in his sandy shorts, with his pregnant wife," was walking along the beach "negotiating with 'trinket guys.' Fucking kidnappers everywhere."

I don't know why he called me, but it was fun.

The Welch Work Ethic

Throughout his tenure as CEO Jack was vaguely anxious that some people around him might not be working as hard as he was.

He once confided in me—*sotto voce*—at seven or so one night, "I *have* to stay here late. If I left at six the whole place would empty out."

Complimenting Bob Nardelli, one of the contenders to be his successor, he said, again fairly late, pointing confidently at the phone, "If I called him up right now he'd be there. His whole team would be there, too."

Nardelli's team at locomotives—and later at power systems—reputedly worked, routinely, until Saturday afternoon every week.

No thanks. I didn't.

Welch seldom did, either, although the business brain never stopped no matter where he was. Early in his tenure he made an artless and ill-advised statement in an interview that he only worked until Friday evening and then "hung out with his friends."

Some GE employees reading this had work weeks that continued into Saturday and sometimes beyond—often to do the work of colleagues whose departure Welch had engineered. That was a maladroit comment; one of the very few bad ones this politically astute leader ever made after getting the big job.

In 2006, Charlene Begley, the highest-ranking woman in GE, and then CEO of the now-sold plastics business, but, at the time, head of the locomotives business in Erie, Pennsylvania, announced in an interview that she did not believe in working on weekends and insisted on spending the time with her family. Her boss, Dave Calhoun, later Vice Chairman of GE, and now CEO of Nielsen, was hit with several calls from annoyed railroad CEOs who probably *did* want to spend time with their families, but were committed to making their businesses successful, which sometimes required working on the weekends.

Charlene Begley is a delightful young woman. She became an officer at GE in the late '90s after assuming leadership of the legendary GE audit staff, the Green Berets of corporate finance. She asked me to speak to her troops at a meeting in Florida, and I did. We had lunch afterwards, and I asked Charlene, whom I knew casually, and who lived in my town, "How are you doing? How are things going?"

"Great," she said, "but I'm pregnant."

"Congratulations," I said to this young Catholic mom.

"Yeah, but I haven't told Jack yet."

"What do you mean?"

"He told me after my last baby: '*No More Babies. That's it. Understand?*'" He's not going to like this."

What Welch was telling her, as politically incorrect as it may have been, and even more so now, is that if you want to be a big player in this game, as Charlene already was, your job has to be the primary focus of your life. The successful women in the company have been told, or signaled:

1. do not have a family;
2. have a husband who will stay home and take care of the children, as weird as that is; or,
3. make the children the second priority in your life and hope they will muddle through;
4. understand that the children will probably be drinking and smoking weed while you are having a dinner meeting in Tokyo or Shanghai.

Companies that overindulge work-life balance are going to be under-competitive.

In their book, *Winning*, Jack and Suzy Welch offer some very good advice for "moms": "So before you open your mouth for a fiftieth time to ask for limited travel and Thursday mornings off, or occupy your boss's time with concerns over your childcare arrangements, know that you are making a statement, and no matter what words you use it sounds like, 'I'm not really into this.'"

I don't know whether it was Jack or Suzy who put that advice in their book, but it should *transfix* women who are starting out in life and career.

I was sitting with a GE vice chairman one Thursday afternoon a dozen years ago, working on a speech for an event he had been "roped into." The event was coordinated by a female GE manager.

"We need more data on this thing. Let's ask 'Barbara' how long I'm supposed to talk. Of course she probably won't be there. The women are always gone for some reason or another. "Marsha!" (shouting out the conference room door to his secretary). Call Barbara and have her come up here."

A minute of muffled phone conversation from the secretary outside, followed by the announcement, "Sorry, she's gone for the day."

We can draw a soundproof curtain over the scene that followed.

"Barbara" had kids, and cared about them, and simply couldn't leave them stranded at school or missing soccer, or whatever. But she's also pulling down a six-figure salary and not earning it on the soccer field.

I've spoken at GE women's meetings on several occasions and always think I can spot the real players by the focus of their questions. The good ones are impatient with all the "women stuff," and will interrogate a speaker on purely business issues, comparing observations on—say—Six Sigma or e-business or sourcing. The drones prefer to whine on about discrimination or work-life balance.

I remember at one of these GE women's meetings—a big one—where the crowd listened to several general-session speakers before heading off to hear people like me in breakout sessions. One of the first in the general session was a female TV reporter who spent most of her pitch complaining about how she was not allowed to go where some of the men reporters were allowed to go in Muslim Afghanistan, and how she raised hell and overcame the obstacles and the male attitudes, et cetera.

Maria Bartiromo of CNBC spoke later about what she usually talked about—investing, the Fed, inflation, and Wall Street.

She is, of course, called the "Money Honey" by the knuckleheads on Wall Street, because of her exotic Sophia Loren–like beauty, but it doesn't seem to bother her. It probably wouldn't bother me, either.

Maria did a fine job in her presentation, but what I remember most about her was her answer to a question posed by one of the "work-life balancers"; an answer to the question of "how she has succeeded so well in the face of all the prejudices and attitudes toward women on Wall Street?"

She answered the question succinctly, saying—as a look of real fatigue crossed that lovely face—"I work *very, very, very* hard."

I don't think everyone in the crowd liked that answer.

I led off my breakout session with a discussion about working hard as a path to success in presentations or career activities in general. I then got carried away and told them that all of this "sisterhood stuff," and conferences like these were a bunch of crap because the most serious competitors for the jobs most of them wanted *were other women*, as often, or more often, than men; and that the sisterhood networking stuff would go out the window as soon as the HR slate for the next big job was drawn up.

I ranted on, making the point that women seldom supported each other at *any* level of the Company, from "admin" to officer and in fact, were much tougher and more critical with each other than the guys *ever* were toward women—or toward other men, where their relationships were generally collegial.

I read faces when I pitch—*and you should as well*—and I awaited the outraged, dagger-launching looks. Or people flouncing out of the room.

Instead I saw faint smiles and even nods and quick, whispered, comments that I could tell were of assent.

But it was Maria who had delivered the keynote, and if anyone walked out with a "take away" from the conference it should have been hers: "I work *very, very, very* hard."

I *did* work very, very, hard when I had to, particularly in my early days with Welch, almost corroding a hole in my stomach in the process; but I could feel the gimlet eyes of Welch on the people who worked for me—my speechwriter group—and upon everyone in the component—corporate public relations—in which I worked. Literally.

The Fist Through the Drapes

My "speechwriter shop" was a series of offices in a row overlooking a garden in the lovely East Building at GE. Across the courtyard, visible from all our floor-to-ceiling windows, were the senior executive offices and the Board Room on the third floor. All those windows were shrouded in expensive curtains and thick drapery.

I had an uncommonly slack, very late afternoon in my relatively plush office down the hall; and I strolled down to see my friend Brooks, a Ph.D. in philosophy from UCLA, who happened to wind up working in my component.

I did the usual, "Are you busy?" thing, and came in and started bullshitting on this and that.

I remember that I put my feet up—not on his desk, out of respect, but probably on a side credenza—and began talking.

I happened to look out the window, and upwards toward the third floor Board Room. And through an opening in the curtains, looking like Jack Nicholson in *The Shining* or a kid looking out from a shower curtain, was Welch watching us as we shot the breeze below.

I looked and laughed and pointed at Welch; and Brooks laughed, and the little face fragment laughed—and disappeared.

And we continued shooting the breeze for maybe another half hour or 45 minutes. It was now after quitting time.

I looked up once again, and the little face had reappeared between the curtains. And the face, while not malevolent, was not exactly warm.

Then a fist extended outward through the curtains so that only his face and arm were visible.

The fist was performing an obscene gesture implying pointless and unproductive activity, as the young Chairman of GE glared at these two speechwriter employees bullshitting, rather than *working* on his vision for the future of GE.

I quickly got up and went back to my office.

As the '80s turned into the '90s, stock options began to turn into real wealth and suddenly people like me, and below me—dining employees, limo assigners, drivers, secretaries, and security people—by the thousands, then by the *tens* of thousands, received these wonderful certificates as the stock soared.

Jack would occasionally fret about how much this was costing the company, but then continued passing them out. But he fulminated against and "Rottweilered" anyone who was living off the fat of the company's performance and *not giving 110 percent*.

He torched all of the secretaries of his senior officers by giving them no stock options one year because he didn't want one of them—whom he despised for her lack of commitment—to get them as well, and he didn't want to anger the senior guy who was this woman's boss.

Lack of an intense Kamikaze-like commitment to this company was a career killer.

Golf was a problem, a problem made more complex by the fact that Welch loved it as much as any of us—more—and probably played as much as any of us—maybe more—and not only on weekends.

A couple of the managers used to laugh at how they would nervously keep one lily-white hand under the conference table or in their pockets when meeting with Jack, to hide the contrasting pallor that resulted from excessive wearing of a golf glove.

Playing too much golf got more than one senior guy in trouble; and it got me in trouble as well.

Welch understood the attraction to the game, and made allowances for those who, on an unexpectedly warm day, would slide past the secretary's desk with some mumbled guidance: "I'll be on the beeper. I'll be meeting some—uh—people and then playing a little golf. See you tomorrow." The secretary didn't care. It meant more time for computer solitaire.

And Welch didn't care—up to the point where he saw a trend developing in any individual.

I unexpectedly stumbled into one of these trends in the mid-'90s.

No reason to be in the office. Had all my stuff done. Early fall day. My beautiful Brooklawn in magnificent condition.

On the number eight green. Got a beer and a cigar going. Driving my friend Dave Dudas around in the cart. Laughing. Playing like crap.

Beeper goes off.

Race to the "half-way house." Call the office. "Mr. Welch just called; wanted to talk to you. I told him you were out of the office. He said he wanted to see you."

Back to the clubhouse. Warp golf-cart speed. Beeper goes off again as I reach my locker. Call the office again.

"Yeah?"

"Mr. Welch asked, 'Is he playing golf?'" She told me with a trembling voice that she had said I was. And he said, 'Don't bother him. It's okay.'"

"Yeah, right."

Brooklawn is less than 10 minutes from GE HQ; and so I was soon seated across from him, sunscreen on my face, running into my eyes, in time to do whatever it was we needed to do. Took a couple of gentle "shots" about playing golf, but we got the work done.

Ahh, but the *next* week was a *spectacular* fall day and I was invited to play at Aspetuck, a nice local club, by a friend, a young but senior partner (and now Global CFO) at Ernst and Young, the accounting firm.

Jack was "out of town."

I hit a wedge up to number 10 green. I'm lining up a putt when the beeper goes off. I am now armed with a cell phone the size of a small refrigerator and am advised that the Chairman "wants me to call him."

The game shuts down and my friends, who know with whom I am saddled, as the "Neutron Jack" legend is now in full bloom, are standing, putter heads on the green, as the cell phone conversation begins.

The conversation was ugly and violent: "You *asshole*. The officers meeting is next week and you're playing golf again? *You asshole*. What are you thinking of? You're an *asshole*."

This phrasing was repeated until I got tired of it, and interrupted him: "Jack. Hold on, okay. We've established that I'm an *asshole*. But the officers meeting is in 'the can.' It's perfect. *Fire my ass if it doesn't work*." (My friends are all pale and gaping.)

"And you know what? I'm never playing fucking golf again! Okay? You got that done."

Then, the Irish sea change. The thaw, the softening. The laugh. "You really *are* an asshole. Finish your game. How are you doing?"

"Fine until now."

"Go play. See ya."

"Bye, Jack. Officers meeting will be *perfect*."

We march silently up to the next tee, and I unleash a magnificent 40-yard shank into a gully to the right of the tee, and let loose a series of shouts, curses, and imprecations.

I am awarded a "Welch mulligan" (another shot), and we finish the round.

Not a great day. But for me, an instructive and memorable one.

Dennis Dammerman, a GE Vice Chairman at the time, told me once that when he was hired by GE, and for years afterward, the company deliberately filled its ranks with Midwesterners like himself because it was believed that they tended to have a strong work ethic. Even today, anyone signing up for the Financial Management Program at GE in hopes of progressing to the quasi-military corporate audit staff, and the almost certain career success that will follow, *must* demonstrate a willingness to expend whatever energy and time necessary to ensure excellence in whatever the task of the moment.

Any perceived cracks in the willingness to work as hard—or harder—than necessary is a fatal diagnosis and seldom reversible.

On the other hand, hanging around the office until all hours for the sake of being seen working late, or in case the boss should make a late call, is considered weak and phony.

Then there was Larry Bossidy. When Larry ran GE Capital he would *never* leave after six, once again, unless there was a *reason*. A "reason" was never the fact that Welch might call at seven.

Larry has nine children, actually knows most of their names, and often told me about attending at least some of their football games.

Let me be clear here. GE and, I believe, most great companies large and small, demand 100 percent of your effort and that you work until you drop when something important needs to be done. Welch torched me on the golf course, not because it was a work day, but because he thought I was not working on making the officers meeting—which I ran—the very best it could be.

Crotonville Turkey Shoot

Welch demanded the best effort from all GE people, at every level, on *every single thing they did.*

We emerged from the officers meeting one year, and boarded a line of vans for the trip to the golf course. About six or seven of us, including Jack, jumped in one chauffeured van after being given, football-hand-off–style, box lunches to be eaten on the 20-minute trip. The van pulls away. We all begin tearing into our turkey sandwiches while listening to Jack comment on this and that—how great somebody's pitch was; some funny observations. The driver is now two minutes out of Crotonville when Jack opens *his* box— *which has no turkey sandwich. Someone forgot to put it in his box!*

"Wait! I don't have a sandwich! There's none in here! Stop the van! Stop! Go back! Turn around!"

The driver turns around, panicked, and roars back into Crotonville and around the circle, past more vans loading officers. Welch leaps out and confronts the transportation manager who, with suicidal thoughts, checks another in the stack of box lunches, verifies the presence of a turkey sandwich, hands it to Jack with apologies, and we roar away once again.

One hundred and fifty people were given box lunches, and he had to hand the one without the sandwich to the one person who could legitimately make a stink about it.

Flawless GE performance? You leave nothing to chance. You check *every* box—or the turkey could be you.

He got the word to the transportation manager who was orchestrating the entire event and handing out the lunches that his missing sandwich was "no big deal."

As he did in the infamous "white trash lunch" incident in the late '80s.

The Facility Manager at GE Corporate and the Dining Manager, my friend George Tonning, decided to be creative in the most excellent employee cafeteria, and after combing a bunch of southern cooking books, came up with "po' boy sandwiches," grits, and the usual stereotypical, heart-clogging crap.

The chefs put them all together, placards were placed at the cafeteria entrance, and in the tray line, announced "White Trash Day" at GE headquarters.

And it was a hit!

Well, maybe not a *total* hit. Or at least not a hit with the *black* employees who strolled into the cafeteria on that *Martin Luther King Jr. Day!*

Martin Luther King Jr. Day was not yet a national holiday so most of the black employees thought it was funny, shook their heads, loaded up on the black-eyed peas, okra, and corn bread, and let it pass.

One or two of the mid-level black HR managers did not. They raised hell with senior management.

George was beside himself; the "facilities people" were distraught, and everybody had a rotten day, until Jack got the word down—maybe just to me (I forget)—that "shit happens," and that trying something edgy and innovative was not a capital offense in Welch GE—even if it led to disaster.

Even the misspelling of his name in the first issue of *The Monogram*—the GE magazine—was so outrageous that he found it amusing. My whole PR component was preparing for a Jonestown-style Kool-Aid social when the mistake was found, but he let the word get down that he wasn't going to kill anyone for it—at least this time.

He let the magazine—and it was a good one—publish a few more years before he blew it up.

He nearly blew it up just a year or two after the "Welsh [sic] incident" when the magazine ran an interview with him and featured *another* story on the cover—about "GE on the Ohio River," or something like that. He communicated his displeasure to our VP of PR at the time, and I went up to see him a short time later—leading off our conversation by saying, "You know Jack, I'm kind of disappointed to hear you're jealous just because they didn't put you on the cover of *The Monogram.*"

I don't know why I say stuff like that on occasion—and I soon wished I hadn't, that time—because he began shouting that he could be on the cover of *Fortune* or *BusinessWeek* tomorrow if he wanted, and this wasn't an "ego thing," but that he was mad because his interview focused on "the direction we were taking this company over the next few years," and that was "much more important than that shit they had on the cover."

Enraged, he then picked up the phone and called the terrified editor of the magazine, berated him for about thirty seconds, told him he had done a "shitty job" and had no idea what was important and what *wasn't* important—"like that shit you put on the cover."

The editor—a great writer and today an accomplished author—sat in a black funk in his office for a day or two, until a conciliatory Welch barged in his office and apologized, as he did to me once for being "too loud." He fluffed up his confidence, and left him with at least the beginnings of a smile.

He regretted some of his volcanic eruptions, as I'm sure Bobby Knight does, because at heart, he did not like to make worthwhile people unhappy.

Some people might laugh out loud at that view.

One of our British vice presidents, to whom I reported very early in the Jack years, once asked me if I thought that the "passion" everyone was already describing in Welch's persona was really that, or "mere sentiment."

I didn't really understand the distinction he was making—or the importance of it being made—and I'm not 100 percent sure I do today.

I have given it a fair amount of thought over the years, based on frequent observation of the habits this remarkable creature, and I think the answer is both: Irish sentimentality and true, visceral passion.

I've seen and felt both.

And neither was fake.

He called me when he heard about my mother-in-law, who, after being taken off an anti-clotting drug to prepare for breast cancer surgery, threw a clot, had a stroke, then another clot and stroke—and died!

I was down—very down, and told him, "You're supposed to *hate* your mother-in-law; and I *loved* her."

He interrogated me on the details. "What drug was it? Why didn't he put her back on it after the surgery?" (He had a hypochondriac's dangerous semi-command of pathology and medicines.) He then concluded: "Doctor fucked up. You need to go home and take care of your wife."

A Pad in Front of You

A few years later I *really* had to take care of my wife; and Jack, and the whole executive office and medical department of GE, helped me do it.

We had gone to the local mall to buy sandals and hats and sun screen for a trip to the Bahamas the next day.

We split up—Beth, with our daughter, and I, with one of our sons—to shop. We decided to meet in an hour, at three o'clock, to go home.

No-show at three o'clock, or for another 45 minutes.

Followed by Tommy, I began to frantically circumnavigate the mall until Regan burst in from the parking lot and told us that, "Mom fainted in the bookstore. But she's okay. They just took her to the hospital to check up on her."

She didn't believe that; and I didn't either, as we raced toward Bridgeport Hospital.

Beth was pretty much out of it when we arrived; tongue severely bitten from the seizure.

Cat Scan. Doctor brings me into a room off the ER, motions me toward a chair—*not* a good sign.

"She's got a brain tumor."

And indeed she had.

A malignant son-of-a-bitch of an astrocytoma.

So we decided to cancel the Bahamas trip and have brain surgery, three days later, then chemo at Memorial Sloan-Kettering, and then radiation in Connecticut, and not a lot of happy outcomes prophesized.

I didn't take it too well. I did my job, but I moped around at work, and at home as well. Tender e-mails from the senior and junior leadership at GE with prayers and thoughts for my beautiful Beth, whom many had met.

And from Jack, his calls nervous and concerned.

One of the GE doctors, Ken Grossman, took us into Sloan-Kettering for the initial follow-up consultation after the surgery.

Months go by. Chemo, radiation, and Beth laughing all the way through it, finally tells me to stop "moping," take a day off and play golf, before the weather gets cold.

So I did, with my rising young superstar friend, Mark Vachon, at Brooklawn.

I'm actually having fun when my beeper goes off on the eleventh tee.

I call Diane—now my admin.

"Mr. Welch called. He wanted to know how Beth was doing. Do you want to call him?"

Jack is now weeks from his retirement date and totally in the background, as Jeff Immelt is wrapping the reins around his hands.

I had gotten strong vibes that they were getting ready to "package me up" because Jeff "didn't want a speechwriter"; and I had become too expensive, a corporate decoration, and not a very attractive one, at that.

I wanted to ask Jack a final favor—my first, actually—and have him weigh in for the best "package" I could possibly get; and so I asked my golf partner, Mark, "should I call him now, or wait until I get my shit together with what I want to ask? He just called to ask me about Beth."

Mark: "Wait until you know *exactly* what you want to say, and have it in front of you." A 43-year-old punk telling the company 'communications expert' how to pitch to the Chairman.

And so I did. I waited.

I finished golf and went to GE. Got a yellow pad and Flair-penned my phone speech bullets.

Called Jack, and I answered his questions about how well Beth was doing, thanked him for his concern. He then asked, "Is there *anything* I can do for you?" I then began my presentation which began,

"You don't owe me *shit*, and I owe you *everything*, but I need a favor."

"I'm pretty sure they're going to 'shoot' me. Jeff doesn't want a writer. I understand this, and I don't have a problem with it. The problem is that I may have to raise three kids by myself because my wife may die, and I need a *great* 'package'—the best I can get."

"Who told you they were going to? Just wait. I'll get back to you, and don't worry. I'll call you in a day and let you know."

"Thanks."

Next day Welch calls. "I talked to Bill Conaty (Senior VP, HR). They're not going to 'do anything' soon, but if they do you'll get the best deal in the company."

It was an exaggeration, but when the shot rang out six months later (I was thrilled), the deal was, as promised, generous.

Rehearse any life-changing conversation like this, at least in your mind, and have a pad in front of you, if on the phone. Never hang up and think "Why didn't I say this?" or "I forgot to tell her that."

Part VIII

If Your Wife Thinks It's Boring, It's *Boring*

Welch got a bit cockier and "Hollywood" as the '90s rolled on and did not rehearse as much. In the '80s and early '90s we would hole up in the Fairfield Board Room and rehearse a speech for an hour or two. I would sit halfway down the board table, recorder running, and he would stand at the lectern. I would hit my stopwatch button and say "go."

And he would *go* while I took notes, sometimes interject, and mostly sit there and get bored during the second run-through. The first run was usually great; the second fine; by the third, the words that had bounced around in my pillowed head for a week or two became a blur.

I would suppress yawns by clinching my teeth. Bored by Jack Welch!

And then my reverie would be interrupted by the high-pitched: "Wait a minute. Why are we saying this? Didn't we already say this in the beginning?" (Papers flipping around on the lectern.)

"Yeah, maybe we did. In a different way. We can take that out. Save some time."

"What are we 'up to'?"

"Seventeen minutes."

"Too long. This is gonna be *way* too long. Maybe we should take out that shit you put in about "Work Out."

"No, you can't, Jack. That's the most important part."

"Okay, maybe. But why don't we take out this stuff about bureaucracy. We could save [Jack counting] three or maybe four paragraphs."

"Okay by me, but we need to do a transition."

"No, *you* do the transition. *You're* the speechwriter. Let's move on…"

He would begin again, and I would sit and act focused as the ritual progressed. Finally, Rosanne would appear quietly at the Board Room threshold, await Jack's notice, and than announce, when he stopped talking and looked at her, that President Clinton or Elizabeth Taylor or the Risen Christ, was in his office and that he was "running behind."

"Okay, Bill. We'll do this later. Maybe about six? That okay?"

"I'll be here," as visions of a "quick nine holes" before home dribbled away and I went down to call the guys and cancel.

Here's a B-school, B-average guy now moving into serious six figures; and he's disappointed at having to rehearse through the late evening with the superstar of global business and missing bad golf with his crazy friends.

Maybe Welch was right. I *am* an a-hole.

But, I am also someone who *bores easily* and will never allow a client of mine, or an audience of mine, to be boring or to be bored.

Rehearsing is essential.

If you are early in your career and cannot commandeer even a few people to listen to you rehearse, and your husband or wife refuses or falls into a catatonic trance after the first thirty seconds, either seek a quick divorce or try this: Do it by yourself.

Find a conference room, or, as I did, the GE auditorium. Lock the door, clock yourself, clear your throat, and begin. For the first few minutes this approach will be surreal—the sound of your voice in the empty room analogous to the tree falling in the empty forest. But drive on and in a few minutes you will get the same buzz as if there were a hundred people in front of you. Suddenly digressions will become apparent, boring passages, unnecessary discussion, rambling, and non sequiturs will ooze out, if there are any. And there will be.

You may stand there experiencing the unusual phenomenon of *boring yourself.* These passages must be hacked out of your pitch after you finish rehearsing. You, and maybe your eventual audience, will be thrilled at the effect the excisions have. You don't think that anything that bores you, the author and speaker, during your rehearsal, will fascinate an audience, do you?

And that is your job: to fascinate. And your job requires that you devote as much time and work and passion so that the end product—your pitch—will fascinate.

Jack's advice to me as I headed for Crotonville to do a presentation: "Tell them to try it out on their wives, and if they think it's boring—*it's boring.* Do it over!

Aside from the obvious male-centric thrust of Jack's advice, it is right on the money. Rehearse any presentation that you have not done before.

Get your presentation into the shape you think you love. And then bring a few of your colleagues, an admin or two, or some random victims into a room of a size approximating the one where you will do the real thing—if practical—and rehearse.

If you can, bring in at least one known cynic who will point out its flaws when everyone else is telling you how great it is. Bring in someone who is senior to you, if you are not the top dog, and listen to his or her views, if you respect him or her.

Pay close attention to opinions that allude to synonyms for boring. For example, "It was great, but I thought it was a little long in places." Or, "I didn't understand why you were telling us about all that analysis and methodology. Will this crowd want to know about that?"

Answer: No! They won't.

And be sure to ask your critics before you do your pitch to be prepared to tell you exactly what they thought they heard you say.

You may be shocked to hear what they perceived as your message—it is sometimes 180 degrees from what you thought you were conveying.

Make adjustments toward radical clarification.

Simplification, benign repetition, emphasis, and on occasion, a succinct conclusion or summary chart may be indicated to enhance your comfort level, although I would never use one, and neither would Welch.

Your next task, after listening to your rehearsal victims, is to "clean this thing up"; to cut out anything that goes on too long or is boring.

And most of the cutting should be done with a cleaver rather than a scalpel. I don't think I've ever seen a presentation hurt by being made shorter—even radically shorter.

Some presentations—even good ones—follow this pattern: A strong introduction and then "padding along" for a minute or so to get to a really great point you really can't wait to make because it's so good, then some more filler to get you to the next big point, and then the next, then on to the end, which is sometimes also good.

Use your rehearsal to cut out entirely, or at least minimize, the transitions from major point to major point, so that when you stand up to deliver it, you—like Welch—"can't wait" to do the thing "because it's so good."

It becomes, in effect, your greatest hits.

Ringo Starr once said that one of the regrets he had of his Beatles days was that when they made The White Album *into two records, they had to fill it up with some crap ("Revolution 9" and "Why Don't We Do It in the Road?" come to mind). He said they should have picked the very best songs and put out just one record that might have been their greatest album.*

Get all the boring and nonessential filler out of your pitch. Rehearsing is the way to find it, to "feel it."

And then remove it.

No business presentation should ever be boring. Even if it's about industrial electronics, circuit breakers, plastics, derivatives, acquisition philosophy, or reinsurance. Nothing need ever be boring, and don't believe anyone who tells you it need be.

If you are providing your listeners with something of use to them, applicable to their business lives, you will never be boring.

Ask yourself, continuously, as you prepare the pitch, "Why should they care about this?"

And if you can't answer that question, or if the answer is, "They won't care," you've got a bad pitch.

Danger: Flying Carrot Fragments

I experienced some difficulty with Welch, by failing to rehearse the things I was giving *him* to look at.

Asked by him to do a "spec" speech, something we could work from, I did just that. Spent a week or so—six or seven hours a day—writing and rewriting.

One relatively long passage in the speech seemed to me just a little off point, but since I thought the passage was good—and it *was* good, and, to be perfectly honest, I had invested many hours in it—I left it in. I violated my instinct.

I sent the speech up to Jack and was summoned to the conference room by the quiet and understated voice of Rosanne, "Can you come up and see Mr. Welch?"

Star Trek door opens. "How are you?"

"Fine. Hi, Jack."

"How's so-and-so doing? How about so-and-so? Is he brain-dead or what?"

Confirmation of a question like that would mean being an accessory to career murder; and I would never do it.

"Everybody can't be a freakin' superstar like you, Jack. Leave him alone."

A flash of anger and annoyance, passing quickly. "I didn't look at the speech yet. Why don't you *read it to me*, and then we'll get started."

This was a different approach than we had used in the past.

I began reading, as Jack, who was now well into his carrot stick phase of compulsive oral fixation, began crunching stick after stick from the glasses on the table and sideboard.

I came to the place—the page I suspected was off-topic—that had troubled me. I should have taken it out, and I felt my face redden as I hurried through it. The carrot crunching increased noticeably in intensity as I slogged through this bog I had created. A faint noise of impatience, even more violent carrot crunching; and then an orange carrot fragment *actually sailed across my vision plane, over the top of my paper.*

He didn't spit it at me. It just flew out of his mouth.

I got through to the end; and we began a new speech, incorporating some of my original stuff. And yes, we deep-sixed the entire passage that had caused the carrot-launchings.

You have to ruthlessly "kill your own intellectual children" if you want to deliver the best of presentations. I had spent hours on the part that I knew did not fit, and what I needed to do was take a Flair pen and put a big "X" through what I had written—but I didn't. And carrot shrapnel and impatience and disapproval were the result.

The question always in your mind must not only be, "Do I care about this?" But, "Will they care about this?"; "Should they care about this?"

Don't walk out there and bore people.

Ringo's Rule

The great thing about this band is whoever had the best idea,
that's the one we'd use. —Ringo Starr

If you don't have a wife or husband, try your pitch on your friends, or even your vice chairman, if you have one. Welch would listen to advice from *anyone* whose intellect he respected, on any subject.

Even me. I was called up to his office sometime in the '90s. He was now living in a brick mansion in Southport with views of the harbor, and across the street from "Sasco," the golf club to which he had been finally admitted after a several-year wait.

"Bill, I need some advice. I've got this place in Southport but it's up on the hill over the harbor and the wind sweeps across it. I thought that if it had a name, 'Windswept,' it would add to its value. I've been told that it definitely does, you know, if the house has 'a name.' But I had a brick wall put around the place down near the street. Do you think that's where I should put the metal plaque that says 'Windswept'? Or would people laugh at that, and think it looks phony?"

People were already making fun of the wall around the house—at least Don Imus, who lived part-time in Southport on the other side of the harbor, had been doing so on the air.

A short time before the Windswept discussion, Imus had announced on the radio that Jack Welch had put up a brick wall around that "middle-school house he lives in," so he could "smuggle in little boys without being seen."

I heard this in the car and almost had to pull over I was laughing so hard. I sent Jack a note as soon as I got to work telling him what Imus had said about the "little boys" and the wall; and I reassured him that our "crack public relations unit" had issued a press release "neither confirming nor denying" Imus's allegations.

My view on the "Windswept issue"—with no qualifications on such matters—was that it could well be ridiculed by Imus and his neighbors if on the gate; and that it would be better placed on a modest monument-style structure midway up the walk to the front door.

He loved the idea and I think he put up the monument, but I can't be sure because I was half-in-the-bag the next time I went over to his house. I was concentrating on staying on the walk and finding the front door, and I forgot to look for it.

Sunday afternoon. Winter day. Mid-'90s. My family, for some reason, was away for the day.

Giants football on the tube.

Giants *ahead* in the first quarter.

The prospect of finding out how they would blow *this* game was unbelievably exciting.

Pour a big Beefeater on the rocks with a little lemon twist. That gets me through the first quarter, so I fire up another one, proving Bob Nelson's borrowed maxim: "There is no such thing as one martini."

Halftime comes and goes, and I vaguely consider the possibility of the *third* shoe dropping. Giants still ahead. My house is quiet.

God is in His heaven and the world is a nice place in which to hang out.

Phone rings. Caller ID reveals nothing.

"Hello?"

"Bill, It's Jack!! I'm right over your house!!"

Oh my God! What can this possibly mean?

(Calmly) "Hi, Jack. Uh… *Where* are you?"

"I'm coming back from Europe, and Paolo and I have some really good ideas for the letter [the CEO annual report letter]. Why don't you come over to my house in an hour. By that time I'll be home and we can work on this. I've got too much shit to do tomorrow and I want to get going while it's still fresh. Is that okay?"

"Sure, I'll be there. See ya." An honest man would have said, "You know what, Jack? I'm half shit-faced. The Giants are winning. And I don't feel like wrestling with a pumped up, jet-lagged alligator for four hours, ruining what I thought was a close-to-final draft of the annual report letter with questionable observations from your smooth dog, pretty boy, English-as-a-second- (or third or fourth) language Vice Chairman.

But of course I didn't say that, and got in my wife's *gendarme*-bait Corvette and scooted, under the speed limit, over to the Welches', about fifteen minutes away.

I drove up the driveway and was greeted by the lady of the house, Lady Jane Welch, who loved the Corvette and raved about it from the open front door.

I mumbled, artlessly, "Your husband bought it for me." Meaning, of course, by making the stock "dance." We're talking about a five-year-old white Corvette convertible with a street value of, perhaps, $25,000.

Jane let that pass, welcomed me in and brought me a diet coke. I didn't have the nerve to ask for coffee. She sat me at a table in the magnificently decorated ground floor room.

Jack descends from upstairs. "Hi. Thanks for coming over. Paolo and I came up with some great stuff on the way back."

"No problem, Jack; just understand that I had a martini before you called." This was not exactly a lie; I did have a martini, but I should have said the sentence twice. "In case there are fumes, they're from the martini, but I'm fine."

(Not interested) "Sure, fine. Now here's the way we need to take this section on Work Out…"

And so we went for three hours or so, while the recorder ran and as I rapidly grew more clear in my thoughts. I left with profound thanks from Jack and we made the letter one of "our greatest" over the next couple of weeks.

My friend and college classmate and GE mate John Connelly, describes his view of the secret of Welch's success as "fanaticism." And that may sound crazy, but it's simply another way of saying what I've already said: never do anything you don't really care about. This is particularly true in communications, where not caring quickly becomes obvious to the people with whom you are supposed to be communicating.

The wonderful craziness of the '90s reached its apogee in 1995, when the stock returned 45 percent to its holders.

We worked and worked on the letter, and I six lost pounds as the weeks wore on. My wife started her routine about being "a single mother" since I was coming home late (but not really *that* late, to be honest).

We got the letter done, as we always did. The 1995 letter started out with *one hundred* drafts, several of them major; and now we were near the finish line. Now the interplay between us consisted of things like this:

"You've got a semicolon here. I like a dash better."

"Dash doesn't really fit here, Jack, and we use too many of them."

"Is it *wrong* with a dash?"

"No, not really."

"Then use the dash. Okay? Humor me."

Then on to the perennial war of the pronouns. "Each manager in this Company must use 100 percent of their intellect focusing on…"

"You can't say that, Jack. It has to be 'his' intellect; or 'his or her' intellect…"

"I hate that. Why can't I say 'their'?"

"Because it's incorrect English, and there should be no mistakes in this letter. I know every one of your colleagues uses it, and all the politicians and TV idiots use it because 'their' is more economical and avoids all the 'him and her' stuff—but it's wrong."

(Angrily) "Okay, but you figure out how to change the sentence around without all that 'his and her' shit."

"Okay." And I would, tiptoeing around each grammatical trap by using plural subjects, such as "managers," which would allow me to use plural, sex-neutral pronouns such as "them" and "their." We could then say: "Managers must use 100 percent of their intellects…"

But it's a losing war with the "his and her" issue.

The Perfect Annual Report

When Larry Bossidy announced he was leaving GE, Welch told me he was distraught and depressed over the weekend after it happened. But on Monday morning when I met with him, he was already looking at the sunny side of the road ahead because of the organizational cleanliness and leanness Larry's departure would bring about: 12 businesses would report directly to the CEO.

We sat down to "back-and-forth" a letter to his 550 top people, and came up with a sentence that read: "for the foreseeable future" all 12 businesses would report to Jack.

We continued to cruise along on the text—and then a pause: "What does 'foreseeable' mean?"

I didn't feel like bogging down on this when we were moving so well, so I said, "a year and a half to two years"—which was my view of foreseeable future.

"Fine." And we moved on. He and the major players, particularly CFO Dammerman, hated generalities unsupported by specific data.

But the "his-or-her" and "dash-or-semicolon" hairsplitting discussions were immensely welcome to me because they were the yellow lights that meant the end was near on this *Oberammergau* journey toward the printing of "his letter."

It meant we were headed toward the final draft!

The journey had begun two and a half weeks earlier. He had returned from our Boca meeting high as a kite from the quality of the discussions and the passion of his 550 top managers. He was thrilled by the learning and insights he had gleaned at the dinners and on the golf course, and was still relishing the "buzz" from the reviews his guys had given on his closing remarks—one of his best and most inspiring pitches ever.

So I was summoned to the conference room. He entered carrying his yellow pad Boca script, assorted other scraps and articles, "idea notes" from people, and stuff he had asked Rosanne to save for this project over the past year.

"How are you?"

"Fine."

"Great Boca. What a team we've got now! Morale is unbelievable."

"Yeah. That's 'cause we're all gettin' rich."

"My close (closing remarks) went well," he said modestly. "How long was it?"

"Fifty minutes."

He shrinks, visibly, with an embarrassed little-boy look. Cringes. I let him suffer—in genuine mortification—for a second or two—and then tell him it "didn't seem so long," and "it was terrific." Which it was.

We get started, with him orbiting the room, sticks of gum being loaded. Gestures. Shouting. Grabbing my shoulders. "Great! Terrific! Did you get that? Make sure you got that! Play it back! Let me hear it again! Yeah. *Yeah.* That's it. Don't touch that. It's perfect. Don't you think?"

And so on, until finally, "Is that enough for a start? Huh? You got enough? Can you get me a draft by Friday afternoon, for the weekend?"

This was Monday, and I said, "That's too much time. I'll screw around with other stuff if I have that much time. Why not, like, noon Thursday?"

"Good. *Good!!*" He liked that, for the honesty in it. "I'll see you then. Thanks, Bill." Warm.

When he is happy and pleased with you, and the way things are going, he radiates warmth like a space heater.

Thursday noon finds me locked in a borrowed, windowless cubicle-type office that was used as a storeroom for Company propaganda. But it is completely enclosed and so peaceful. It has a little table and chair, no distractions, and no phone.

I'm writing furiously, and cursing my stupid macho deadline change because I know that the "Hound of Third Floor Heaven" is probably starting to wonder, "Where is it?"

Then I hear the high-pitched voice out in the corridor: "Where is he? He's in *here*? Where? In *here*?"

Door flies open, "What are you doing in here? (Laughing) This looks like a place where a grunt works."

"It is. *I* work here sometimes when I don't want to be bothered. Obviously it doesn't work all the time."

"How are you doing? You going to have anything for me? Doesn't have to be perfect. I just want to get started looking at it." Uncharacteristically apologetic.

I basically threw him out. "If you will leave me alone for three hours, I'll give you something that's a *lot* better than just a draft."

"Okay, see ya." Out the door and kidding the secretaries—who are fluttering around—laughing and bragging about how he was able to "track him (me) down."

Then, after spending three and a half hours frantically flogging my poor Diane, I send him up a draft with a note to help sell it, which said, "I am not at all embarrassed by this, as a draft. I think it's *very* good."

About a half hour later I'm summoned up and I scoot into his office.

"Well, what do you think?"

"It's the *nuts*! I *love* it! You *nailed* it." Wild enthusiasm and then, "I'll take it home and we'll get together tomorrow and polish it up. Thanks, Bill. Thanks. This is terrific."

He can make you feel like a billion bucks.

Ninety-nine(!) drafts later, we were nearing the end.

I know with precision how many drafts there were because the secretary would type "WKL-14"—my initials plus the draft number in the corner, and save a paper and electronic copy of each. At least we did that for a while until I started getting cumulonimbus-faced questions from Welch such as, "Why does it say 'WKL-38' up here?" pointing at my initials as if at a melanoma. "Those are *your* initials. This is *my* letter. Why do you have your initials on it?" Clearly it should have been "JFW-38," in his mind.

I dumped the "WKL" shortly thereafter, and just left the date and draft number.

And the drafts continued all the way through to the "dash vs. semicolon" session; and then he leaned back in his chair and said to me across the desk, "Bill, it's done. It's wonderful. I don't need to see it again. Tell them to print it. Great job."

So I went back down to my office. The annual report editor, Ray, a friend, came in, thrilled that he could now go and print the GE "book" within our booked time at a huge printing plant in Oregon.

Ray is thrilled; I am full of myself, recounting amusing Welch stories of the past few weeks, and I go home at 5:30. Ray heads out to Oregon on a red-eye that night with the electronic files for the grueling four- or five-day grind at the printing plant.

I'm still perched in my swivel chair two days later, feet up on desk, dreaming of tees and greens as I look out at the barren winter Connecticut landscape.

The phone rings—a Welch ring—or more precisely, a Rosanne ring…

"Can you come up and see him?"

"Yes!!!" Visions of management awards, more option grants, and warming Irish effusions of praise cheered me on my way up the back stairs to his outer office.

Rosanne points wordlessly to the inner office.

Welch is at his desk, annual report letter and yellow pad in front of him. Flair pen in hand. Scowl. *Serious* scowl.

"Jack. What's the matter?"

The helicopter is down the hill, warming up on the GE pad, stinking up the place with kerosene fumes, and giving the few Vietnam vets on the campus just a little bit of a flashback to the smells of our "Hueys" in 'Nam.

Jack is supposed to be at Crotonville in a half hour or so. His plan is to "preview" his annual report letter to two or three combined classes in The Pit—the ultimate "inside baseball" for a bunch of GE managers, who know that *USA Today, Washington Post,* and other papers would practically bid to get the first shot at it. And *they*—the Crotonville "kids"—will be privy to the guts of it, a week early!

But he's sitting there, angry and unhappy, yellow pad next to the typeset annual report letter, jotting notes that he would use to speak from at Crotonville.

"What's the *matter?*"

"It's not *logical;* it doesn't flow right. We talk about boundaryless behavior; then about Crotonville and management selection—the 'four types of managers;' then all this shit about 'Work Out,' and 'self-confidence,' and 'simplicity.' All this stuff is good, but it doesn't flow." He changed his mind when he began to organize it into an oral presentation. That discipline illuminated the letter's flaws in how it flowed.

"Well, you've got a half hour before you talk. Let's change it. I'll go with you in the helicopter."

"What? What are you, a fucking idiot? I'm not talking about Crotonville. We have to change the *Annual Report.*"

Approaching hysteria, I said, "Jack, they're printing *two million* of these goddamn things right now. We *can't* change it."

Levitating, space shuttle smoke rising from his chair: *"I don't give a shit if it costs a million bucks! Or if we lose our place in line at the plant! Or if they never print the fucking thing! We're going to make this right!"*

"When I arrive in the morning we'll get together with [two or three senior VP's—Ben Heineman, General Counsel, and a few others] and make this work. Now you go down and you think this through."

I don't remember exiting the office, but I do remember picking up the phone and getting Ray at the printing plant in Oregon, and telling him, "Stop the presses." I had seen this done in 1940s B-movies and old *Superman* episodes, and it was kind of a minor power trip.

But trauma lay ahead.

Ray made a groan of pain, but then brightened and said that, because the annual report, for some reason, was being printed from back-to-front, he could continue printing, but we had to get the CEO Letter done fast so we wouldn't have to shut down the presses.

I began revising and "re-transitioning" the letter without messing with the thoughts and the phrases with which I knew he was enamored. Five or six hours, and five drafts after that, I had a copy up to Welch. He generally liked what I had done, but came down to our "shop" to "fine tune" it on the huge and powerful Mac computer that produced the final files.

So, with a sweating computer operator from the GE basement graphics netherworld pounding the keys, Welch and I, along with Joyce and Ben Heineman, yelled out "change that;" "move that over there;" "No, *No*, not there. Over here." Fingerprints all over the monitor.

All of the inhabitants of the open bays had evacuated to less turbulent areas of the second floor. All of the glass office doors had been shut, while the denizens whispered to their husbands or wives on their phones, "Jack Welch is outside my office yelling and screaming at the computer guy" (mistaking Jack's intensity and excitement for anger, which it was not).

We got it done.

I realize all this thrashing around and the tempest in the teapot of corporate communications is the stuff that soldiers, cops, and firemen laugh at as an exercise run by—and for the benefit of—a bunch of pale, overpaid, soft-handed business people—"thrills, chills, and broken yo-yo strings."

But I went home that night, as I did many nights, with a buzz of exhilaration that lasted long after I had bored my wife to death, and closed my eyes in search of a sleep in which I was not really interested—while replaying paragraphs in my head and wondering about whether some company whose name we mentioned "was hyphenated or not."

"Beth, remind me to check that in the morning."

But the tempest in the teapot had, once again, produced the world's best annual report letter, generating above-the-fold headlines on several of the business pages. The stock got a kick and continued to move upward. And I had been a part of it; and Welch made sure I *felt* a part of it.

Anything signed by him or spoken by him had to be *owned* by him—had to be his.

If you are a CEO, or leader of an organization or component and merely "sign off" on your communications, or read things written for you; or sign messages to your employees put in front of you; you are probably not a bad CEO; but you are not a "fanatic"—the best leader you can be. If that's okay with you, that's okay.

Do you just sign things or say things that are put in front of you? It may be kind of an ego trip, cool, and even regal, but it's not the stuff of which transformational leaders are made.

"Not a Pennyworth of Difference"

"Sometimes I sit there for 20 minutes and wonder, 'why are they telling me all this shit?'"

That was the utterly candid and wonderful Larry Bossidy, who actually never *really* sat still for as long as 20 minutes listening to someone tell him "all this shit." And I'm positive he never sat there for 20 minutes when he became CEO of Allied Signal—and later Honeywell.

Larry, as usual, hits it on the head, with the question every audience member should ask as the droning from the stage or the end of the conference table continues. "Why are you telling me this? Why should I listen to you if you are not 'feeding' me, giving me something I can take back to my business or my job, and *use*?"

Can you answer that honestly? Or would you offer these lame protestations?

- *"Well, it's pretty good background on this project we've been working on, with some new data."*
- *"Well, they asked me—the boss asked me—to report out on our new router product (or locomotive, or spaceship, or whatever)."*

That's fine, but why should most of the people in that crowd give a rat's ass about your locomotive? What does what you're telling them do for their jobs, their products, their problems, their lives? What does it do to make your company *faster, more competitive, smarter*?

The most "spot-on," as the Brit's say, summary of the utility of presentations and shared information comes not from Welch, who arrived at the insight about a century later, but from Sherlock Holmes, the detective creation of Sir Arthur Conan Doyle.

Dr. Watson, Holmes's eventual friend and chronicler, is evaluating the intellectual strengths and weaknesses of his new acquaintance in their first detective adventure, *A Study in Scarlet*:

His ignorance was as remarkable as his knowledge. Of contemporary literature, philosophy and politics he appeared to know next to nothing. My surprise reached a climax, however, when I found incidentally that he was ignorant of the Copernican Theory of the composition of the Solar System. That any civilized human being in the Nineteenth Century should not be aware that the earth traveled around the sun appeared to be to me such an extraordinary fact that I could hardly realize it.

"You see," he explained, "I consider that a man's brain originally is like a little empty attic, and you have to stock it with such furniture as you choose. A fool takes in all the lumber of every sort that he comes across, so that the knowledge which might be useful to him gets crowded out, or at least is jumbled up with a lot of other things…"

"Depend upon it there comes a time when for every addition of knowledge you forgot something you knew before. It is of the highest importance, therefore, not to have useless facts elbowing out the useful ones."

"What the deuce is it to me? You say that we go around the sun. If we went around the moon it would not make a pennyworth of difference to me or to my work."

Why tell people about things that are of no practical use to them? Why, as a leader, do you tolerate your people hosing you, or each other, down with reports and "background" and "updates" and "analyses?"

If you embrace the following maxim, you will never do another bad pitch: Any presentation that does not give the people in the audience something they can take out the door with them and use is a failure and a waste of their time.

Part IX

Bore Wars Continue ...

The "paper ball revolution" occurred in 1986. A few months after our Crotonville "graduation," Welch and I put together the agenda for the corporate officers meeting in Phoenix.

It is worthwhile, in my view, to show how presentation philosophy had progressed under Welch by that time.

If you recall we had, in 1980, "A Vision of the Industrial and Consumer Businesses, 1980–1990."

"A Vision of the Energy, Technical, and Materials Businesses 1980–1990."

And on and on. Nothing *shared*, nothing gained.

Spin forward to 1986 and the officers meeting. Here are a few of the new generation of agenda topics:

"Alliances for Strategy: Plastics."

"Alliances for Strategy: Factory Automation."

And then Gary Wendt—the "cup-munching nut"—with, "Acquisition Integration: How to Make One and One Equal Three."

Then, *this*: "Let's put the European medical systems guys on the program. Give 'em twenty minutes. They had a great year. *Twenty minutes*. Got it?"

"Jack, that's too long."

"*Give 'em twenty minutes to tell their story. They had a great year. Twenty minutes!!*" he repeated.

Then he got quiet for nearly a full minute as if I were no longer in the room and stared down at the table with the semi-scowl that meant some kind of processing was going on. This phenomenon did not happen that often with other people around; but even the senior people in the company, those closest to him, would sit quietly until the internally tempestuous little reverie worked itself out.

Then he spoke loudly and decisively: *"No, no, no! We're not doing this any more. No more 'reports.' We're sick of reports. The only pitches that are worth anything are when you tell people what they ought to do. Otherwise it's just a waste."*

And so it began, gradually and then with increasing momentum, that GE began to move from a typical, pompous, self-absorbed corporation to what Welch would later describe, with as much pride—and even love—as I have ever heard in his voice, as "a real *learning* company."

We became a company of teachers and students, everyone playing both roles; sometimes playing both on the same day.

The best practices idea that Mike Fraiser—the red-headed "Opie" kid— had surfaced in that magical pitch that supercharged his career, began to consume Welch's imagination, and he began to describe it as "the ultimate competitive advantage" a company can have; "the ability to embrace great ideas from anywhere, spread them across the organization and get them quickly into practice."

We no longer had the time or patience to listen to blowhards, braggarts, bullshitters, politicians, or bores. Everyone on the program had to have something of interest and use to say. They were no longer on the program because "they had a good year," or because they were big shots. There were no more "reports"—except for maybe two.

The first "report" was the executive compensation update, which was always a big hit, delivered by the head of HR. This consisted of the announcement of "breakthroughs" such as permitting officers to lease foreign cars as part of their "deal," rather than the previous policy where the company only paid the leases on American cars. This policy caused me to begin referring to GE corporate officers as "Lexus jockeys" as the East Building garage began to fill up with that trendy vehicle.

Deferred salary plans at 14 percent a year *thrilled* the crowd. Deferred bonus deals held everyone's interest. They certainly thrilled *me*.

The various option package descriptions and how they had performed since the meeting last year, had the crowd gasping and reaching for their option spread sheets and calculators.

And then the new officer "free GE appliance" updates were reported. This didn't apply to me, so I lost interest.

By the end of this pitch there wasn't, as we used to say, "a dry seat in the house." I, as the only non-officer in the room, sat in the back and made jealous grunting pig noises, to the amusement of the boys—and by now, girls—around me.

Welch used to laugh and make "pig" references before these reports began. But these people were *delivering*, and they were now getting *paid*, big time.

And they should have been.

The other report—usually equally thrilling—was the "Financial Perspective," then provided by the CFO, Dennis Dammerman, and now, for years, by Keith Sherin.

When I make the case for "no more reports" in the talks I occasionally give, the older members in the crowd will ask, understandably, "You mean you don't have a financial "state of the company" report at GE meetings?"

And my truthful answer is, "No, we don't," but when we walked out the door from these reports at Boca, we knew a lot of wonderful financial things about the company. But we also knew:

- *Inventory turns are way up,* but not matching the pace Jack has been promising the analysts. *Go back home and make this your Monday-morning priority.*
- *Your second agenda item needs to be plant and equipment spending. It's too high. Figure a way to reduce it by x percent and report precisely to us on your efforts, and your success, at your next operations review.*
- *Travel and Living. Out of control. People taking trips to run up their personal frequent flier miles! I once asked Welch why we couldn't "recoup" all those miles—because I considered frivolous travel at company expense to be an integrity violation—and he gave an uncharacteristically tepid answer that "we just can't do that." "Report back by (date) how much you have reduced T&L spending in your organization."*
- *Look at "this" in your business. Look at "that." Report back. "We cannot sustain this trajectory we are on, with earnings and stock price, without your attention to this."*

The pads in front of the attendees were scribbled on for two days at these meetings, and the pages torn off and brought home when the meetings were over. Homework assignments. No platitudes and inspirational bromides.

Thousands of hours of human lifetime entrusted to us. And to give them nothing more than "tone" or "impressions" or atmospherics was a raw deal for our mates.

We changed that by enforcing Welch's philosophy of "*telling people what they ought to do*," rather than the playacting of reports and "visions."

GE executives almost immediately became very comfortable with the new view of the purpose of presentations. Most of them—not all—hated the sham and fakery of the old-style dog-and-pony shows, and really wanted to share the same kinds of things with their mates from the podium that they shared in the bar or on the golf course.

Once it became clear that Welch was not writing down the "mistakes" they had made—he knew them anyway—some remarkably "un-GE" presentations began to capture the interest of the 500 Boca leaders.

People began to take notes!

What are your meetings like? Does Betty Creamcheese, the HR bore, and Joe the technology knucklehead read a bunch of illegible PowerPoint charts while their victims Blackberry each other with their suicide intentions?

Or does somebody from somewhere in the organization—maybe not even a big player—stand up and say, "You know, we in the XYZ division just ran into a problem with our customer base—a problem that each of you may have to face someday, sooner rather than later. I'd like to spend my ten minutes telling you how it hit us and the pain it caused, and how we got the right answers. You need to walk out the door today aware that this thing is 'out there' and can bite you in the ass at any time. But if you can avoid the mistakes we made it, will not be as painful."

Or perhaps, "Six months ago Steve, our VP of Customer Service, got a call from Shaminex, our number-three customer, who told him: 'You're fired.' That was not a pleasant day, and what we learned from talking with our customers was even worse. Our products are loaded with yesterday's technology and broke down more often than all our competitors." And so on.

Some of the very best presentations I have ever heard—like the one Jim Bunt made to me about diversifying out of equities on the day I got "packaged"—are warnings. And warnings should not be subtle. At GE the warnings were all stark, scary, and dramatic, like Paul Revere's horseback presentation. They were largely devoid of background, analysis, subtlety, nuance. Simply, urgently: "The British (or Japanese or Chinese) are coming!"

Some may say, afterwards, "he's trying to scare us to death." Most won't say that, and I guarantee that not a soul in the room will wonder "what the point was" of that pitch.

Want to get the stark and unsubtle tone of a good "warning" presentation? Take a look at the warning placards and labels on a large professional wood chipper—the kind landscapers and arborists (and wife-killers in Connecticut) use.

I ran a GE volunteer project that involved brush clearing, painting, carpentry, et cetera, and decided I would help with the brush clearing, and use the wood chipper—until I read the warning: STOP! THINK! DO NOT PUSH BRUSH PAST THIS LIMIT. LOOSE CLOTHING CAN BE CAUGHT IN BRUSH AND WILL DRAG YOU INTO THE BLADES OF THE MACHINE. THERE IS NO ESCAPE.

I decided to work with the painting crew.

Lloyd's Law: A Learning Company

Lloyd Trotter, now a Vice Chairman at GE, once stood up at Boca and described the "puffy" (a Jack word meaning pleasant) day he was having at his business—everything going well—when the phone rang and he was told of an environmental mess at one of his sites.

His presentation: How he dropped his coffee cup when the call came. What he *did* first. Whom he *called* first. Whom he *should* have called first. What he would do first next time. What he did right and what he did wrong. What *you* should do when that phone rings.

This is called "sharing," sharing what two or five or 30 years—or one disaster—has taught you; sharing what your mates *need* to know.

People will listen to a promise, from an experienced teacher, that what he is going to tell you will be useful and important to them. They really will.

Do they listen at your meetings? Do you start all your presentations with a promise of something of use to your audience? And do you deliver on that promise?

Lloyd was on the program, once again, at the officers meeting, with a humbly presented "matrix" he had invented to help manage his business. This matrix—the "Trotter Matrix," as it became known—spread across GE, and is widely used today.

The Trotter Matrix is a "forced ranking" around the leaders' goals, for both organizations and for individuals within those organizations. It is, to be candid, a procrustean managerial torture device in which achievers (typically those 5 percent over the "goal") are circled with what have become known as "halos." Those 5 percent *under* or more have rectangle shapes around them, which became known as "coffins."

These matrixes are updated practically in real time, and are visible to the entire organization.

One does *not* want the funereal rectangle around one's name or component for too long.

Lloyd offered his little matrix as a gift. Many in the officer audience walked out of the room, called back "home," and spread it across GE.

That's the way a "learning company" works. Jack didn't use devices like that, but he was thrilled at Lloyd's contribution.

A VP of Sales for the plastics business stood up and announced: "We just lost one of our biggest accounts, General Motors. We tried to raise prices on the 30 to 40 pounds of plastics per car we sell them, and they said, 'no.' We pressed the issue and they fired us. Seriously fired us. Jack and their CEO were drawn in. We thrashed around; and we finally got them back, although at a much smaller increase than what we had wanted. Both of us lost a lot of time and a ton of money in the time it took us to get it right. It was stupid and wasteful, and we went about it just wrong.

"What I'm going to tell you over the next 12 minutes is how you can avoid getting into a mess like this by avoiding the very simple—but critical—mistakes we made; and if you *do* get into this type of mess with a customer over a price increase, how you can get out of it."

Twelve minutes of 500 people scribbling notes—500 people, most of whom would some day have to raise prices on a critically important customer. Here's a guy spilling his guts to his friends; and I, a non-business guy in the back of the room, remember at least the gist of his pitch 20 years later.

Has anyone in your organization ever delivered a pitch that someone remembered, and referred to, and even cherished, a year later?

Have you, as a leader, made it clear to your people that it's okay to stand up and say "We screwed up. Here's what we did wrong. Don't you do this! Here's what we learned."

Welch made it clear that he understood people made mistakes; and smart people learned from them. And they shared what they learned with their friends.

Dave Nissen is a GE business leader who basically created one of GE's best businesses—once known as "Global Consumer Finance"—through a series of acquisitions. At one point the business—now known as GE Consumer Finance—did *no* business in the U.S.

Jack wanted him on the Boca program to talk about acquisition pointers and techniques, and I spent just a little time with Dave learning about the business.

I sat with Welch talking about the upcoming Boca program, in the late '90s, and I couldn't say enough about Nissen, whom I had gotten to know just a bit.

"Jack, this is a great man."

"Yeah. He's kind of an odd duck. But he *is* a great man."

And he gave *one of the greatest business presentations I have ever heard* at a Boca meeting in the late '90s. It consisted of a one-minute description of his business, which was a 10- or 15-billion dollar cash machine he had created. And he then said, "We built this business through acquisitions. We did a lot of smart things and a few dumb things; and, over the next 10 minutes I'm going to respectfully suggest to you what to do and what not to do when making an acquisition."

- *"First thing: Due diligence. Look for this. Look out for this. Don't do this.*
- *Combining 'back rooms.' When to do it.*
- *HR issues. Watch out for this. 'This' is what you* must *do. Never do this."*

This was nine or 10 years ago, and while I've garbled Nissen's points, I remember sitting in the back of the Boca hall thinking, "This is the way *all* presentations should be."

Maybe I need to "get a life," as they say, but I sat there watching 550 GE people, all of whom would someday, in some way, be involved in an acquisition, writing furiously, while the master of acquisitions laid out for his mates what they needed to know about how to do it.

The Blackberries were out of sight, and a thousand eyes and ears were riveted on this quiet, self-effacing "odd duck," as he told them things that could make or break their businesses and careers and lives.

A teacher; a team guy; a contributor. A great man.

It is perfectly acceptable to stand up and "blow" about a great success, for a minute—max—and then go on for eight or nine more minutes explaining why that success occurred. What you did that was right, and what you did that was—maybe—wrong. Every one of us, in retrospect, would do something differently. Those things must be part of your presentation.

The Bore Test. Are You Relevant?

Welch and Frank Doyle—our Executive VP, Relations—adopted a criterion for speaking at the GE Corporate Executive Council—the quarterly meeting of the top 30 or 40 players in the company. It was called a "bore test"; and before anyone was put on the program the question was asked and answered: "Will this subject be boring to anyone in the room?"

And if the answer was "yes" or "probably," that individual was not invited to speak.

How difficult is this?

Ironically, but appropriately, the injection of specificity, best practices, and "learning" into the agendas of our big meetings—the ones I ran—cost me part of my job, that of helping write the agendas and picking the speakers.

Gary Reiner, our Senior VP and CIO, was now charged with putting the agenda together for Jack's approval (I was kept in the loop) based on the truly intimate knowledge he had as to the best of what was going on around the company, and outside of it—particularly in Six Sigma and IT.

Gary, another relatively young guy with a scary IQ, would pick from around the company people who were out in front in some area *of general interest and usefulness to virtually everyone in the room* and propose them to Jack, who invariably *knew* them, or knew *of* them.

Some of the speakers were officers; and some, such as myself, were as junior as "Executive Band." Rank became utterly irrelevant; the quality and usefulness of the "thoughts" and teachings trumped rank. Bad presenters, disproportionately engineers, were labeled "awful" and were not allowed on the program. Some missed their big chance to stand up, at age 33 or so, and "teach" 150 GE officers in "The Pit" at the officers meeting.

More than once, a month or two after the meeting, those who were put on the program got their own "stripes"—a GE officership—following their having "knocked it out of the park" at the meeting.

Would you consider a "bore test" in your organization? At your meetings? At any level?

Do you have a communications person setting up your meetings and agendas with little or no input from you? And do you then just go there and be a big shot and snooze through all this self-serving crap and have your ass kissed during cocktails and dinner? Is this your view of communications in your company, and of the role of its leader?

Seize the agenda. *We're only talking a couple hours of work here. You don't have time?*

Are you a "game-changer" in your company? What are you doing that everyone needs to do? Are you missing an opportunity to pitch to those who can make you a star because you are considered "deadly," "detached," "too cerebral," "too theoretical?"

Do you turn and read your unreadable PowerPoint charts full of arcane analysis and footnotes, while your audience fires up Blackberry devices and tunes you out, as if you were static from somewhere outside the solar system?

Teach them something; give them something they can use, and you will never do another bad pitch.

Larry Leaves. Lane Grieves.
(On the Way to the Bank)

I never got totally "comfortable" with Welch, but I did begin to get comfortable with Bossidy and some of the other "players"—maybe *too* comfortable.

I understood this one day in the '90s.

I had set up a meeting to talk about the Boca agenda with Welch and Bossidy. It would have been late November, or very early December.

A couple of weeks after I had set up the meeting, "The Idiot"—and I don't mean to rip off either Dostoyevsky or Johnny Damon—wanders by his secretary's desk, probably on the way back from the gym.

"Oh, Bill. Did Mr. Welch and Mr. Bossidy reschedule?"

"What do you mean?"

"Don't you remember? You were supposed to meet with them at eleven o'clock."

It is now 11:35.

"Oh, my God. Has anyone called?"

"No."

I rocket up the back stairs and aim myself at one of Jack or Larry's conference rooms.

I barge in—acting cool and self-possessed, and say, "Sorry. Something came up; you wanna figure out this agenda? Shouldn't take too long."

I slide into a chair and they turn their attention to me. They have been engaged in billion-dollar dialogue, hirings and firings, in the privacy of a conference room with no interruptions, and have not even noticed that the grunt who called the meeting hadn't shown up for it.

Bluffed my way through that one.

But I *did* get comfortable with both Larry and Jack on the golf course.

Larry Bossidy was arguably GE's greatest Vice Chairman, after first growing GE Capital into the behemoth it has become (in fragmented form) today. Welch once told me, jocularly, that "a GE Vice Chairman's most important job is to play golf with the Japanese."

But Larry became Jack's "soul mate" and one of his "indispensable" men. Welch simply loved the guy for his toughness, his cynicism, his impatience, and the different kind of high IQ he brought to this all-star team now running GE.

Larry left GE in 1991 to become Chairman of Allied Signal.

I was seated at my desk one morning when he called.

"Bill, I'm leaving. I just wanted to let you know."

"Where are you going?" I thought he was leaving to deliver a speech we had been working on.

"I'm taking over at Allied Signal. I thought it was time I ran my own show."

"Larry," I said, "I'm sorry to hear this. I'm gonna miss you. We worked well together."

"I know. And I want you to know that I want to stay in touch and get together and play golf and stuff. Let's stay in touch."

"Sure, Larry. And good luck. Let me know if I can help."

I hang up and walk down to my boss, Joyce Hergenhan, who had already heard the news.

"Joyce, Larry just called me. He's leaving GE. This is a big loss."

Joyce was as politically astute as anyone in the company. She tells me, "Don't you do *anything* until you talk to us. Do you understand?"

I wandered back to my office in a naïve fog. What the hell is she talking about?

Ten minutes later, maybe less. Phone.

"Can you come up and see Mr. Welch?"

I get the "go sign" from Rosanne and barge into his office, beginning the conversation at the threshold: "Jack. Larry just called me. I can't believe it. He's leaving."

Welch: "Don't even think about it!"

"What do you mean?"

"You've got a big future in the Company. You're going to be Director of Communications. Don't even think about it."

"Jack, (this is *really* stupid on my part) I'd *never* leave GE."

"Just don't do *anything*. And come up and see me in the morning and we'll talk."

I went home and told my wife and asked her if they "really thought I could ever leave GE," and she said, "That's apparently what they are worried about."

I was summoned back up in the morning, and subjected to what I can only describe as an Irish intensity I had never seen in him before—brooking no argument or opposition to his will. Tens of thousands of shares of restricted stock and another load of stock options. I didn't even understand the concept of "restricted stock," which is one of the ultimate perks, usually given only to big shots. It involves an award of thousands of shares of stock which you own and collect dividends on, but cannot sell until certain multi-year milestones have passed, and which you lose if you leave the company—hence the term "golden handcuffs." Some of my officer friends were miffed when I told them, since they had never gotten any.

This "pile," delivered at the beginning of the headlong GE stock rush of the '90s, and followed by huge (for me) reinforcing option grants, wound up amounting to several million dollars when they were all exercised, and cashed, a few years later. Not bad, for a stumbler-through-life, as I told my old friend, the colonel from the Pentagon, who basically ordered me out of the place and into the arms of GE.

"They like me! They really like me!" I told my wife, imitating the idiotic Sally Field speech at the Academy Awards. And shortly thereafter, over at Jason Robard's house in Southport for some GE-connected charity event, I grabbed a *real* Oscar from his mantelpiece and began doing the same routine, amusing no one but myself, and maybe my wife, a little bit.

But, from a greedy, piggy perspective, I may have left some on the table. When I went up to see Welch on day two of this conversation, I should have had some specific, rehearsed questions in my head, like, "Uh, Jack, you say I will be 'Director of Communications' for the company. Will that be a *Senior Executive Band* job?" The answer would have been yes, at that point, but I never asked the question.

But the truth is, and was, I could never leave GE. Years ago, to the amusement and disbelieving smirks of friends, I would describe a draft of my proposed tombstone—not in Arlington Cemetery like those of some of my friends—but somewhere. I used to say it would have three symbols: the Cross of Christianity, the flag of the United States, and the GE logo—the Monogram.

So the Monday after the Bossidy announcement and my windfall, I was up with Welch again as he alternately fretted and exulted about Larry leaving. "Bill, I was a wreck when he told me. I didn't know what we would do without him. But after the weekend I just see this place as more logical and 'cleaner' in an organizational sense. Now it's just 12 businesses reporting right into 'here.'"

And then he said, sadly, "I'm glad Larry got the big job. He deserves it. But I wish it was at a better company."

"Allied isn't any good?"

"It's a toilet. And it's run by a bunch of bozos."

Larry, of course, flushed "the toilet" and turned Allied into what I at first thought was a hokey appellation: "A premier company." A bunch of us bought some stock (legally), and, like Larry and his employees, did very well.

For Larry's first annual report letter he simply took Jack's last GE epistle, modified it slightly, kept all the neat phrasing, and signed it. Jack read a copy and sent it back to Bossidy, with a copy to me. His note read, "Larry, this is utterly shameless." He actually thought it was hilarious.

I would see Larry every now and then, and talk to him on the phone; and had him come back up to GE to speak to my Elfun volunteer group.

Larry packed the GE cafeteria for the Elfun meeting. Standing Room Only. He agreed to come and talk to us if I would write his speech, which I entitled something like, "Life after GE." Before the meeting, he even sent his helicopter to fetch me at GE for lunch and a conversation—at Allied HQ in Jersey—about his talk, and then had it bring me back home.

At the Elfun meeting, I introduced Jack, who introduced Larry, and we had the "big time" night of all Elfun meetings.

Larry asked me, afterwards, if I was "still happy" at GE. I said "sure," and rambled on about how great things were.

My wife, who was listening to the conversation, said, "He keeps asking you if you're 'happy.' Why is that?"

Naiveté, even by marriage, runs in our family.

Finally, from Larry, "Bill, okay, as long as you're happy. I would have brought you with me, but Jack would have cut my nuts off."

I guess the point of this is not how some average guy from nowhere got so lucky, but how the smartest business, organizational, military, and political people in the world value the ability to communicate, and value anyone who can help them do it better.

Welch didn't really need me. He was a "natural," but I helped him to be even better, and I saved him a lot of time.

Bossidy *did* need me, or someone, because, while he did not share Welch's view of total commitment of time and vital force into a pitch, he did understand the importance of never, *ever* giving a bad one.

If you suspect that "they" are concerned that you might leave, have a well-thought-out, even rehearsed, 20-second wish list of what you want. Don't be caught off-guard, as I was, needlessly, with a night's warning. Put him or her off-guard with a big, but not phantasmagorical, condition for staying. You probably won't get it, but you'll do better than playing the grateful golden retriever, rolling over for proffered treats.

The Inevitable (But Very Short) Golf Section

I played golf with Jack a couple of times; and with Jack and Jane once or twice. Welch had parked himself at "my" club, Brooklawn, in Fairfield, Connecticut while awaiting admission to The Country Club of Fairfield, which had a beautiful course on Southport Harbor, across the street from the brick home that Imus enjoyed referring to as the "middle school."

The Country Club of Fairfield is not known as a "rich guy's club," but it is very inbred and admission of outsiders is infrequent, since the children of members move to the "head of the line."

Welch languished at the "middle school" across the street, waiting for the call from the Admissions Committee.

But in the meantime, Jack, when not at Augusta, Seminole, or Sankaty Head on Nantucket—or one or two others—he might play an afternoon round at Brooklawn, and would bring the Board of Directors there when the July meeting was held at headquarters in Fairfield.

The fleet of limos from HQ would pull up at the club, disgorge the Board, and play would begin—after the pro shop had been stripped of anything desirable, and the tab slid onto the GE account. The pro, who ran the shop and whose income depended, in part, on its revenue, prayed on his knees for fair weather on the Board outing day, so that it would not be canceled. The locker room attendant—a genuine character named Bruno—accosted Welch one year and told him that "Mr. Akers"—CEO of IBM at the time—had tipped him generously, and that he wondered if GE—"a much better company"—could do even better than that. Welch asked him what his friend Akers's "number" had been, and he doubled it, appreciating Bruno's brass—and a challenge—no matter the direction or level from which it came.

Welch would fill out the foursomes of board members and invited guests to the golf outing. Most were officers, but I got "the nod" a couple of times, once to play in a foursome with Sandy Warner, J.P. Morgan's CEO, and Reg Jones, Jack's predecessor. We had a nice round, with Reg saying, "That's good" to any putt in which the hole was visible on the horizon. I've mentioned it before, but I was thrilled to play with this man, who had the self-confidence to pick what should have been a 30-to-1 shot: a noisy, wild outrider in the management statistical spread, to run the crown jewel of American capitalism. It was the gutsiest and most underappreciated succession call in American business history.

I, and everyone else, was intensely curious 12 or 13 years later as to whom Jack would turn to as *his* successor.

Tough Jack to Follow

It was obvious to me early on that Welch was not going to pick someone to succeed him—as Reg did—who was his temperamental opposite. He did, however, go for his *physical* opposite—a big, tall guy with a lot of hair.

For many years I would be able to spot Jack in a reception crowd by looking for an extended circle of people looking downward. The few times I saw Jeff at similar functions, he was surrounded by a crowd looking up, like tourists in Muir Woods gawking at a redwood.

For years Welch had identified, among the characteristics of a "transformational leader," something he referred to as "edge." We struggled to define "edge" in terms that made sense, in talks and annual report letters, and didn't do a very good job, because as we defined the personal characteristics that described "edge," we always wound up describing *Jack.*

I eventually boiled "edge" down to meaning "like Jack." He found that amusing on the couple of occasions I mentioned my definition to him, but shooed me off for pursuing such a simple and shamelessly immodest formulation. But everyone would always wind up defining "edge" the same: "You know—like Jack."

But, in my view, there was not *yet* another "Jack" in the deck, at least in the three-card monte the succession game came down to.

All three of the finalists in the CEO contest were workaholics; although that is a meaningless datum in this day. All of the best are, or they don't last long.

Jim McNerney, whom I like a lot, was just fun to be around.

Bob Nardelli had a quiet three-yards-and-a-cloud-of-dust determination to work any problem to death. We all found it hilarious, and "typically Bob" that he had taken his Sunday "day off" before the officers meeting, to spread mulch around his yard.

Jim McNerney, I think, lacked the visceral craving for the big job that the others had. He did not seem to have the messianic mindset that he was "The One" the company must anoint to ensure its future.

Jim had gone from business-to-GE-business, adding value to each; and when he stood up on the stage at Boca to rehearse for me, after moving to aircraft engines, he began with this little introduction, for my amusement, and his own. It went something like, "Two years ago I was the world's leading expert on GE Asia-Pacific. Last year, I spoke here as the foremost expert on lighting. As of today, I am now the global expert on the subject of aircraft engines, on the basis of my last four months of experience in the business."

He did not use that dry and self-deprecating opener in his actual pitch the next day, although he should have, but it illustrates a failure to take himself too seriously; an endearing trait in an important man, but maybe a disadvantage in a CEO race. As Welch recounts, when Jim was given the bad news that Jeff—his competitor—had gotten the big job, he began joking about a "recount."

Immelt also has some of this endearing willingness to not take himself too seriously, which is one of the reasons why everyone seems to like him.

Bob Nardelli takes himself *very* seriously, and was—and is—in some ways, the opposite of Jack, relying more on iron-handed discipline and endless work to get things done. And he *did* get things done. As Welch once recounted, when Nardelli was given the news that he didn't get "the job," he clouded over and asked, "What more could I have done?" In other words, the same tough question he would have asked a subordinate after a presentation: "Where's your data?"

So Jeff got the job, as most of us around the flagpole figured he would, because he, in our view, was "most like Jack." As the decision neared, several of the real insiders in the analyst community were saying it was "Jeff's to lose." We asked them to please stop saying that, as it was ruining the suspense; but they had it right. And Jack was absolutely, and uncharacteristically, oracular—not a wink, nor a slip, nor a clue.

The guy who was really the most like Jack, never made the "final three"—Dave Calhoun, featured on the *Fortune* cover as "The #1 non-CEO Businessman in the World." He became a Vice Chairman at GE; and has since taken over, for $100 million dollars, as CEO of The Nielsen Company.

Dave did not make the cut despite being a favorite of Jack's, who told him early on that he wanted him "in this thing." He has diabetes, a serious strike against a potential 20-year GE CEO, when it, ironically, would not be against an American presidential candidate. Dave later told me that this was not the deciding factor why he was *not* a factor. Calhoun was also "snakebit," landing in three struggling businesses—lighting (old, no growth), reinsurance (disastrous hurricane magnet), and then on to aircraft engines in time for 9/11.

At one Boca meeting, a little more than four months after that horrible day, 150 GE golfers streamed back through tight security at the hotel. We had been told to "have ID," which was checked as we headed back to showers, dinner, and $100,000 worth of Rudy Giuliani.

I didn't play golf with Calhoun that day; but I was hanging with him as we hit security. Dave had forgotten his ID; and I, helpfully, vouched for him to the guard saying, "I know this man. This is Mohammad Al Calhoun from our Syrian operation." Dave didn't think this was particularly funny, but his blondish hair, and our laughter, got him through the checkpoint in time for drinks, dinner, and to hear "America's mayor" make his speech—the gist of which was that the U.S. should lobby to take away Yassir Arafat's Nobel Peace Prize. Why he thought we would have the slightest interest in that has always escaped me.

Every single one of the men who were in the original field of 23 potential GE CEOs is a good-to-great "presenter." Some have some weaknesses, usually related to PowerPoint, but none could ever be described as "deadly."

You simply cannot get a job at this level if you can't stand up and teach, and persuade, excite...and lead.

Know Your Potential Enemy

Okay. You've begun your investigation into your audience, and you've begun constructing your pitch. With something like the Welch "black cloud" presentation, weeks may be required. With most, little more than some hard, self-critical analysis and quiet thinking will be needed since you know what your boss needs, or hates; as well as what would be *useful* to your colleagues.

Thought game: "I like these people; I really do. Some are my friends, but all are giving me 15 minutes of their lives. A few—Terry, Pete, and Jesse—may well have a say in whether I get that job that will open up after they fire Steve. What, specifically, can I tell them that they can use in the projects or functions they are working on?

Do you know what the key players' interests are? Their problems? Their needs? Not difficult to find out; a few five-minute phone conversations with a few people you trust can help a lot.

Then, ponder how well it's going to go over when you turn to Sue within minutes of opening your pitch, and tell her, "Sue, I know you and your team are struggling to get that T&L spending down without losing that customer touch. Look what we found that might be a way to do that by using this fairly simple algorithm my team came up with." Quick example, and then: "Jesse and Connie—this might well work with that issue you've got going in Sheboygan. You're not going to believe what we found. See if some of this might work for you…"

Sue and Jesse and Connie, and however many others you can bring into this corral, will hang on your every word, will interrupt with questions, argue with each other, ask if some of their other issues apply. Your pitch may develop into a wonderful food fight. You may go overtime. But it will have been the best presentation you have ever done in your life; and you will know it as you, hoarse and flush-faced, stumble off in triumph for a bottle of water.

Welch always advocated this type of pitch: short, with maybe a couple of charts, some big thoughts, some advice, and then a raucous interchange. An Italian family around the dinner table—loud, emotional, loving.

And you can probably guess who may well get that job once Steve gets fired.

You scored, and there's no reason why you can't do it every time you walk up there.

You can do this, can't you?

Out of the Gate and Serious

Okay. You've got this pitch; you can't wait to do it. It's important, and you know it's good. You don't need to actually memorize your presentation—a mistake—but you do need to memorize, and savor, and roll around on your tongue 20 times, or so, that first minute. You need to walk up to the lectern with a serious face—even a scowl is okay. Have nothing on the screen. The aura that needs to waft over the group is that "this is a serious individual with something important to tell me that I need to listen to."

If you wear glasses, fine. Wear them to your pitch. Do not put on a pair of reading glasses; or, God forbid, half-frame things that sit on the end of your nose, like Senator Schumer. You will look like a wimp and an idiot.

Look into something called "monovision"—a single contact lens that allows you to read "type" with one eye and see for distance with the other. Some people's brains cannot handle this separation of ocular responsibility.

If that is you, make your speaking notes in huge type so you can read them. Don't do the "four eyes" thing if that is not your customary persona. It will distract the audience.

If it is a senior individual you are addressing, you should start by saying something like, "Joe or Mary [if it is a first-name company like GE], I only have a few minutes of your time, but there's something I think you need to know about…"

Or "Ted, I need 10 million to expand this plant. I know you don't have it, but hear me out…"

Ben Heineman, our General Counsel, would ask presenters, *as they walked into his office*, "Why are you here, and what do you want from me?"

Those two jarring questions focus the mind. But the mind should have already been focused, days before. Weeks before.

You make it, or lose it, in that first thirty seconds, or minute, you are up there.

Sell it: "This is important."

Sell it: "I only have a couple of minutes and a couple of charts."

Sell it: "This is how we see this issue, and how we think we need to address it. I need to know what you think.…"

Never stand up with a big grin on your face and make some stupid "humorous" remark to begin your pitch.

If you are the boss, forego the jocular crap and be serious in your demeanor. You can revert to your jocular, friendly self at cocktails or in Q&A.

Never stand up and tell a joke you heard somewhere, no matter how funny you think it is. You may get a laugh—putting you on the "comedian" career path at companies like GE. Not a big future.

Or, as is most likely, you'll get a few twitters, or total silence—embarrassing silence—as you feel the blood draining out of your face and the pity on the faces of the people to whom you are speaking.

You've trivialized your talk. You've sold your soul for a few gratifying magic beans of laughs—and maybe you didn't even get those. The boss thinks you're a lightweight.

Do not ad lib something that comes into your mind as you are being introduced. Ad-libbed stuff almost never works, which is why Jack and I worked so long to have a canned nuclear zinger to drop on Warren Buffett. That would have been okay at his level, because the audience knew a deadly serious and pointed message would quickly follow. If they don't know you they don't know that, and you can lose them early.

A 90-caliber big shot can get away with jocularity as he or she begins. He or she has the credentials and the gravitas to get away with it.

But, you know what? I still don't like it, at any level.

Welch, as the years rolled on, actually did start off some of his pitches with a humorous play or two, but never a stand-up "joke". He rolled into a Crotonville "Pit session" on the way back from a meeting in Manhattan—dressed in his $2,000 suit, blue shirt, and $200 yellow tie; walked in from the helipad, looked at the business-casual dressed crowd of 150 or so, and said, deadpan and with mock menace, "I guess you people didn't get the word on the dress code." Laughter, but a few nervous giggles.

When you get to *his* place you can afford to be flippant at the start of a pitch. *Once again, if you're not there yet, you can't afford it.*

Jack did throw in a few humorous ad-libs on occasion, but never got hurt by them as you and I would. One time he walked on stage at a GE Women's Network meeting to a tumultuous, adoring ovation; laughing, he waved it off and said, "Where were all of you when I couldn't get a date in high school?"

They laughed even louder. *But don't you dare try something like that.*

Welch kicked off his first Boca as Chairman with the line, "How do you like having a stuttering overachiever as CEO?" But there was a little touch of menace in his delivery of that line.

"Their worst nightmare" was grinning down at them from the podium.

Jack was a master of the killer anecdote. Here's one he used: "Just last Thursday I was in a plant to see a 'Best Practices review.' Four or five people were in the room to make a presentation. All hourly people. Fella gets up, all prepared to make the pitch. I said, 'What do you do?' He says, 'I'm the Manager of the Boiler Operation.' I said, 'Who do you work for?' 'Over here.' "Who's that?' 'Manager of Utilities.' Said to *him*, 'Who do you work for?' 'Manager of Plant Services.' I said, 'Wait a minute now, Manager of Boilers … who works for you?' 'The Supervisor of Boilers.' We had five layers in that room and we hadn't reached anywhere near the Plant Manager. (Officers laugh) Now you laugh, but I bet every one of you can go find that somewhere in your operation."

Start off strongly, with a hint of urgency in your voice. Memorize your opening. Sharpen it like a spear and then fire it into the hearts of the audience after you bound up to the lectern to do your pitch.

And, if there is a particular anecdote that set you off on this subject and frames your thinking on the subject you are about to present, tell it. The dramatic effect of a powerful anecdote is immense. Grab them by the throats; pique their interest and their curiosity in those first seconds.

Part X

Tell Me a Story

Gene Murphy came to GE from RCA when we acquired that now ghost of a company in 1985. He was, and is, known for being a tough, hard-nosed businessman. He ran our aircraft engines business for a while, and later was a Vice Chairman of GE.

Gene was, and remains, a consummate gentleman and an unabashedly devout Irish Catholic who was sometimes heard by visitors praying quietly, but aloud, *on his knees* in his office.

Picture, if you will, the quiet, but audible, prayers wafting out the door to the third floor hallway: "Hail Mary, full of grace..." And then contrast this with the bloodcurdling shrieks issuing from the Chairman's office down the hall: "You asshole! You're in deep shit! You get this cleaned up or you're outta here."

Yet you can't get any more Irish, each in his own way, than either one of these characters.

Jack increasingly used Murphy on the Boca and officers meeting programs to speak on the subjects of compliance and integrity—something Welch never wanted off the front burner, even if people were getting tired of hearing about it—pre-Enron.

At one Boca meeting Gene was again scheduled to speak on the subject, I worked with him on the pitch and rehearsed him in the Fairfield auditorium.

One line I had put in—which I believe had been "suggested" by Jack—stood out powerfully. Gene was to look out into the sea of 550 faces in the Boca ballroom, and say, "You know, there were three people, one of them an officer, who were in this room *last* year, but are *not* in it today. They committed one-strike-and-you're-out integrity violations—and were removed."

Welch had consummate integrity. I'm not sure whether it came from an innate moral compass, or from the certain knowledge that one major slip could doom the company to death—almost literally. He would have killed himself before ever allowing that to happen.

During the '90s, Jack had even shaved the top of his head—or, rather, clipped off his comb-over. I remarked on it the first time I saw it—I didn't like the change—and he replied that it was his "integrity haircut." No cover-up; no fake; no comb-over.

We did an annual survey of all professionals in the company and braced for the results. I wrote the first survey, which consisted of questions such as, "We're asking for input and 'voice' on the way we run this company. Is this real or fake? Do you think we really care about what you think?" I deliberately invited a sucker punch.

My view was that we should tag these paper surveys with some kind of code that would indicate which *business* the response came from, not which *individual.* I suggested this to Welch, whose eyes lit up at the thought; but then he said, "No. That would be an integrity violation," which it would have been. I didn't think of it that way at the time.

But back to Gene Murphy's speech…

First Boca morning—6:30 or so—and Murphy finds me as I fret around the sleepy, still-empty meeting room, annoying the staging people and checking and rechecking everything.

"Bill, I've been thinking about that part where we talk about the three guys who got fired for integrity violations. Everybody in the room will know who we're talking about, and I just don't think it's the gentlemanly thing to do. I'm going to take it out. Will you tell the staging guys, so they can 're-cue' the speech?"

"Okay Gene, but let me run that by Jack before you change that. That's an important part of the pitch and he wanted it in there." By now my instincts had long become trustworthy, as had my feel for the Tasmanian Devil.

I tracked him down and accosted him outside the room an hour before the meeting.

"Jack, Gene is taking out that part about the three guys getting fired. He thinks everyone will know who he's talking about and that it will be unnecessary, and unfair to 'pile on' about it."

"What? Are you out of your mind? Are you nuts? Don't you know anything about communications? These people need to walk out of that room knowing that three guys, including an officer, got sent home for cheating.

That's the whole story. The rest of that speech is all bullshit. Put it back in."

"I think I understand your view on this issue. I'll tell Gene."

I told Gene. The anecdote went back in. And it was, as Welch predicted, the big "take-away." Guys at dinner rehashed the fate of the three unconnected executives, none of them bad guys, but people who had slid, stupidly, into integrity traps—expense account stuff—that wound up ruining a big part of their lives.

And it's true. One real-life, chilling, or eyelid-elevating anecdote—a vignette that lights up the issue like a flash of night lightning, is worth a hundred, or a thousand, pages of truisms and generalizations.

The Dogs Are Your Friends

How do I know this about the power of anecdotes? It goes back to my Vietnam days when I was asked—told—to go to Saigon and give a presentation at a "Night Operations Seminar" at Military Assistance Command headquarters.

I was a first lieutenant with a master's degree, which apparently tagged me as some kind of intellectual; and I had that Combat Infantryman's Badge on my chest—the same one Audie Murphy wore (his for just a bit more combat activity).

I had never done a presentation before; and this was to be before a fairly large group of senior officers, none of them from Special Forces. A few were not too fond of people who wore berets, guys who did pretty much whatever they wanted and seemed to get all the publicity.

The only "F" I got in college was one in Military Science—ROTC—and I always hated all the map reading, "small unit tactics," and patrolling stuff, so I never paid much attention to it. I obviously wasn't going to impress the brass with military jargon and tactics.

I just sat down and thought through what I knew about ambushing— how it was an economical way of keeping the enemy off balance; and on defense—how to determine where the best locations to insert ambushes were; and what my team and I *had learned in fielding thousands of ambush parties on my watch and in the years before.*

I asked all my sergeants, some of whom had four or five Vietnam tours with Special Forces: "What's your best advice on ambushing, 'Top'?" (A respectful nickname for the team sergeant.)

In any case, probably due to both instinct and serendipity, I put together the exact kind of presentation I am urging you to use: Here's what we do. Here's what we do right. Here's what we did wrong. Don't do this. Don't *ever* do this! Try this. Watch out for that.

Despite my very junior rank, I had a little bit of arrogance and cockiness born of having seen a fair amount of action during Tet and one or two occasions afterward. And a bit of the smugness that comes with that green hat, as well as with the chromed, sawed-off Winchester 12-gauge pump shotgun I carried in a specially made holster on my hip. I was told that no weapons were allowed in the presentation room—a bunker—and that they would "hold it for me" until I was through.

So I started, quickly establishing my *bona fides*. Our "A team" had as many kills as any other team over the past year. Most of what we did for a living was ambushing; and I planned to spend *the short time I had with them* giving them the results of what we had learned about the art and science of night ambush. So I did, and I told them about:

- *Meandering around almost aimlessly until dark fell, so no inform-ant in a village could possibly point, for sure, to the place you had set up.*

- *Benzedrine, if done moderately, would keep you wide-eyed until—in our case—3 a.m. when there was no further possibility of "con-tact." You could "hear the rice growing."*

But my biggest "take-away"—at least so they told me—was about *the dogs*.

"The dogs are your friends."

You set up in the warm darkness. The bennies are working; the rice is making a lot of noise growing. And then you hear it, maybe a quarter mile away. A dog barks. Then another and another.

Then, quiet for a few minutes, then another and another in a slightly dif-ferent direction. Then quiet, then more barks, and the direction is now clear.

There is no doubt about what you are hearing, because no sane civilian is out at ten o'clock at night in this exotically beautiful madhouse of bullets, shrapnel, and sudden death.

The hair stands up on your neck.

If you think they are moving toward you, you whisper to the radio bunker at the team house that you "might have something going," and you get the Vietnamese mortar crew in the camp up and ready to fire illumina-tion—flares—at a location already programmed. And then you wait.

And if the dogs start up again, and their irritant seems to be changing direction, you decide whether to pick up and move to another spot where you think they might be headed—usually 200 yards or so—and set down again and wait, hearts pounding.

What you must *not* do is walk into another ambush by your mates, who *should* be monitoring the radio and know that you are moving near them, but maybe are not.

But you'd move, rather than let the enemy—if it was the enemy—slip by.

And sometimes the dogs got quiet, and either the enemy went somewhere else, or turned around, or were not there.

And sometimes you would nail them. But after 3 a.m., still with no "bites," we'd post a guard and lie out under the stars without a blanket in the warm night. And we'd sleep, waking at dawn and returning to a meeting place with a "deuce-and-a-half" truck meeting us to take us back to camp, but *never by the same route we came*, because then we would be subject to ambush. That was another "lesson" I preached.

So I did my pitch to the brass in Saigon and they loved it, citing its "practical advice" as extremely useful.

But I should have heeded my own advice.

A month or two after my presentation, I left with the major and two sergeants in one jeep. Four other Americans followed in another jeep; and we went to one of our outposts, a few miles away, and, for some reason stayed too long. We retraced the same route we had taken, now in pitch darkness with blackout headlights on, on the bumpy semi-paved road. I was violating every rule the smug lieutenant had taught in Saigon. I told the major we were nuts doing this. He agreed, and we peered nervously into the darkness.

The major was driving, and had his M16 out of easy reach on the floor of the jeep. The weapons of the two guys in the back were blocked by the jeep frame and canvas roof. The only useful weapon was my chrome plated shotgun pointed out into the night.

The dark smelled like danger and death as the jeeps roared down this road that the enemy "moved battalions across," as the major used to say.

The jeep with the other Americans was a few hundred yards behind us when the blasts went off—mines, Chinese "claymores"—on either side of the road. They slammed the driver and passenger side occupants into each other. My head hit the major's. The major's foot came off the accelerator for a second or two and the place lit up with automatic weapons ripping through the jeep windshield and the canvas roof frame an inch from my head. I pulled the trigger on the shotgun and nothing happened.

The hammer wasn't cocked.

I cocked it, yelling and screaming incoherently, and in the muzzle flashes and other lights saw a North Vietnamese soldier in khaki stand up and fire at me from 20 feet away with an RPD—a light machine gun. He fired high, as they typically did. I almost closed my eyes as I spasmodically let go with the 12-gauge and saw him fly backward and toward the ground.

We found pieces of his skull and brains the next day.

The major, who had been shot many, many times in Korea and Vietnam, had recovered from the blasts. Cursing, he slammed his foot back on the gas and we shot out of there with bullets still ripping through the jeep.

Our teammates in the jeep behind us had slammed on the brakes and bailed out before the "kill zone," when they saw the ambush go down. They ran into a village to hide and "exfiltrate" back toward camp in the darkness.

I was pumped at this point, and kept blasting everything I could see, reloading from my pockets. As we moved closer toward camp, one of *our* troops, a Vietnamese, moved out of the darkness and I shot him, fortunately hitting him in the leg within only a couple of the .32-caliber slugs in the shell. I would have shot my mother had she popped out of the dark that night.

A massive assault by a relief force from our camp rescued our second jeep crew from the village they were moving through, and the enemy melted back into the night. We had 12 or 14 bullet holes in the jeep and not one of us was wounded—except for days of ringing in our ears from the mines.

The major said, "Bill, you need a Purple Heart for this." He already had a bunch of them. I said, "Sir, I'm not wounded." And he ripped out his Bowie knife and said, "Hold out your arm." I laughed and pulled away.

He was serious.

That's it. That's pretty much all of my relevant Vietnam stories. I saw maybe 10 or 12 days of violent combat and maybe another month or so of slogging through the mountains and calling artillery and air strikes in on the enemy, with few shots fired at me, personally. Got mortared in the camp, ineffectually, two or three times.

But I did make a great presentation in Saigon. I told them what to do and what not to do; I told them to *take amphetamines and listen to the dogs.*

Do they walk out of *your* pitches with any advice as specific as that?

What You Face If You're Black, Asian, or a Woman

Most senior corporate people I have spoken with on the subject of presentations, which many of them listen to every day, have offered this piece of advice:

"State clearly what you want right away. Give very little background. Offer very little methodology. Be clear about *what it is you want them to know.*"

And now we must confront what you are up against; and the impression you will make on your friend or enemy—the audience—during your presentation.

If you are a white male...

As a white male, you start with a clean slate. A "level playing field," as the cliché goes. You've got 90 seconds, or two minutes or so, to establish your territory and credibility. Start with no smiles, no persiflage, no indication that you are anything but a serious individual with something serious to say. Look serious—even intimidating—if you choose. *But you have to deliver.* And doing so involves a lot of work done days and weeks in advance.

If you are a black male...

The same rules apply, and your audience will be sincerely rooting for you to do well, hoping that you are not up there because of some affirmative-action boost, and out of your league. Even if you do terribly, nothing will be said, although the data will be filed away somewhere in the back of some brains, and will affect—fairly—selections for jobs down the line.

Black males are generally perceived as eloquent, and as strong leaders. They are very good Army officers. The lurking, unspoken, awful question is about competence. I don't like saying that, but I have resolved to write what I perceive to be the truth.

GE is a place, in my view, where a brilliant and self-confident black person *has* to go. Welch would never hand over a GE business to a minority, or a woman, to get a check-mark on some "diversity" questionnaire—and everyone knew it.

Lloyd Trotter, whom I have cited a couple of times for doing memorable presentations, is black. I had hoped to avoid mentioning that.

Most of the senior people in the company have admired him for "getting cost out continuously from a bunch of shitty industrial businesses"—which is what he did, and does.

Lloyd is also *not* a naturally eloquent speaker, but always followed Welch's command to "tell people what they need to do."

I've done a speech or two for Lloyd, I like him, and recognize him for what he is: a great leader and a good businessman who happens to be black. There are a couple of other senior black men in GE, who wear their rank and compensation with the mantle of merit.

No black males were removed in profit-and-loss jobs, that I can remember, but a few in senior staff positions were eased out, gently.

If you are Asian...

I've spoken to one or two meetings of the Asia-Pacific Forum at GE, and have been told, "We are stereotyped as 'bright,' 'brainy,' 'brilliant'—not bad so far—but also as 'bad leaders.'" And at least their GE record would support this view.

I never thought about this much, one way or another, but they may have a point.

Leadership of U.S. GE businesses by Asians is nearly nonexistent, and, in the one case I can think of, unsuccessful.

Asian males need to stand up, look serious, and forcefully establish the importance of what they are about to say. You need to look and act as western as possible if they are looking to move upward in the West. Stop the incessant public smoking.

You must be up-front, clear, logical, and forceful. No apologies; no equivocations. Tell 'em what you want, and what you want them to do.

If you are a woman...

It is women who have the toughest job of all in scoring high marks in presentations, in my experience.

At Boca, we would sit around the dinner table and discuss some of the day's presentations by the men—but *all* that were made by the women. Why is that? There were many favorable comments as well as negative; but why did the boys feel they had to evaluate every female on the program when they did not subject all the men to the same analysis?

There is a streak of something male, reaching back to the primordial pit, that I am not qualified to clinically evaluate, but I do have some observations…

In the early days of the Jack era, there would be one woman on the program or *none*, out of as many as 25 speakers. So she naturally had enormous attention and pressure focused on her. My boss, the VP of PR, was put on the program by Jack. She rehearsed more times than any speaker I have ever worked with in twenty years, and did a good job reading her pitch in the cavernous hall.

She was, however, visibly nervous, and her nervousness was the dinner table subject of the evening reviews by the boys, whereas the subject of reviews of the men's talks was *content.* This is not fair, but no one has ever claimed it was, or is.

In the latter years of Jack's tenure, he would insist that at least five or six women speak at the meeting, choosing them himself, or having Senior VP Gary Reiner search for some who had something worthwhile to share with the group.

They, of course, were each evaluated over the veal, chicken, and swordfish Jack had selected for the three evenings' dinners. Why? Two reasons: There was the persistent and not unreasonable view, sometimes stated aloud, that "she's on the program because Jack wanted more women." On rare occasions, an older, totally secure player would assert that "she's in that *job* because she's a woman."

Statements like that are heard in quiet conversations with people one knows personally and one can trust never to repeat.

Women—*most* women—are not thought of by men as *real* leaders. Their intelligence is not in question. Their commitment is usually not in question. Their ability to lead largely male organizations that are still faintly patterned on World War II military organizational models *is* in question.

A few of the best *staff* officers at GE have been women. The record of the business—profit-and-loss—leaders has not been so good.

And it matches their relatively dismal record across the Fortune 500, particularly as the bubbles from the sunken flagship SS Fiorina continue to rise to the surface.

So, given the often unreceptive audience of troglodyte males—*and often jealous and unsupportive females*—how should a woman approach, and deliver, a presentation?

1. You need to say what you have to say with *confidence* and *authority*. I have spoken to several senior women who present, successfully and frequently, who have told me that they have to catch themselves before they say something like, "I may be wrong on this..." Don't do that. Make sure you are right, and then assert it as fact.

2. Be cordial and feminine with the audience, but don't smile too often. Your "aura," as with the men, should be, once again, that of a serious individual with something serious and important to say.

3. Don't speak too harshly, or too loudly. You, unlike the men, are not allowed to attack the audience with the ferocity the men can, even if the audience deserves it. Taking your comments and your manner beyond "firmness" will produce men's room critiques such as "shrill," "pushy," "bitchy," as well as occasional speculation—*speculation I have heard*—on whether you should be allowed on the program "when it's that time of the month."

4. Above all, and more importantly than all of the above, you must construct a presentation that is so useful to these people in their jobs and lives that they will walk out the door with your gift to them on their yellow pads—a best practice, a customer insight, a way to change a process, a fix to a problem they may be having, a warning—anything of real use to them.

I wish I had a magic bullet for this issue, because it really isn't fair. But I don't.

Women simply have to be better presenters than men, and that involves preparation and content, rather than whether you should wear pink or have your hair pulled back.

Putting together a brilliant, useful presentation is worth more of your time than all the "networking sessions" and women's forums put together, when it comes to scoring big in front of a roomful of people, some of whom have their doubts about you.

Ten Minutes! No More!

Toward the mid-'90s, Welch's "best practice" that we applied to the Boca and Officers Meetings was "10 minutes." He would then shout, excitedly: "Ten minutes! No More!"

Ten minutes is more than enough time to present effectively on most subjects, *if* you think it through and extract every non-contributing thought or word. The old line, "If I had more time I would have written you a shorter letter" applies in spades to business presentations, as well as CEO annual report letters.

I used to construct the programs for the Boca and officers meetings, and allot people times for their presentations based on Jack's instinct—"Give him 20 minutes," Jack would suggest during the mid-'80s; or it might be based on my need to fit in coffee breaks and other housekeeping nonsense. Neither Jack nor I had seen the presentations, at that early point. So, out in the field somewhere, some poor guy who had a perfect nine-and-a-half-minute pitch planned was now stretching it out to 20 minutes because some bureaucrat in Fairfield told him to.

There is nothing worse than sitting in a large room, as I often have, where some bore has just gone 25 minutes over his allotted time and is showing no signs of wrapping up; you can feel the palpable impatience and hostility of the crowd, who would probably enjoy seeing his PowerPoint projector explode in flaming shrapnel and the screen fall on his head.

Once again, you should continuously signal the audience that what you are saying is important, and that you only have a few minutes to get it across. Avoid signals that audiences, who are extremely sensitive to "time messages," will interpret as implying they're going "to be here for a while." Things like, "I'd like to begin with a review of the year's financial performance." Beware of the word "begin."

Also avoid saying, "Later on I'll talk about, in some detail, the analysis behind each of the 10 conclusions our task force produced..." Or, "But there are other challenges we faced when we began this project a year ago..." (No, the only challenge I face is how to get the hell out of this room without being spotted.)

Use your authority.

For reasons I don't fully understand, a speaker or presenter has an aura of authority—the potential to intimidate—even those vastly superior in rank. This aura can be surrendered—within seconds—by a stupid humorous reference, a nervous smile, or an obsequious demeanor.

Don't fail to wear that mantle of authority, and use it to make people listen to what you have to say. Look at them intently. The minute you turn your back to them to read a PowerPoint chart, the mantle of authority begins to slip from your shoulders, and your pants begin to slip, revealing your ass.

I am a fairly warm and friendly individual by nature, but I maintain that invisible license to intimidate until the end of my pitch.

I have, even actually *practiced* intimidating people.

Well, maybe one person.

Up in Welch's office one day I was finishing up a speech or annual report letter and getting more than the usual number of pats on the head—"Great job, Bill." "This is terrific." "Bill, this is wonderful."

He was using me to compliment himself!

Rosanne appears in the doorway as I'm taking my leave. "Mr. Welch, Bo Dietel is downstairs in the lobby and would like to come up and say a quick hello."

Jack, with an amused half-smile, said, "Sure, why not."

Now, Bo Dietel is a former New York City cop—and a tough one by reputation—who was doing *shtick* occasionally on the *Imus in the Morning* show before Imus, with Bernie's help, ad-libbed himself into temporary oblivion. Bo had become one of the most accomplished ass kissers—group and individual—on the planet; overtaking even Imus, the master.

Now, had I run into Bo Dietel unexpectedly, I would have probably broken into a big grin and said hello; and maybe even introduced myself, as I did when I ran into Henry Kissinger in the elevator coming down from seeing Jack.

But this time I knew I would be walking past Dietel in the silent third floor corridor that led to Jack's inner sanctum, and for laughs, I decided to see if I could intimidate this tough semi-celebrity.

After I said good-bye to Rosanne and Sue, as I always did, I began walking down the hall toward the elevator when I heard it open, and saw Dietel turn the corner and begin walking toward me. The scene—minus art deco—reminded me of the ominous walk Luca Brazzi makes down the corridor in *The Godfather* on the way toward his nap with the fishes.

I'm fairly good sized, and I puffed myself up like a toad as big as I could get. I then walked, unnaturally slowly, and began looking Dietel up and down, from shoes to face, and back down again, like a secret service guy.

I continued to look him up and down as we approached each other, and I then put an obviously-fake cold smile on my face and said, "Good afternoon." He had a sickly, nervous smile on his face, scooted just a little bit sideways—out of my path and said, "Hi," or something.

It was an extremely successful intimidation!

This is admittedly pretty pathetic, and Dietel may have been able to kick my ass (or maybe not), but I am trying to make a point I know to be true. *You* have the power to hold your authority—to "hold the talking stick," as the Indians say, for your *entire* presentation; even if pitching to the most boorish pack of pompous, bored, ADD-afflicted corporate asses imaginable.

You can maintain that authority by doing the following:
- *Walk into the room with a crisp, captivating, valuable presentation that you know is "so good that you can't wait to do it," as Welch would say.*
- *If you don't have one, call in sick.*
- *Walk to the lectern; stare very briefly at the group with, at the most, a faint, cold, smile of the type I fired at Bo Dietel.*
- *Begin immediately and urgently to sell what you are about to say— stressing its importance and its brevity.*

And then deliver.
- *The discussion may get loud, and even rancorous. They may hate what you are saying, but when you finish and walk off, every soul in that room will know they have been in the presence of a* player; *a confident, well-prepared advocate of a case for some behavioral change on their part. A leader. Someone to be reckoned with.*
- *Ignore all imposed time slots allotted to you on the program. For example, if "Coping with Deflation in a Materials Business" is slotted for Mary Smith, 9:40–10:00 and Mary, through rigorous thought and intense preparation, finds herself at rehearsal at nine minutes rather than the 20 minutes allotted her by the bureaucracy, she can do one of two things: She can add 11 minutes of "hamburger helper" to get her to 20 minutes—and by doing so ruin what could have been a great presentation—to obey some stupid, bureaucratic edict.*

Or, she can leave it at 10 minutes; maybe even shave another minute, deliver it powerfully and then sit down, leaving the audience stunned with her insights and advice and intensely grateful for her brevity. That approach is one that inevitably draws the comment—at the urinals or over dinner—of "Mary's was the shortest pitch on the program... and the best. That asshole, Harvey, ran a half hour over and, as usual, had nothing to say."

- *Disobey the bureaucrats and delight your audiences by refusing to use all your allotted time.*

PowerPoint Is the Enemy. Never Surrender.

There is a way to be quickly taken for the opposite of a leader, and to be typecast within seconds as a dork, a dweeb, a jargon-monkey, a bore, or an assembly line management ether-salesman.

It's called PowerPoint.

This technology, which could have been a real asset to business communications, has become a hideous thing of evil. The medium has become the message. And the message is boring, complicated, and often unreadable.

One year, Jack made a typically passionate plea for simplicity, both at Boca and at his officers meeting:

"Let's simplify all our communications with each other and all our constituencies," he told them, "from those gobbledygook plant newspapers to everything we say to people. Simple, straightforward communication. Let's commit ourselves to making all our internal meetings—*all* our presentations—simple and clear. Many, many fewer charts surrounded by a rich discussion of real issues."

As much as Six Sigma improved the way we did things, and brought us so much closer to our customers, it was an elixir of mental discipline. You couldn't wing it anymore, or throw up the kind of generalizations that Dennis Dammerman and Welch hated.

Well, they got the analysis and data they needed; but in typical GE fashion it went *way* off the deep end, to a point where it began to hurt the whole crusade. We began to drown, visually, in complexity and mega-data.

Welch got up at our corporate officers meeting in "The Pit" at Crotonville in '98, and said:

> We have managed to create more complicated charts with Six Sigma than any group of human beings could ever have been expected to do. The purpose of these presentations has become the demonstration of how smart we are about Pareto analysis, or how much work we have put in on a project, rather than the sharing of useful learning experiences. Our charts have become mind-numbingly complex.

I was back at my desk late one morning, getting ready to go to the gym and lunch, when the Man called in a grumpy, cranky mood about something we were working on that he didn't like and didn't want to do. He started chewing—small bites—out of my ass because it was the only ass within reach. I endured the chewing and the whining, up to the point when I told him, "You know, the stock is up over two points and it's not even noon; and you don't need to be kicking my ass for no good reason. If you *really* want to get angry you need to come with me and listen to your new managers at Crotonville talk about how these shitty presentations and stupid charts, which are *required* by their managers, are *ruining* Six Sigma. They hate the presentations; they hate the charts. The charts are so busy that no one can even read them. Your senior guys are ignoring all the stuff you told them about charts at the officers meeting."

This provoked predictable pyrotechnics: "It's *unbelievable.* I'm seeing more and more overdone, complicated, cookie-cutter charts. It's phony. It's corporate misbehavior at its worst. I refused to look at a guy's charts today. Filled with complicated bullshit. *I made a scene.*"

He rumbled off, like a summer thunder-boomer departing; another minute of smaller booms and dimmer flashes, and politely said a friendly "bye," as he always did. I got up, with a head full of discord and bugs flying around; the usual aftermath of a loud conversation with Welch. I began to get a plan together to move toward the gym.

Then the phone rang again.

It was the guy with the charts filled with the "complicated bullshit."

The guy was Lonnie Edelheit, Senior Vice President and Chief of Research and Development for GE, whose home was the GE Research and Development Center in Schenectady. Lonnie was a large, bearish Jewish uncle kind of guy, friendly and pleasant with a bumbling scientific manner. Welch found him endlessly amusing; he was obviously fond of him, but picked on him mercilessly at corporate executive council meetings and other senior gatherings.

Today he had been more than picked on. He had walked in on Jack in a foul mood, had begun a presentation, and been summarily thrown out of Welch's office as the first few charts hit the screen. Jack had indeed "made a scene."

"Bill," Lonnie moaned at me on the phone. I thought for a second he might even be sobbing, his tone was so mournful. "Jack just kicked me out because he didn't like my charts. He told me not to come back until I fixed them. I don't know what he's talking about. Can you come up and help me?"

So the gym was put aside, and I walked one floor up the back stairs to the visiting VIP office to which Lonnie had been banished after Jack's tantrum.

He came out from behind the desk with a paper copy of his charts, looking as if he'd been beaten. "Look at these. He ridiculed them. What's the *matter* with them?"

He held one of his charts out for me to look at, and God help me, I lost it. I busted out laughing. "Sorry, Lonnie," I said as he showed me the next one and I laughed even harder. "Lonnie, are you kidding me?"

The charts were a horrible mess of "wiring diagrams," boxes with arrows pointing to other boxes, scientific jargon, acronyms, and hundreds of words squashed into every available white space, leaving only room for the footnotes(!) at the bottom.

Dilbert material.

"Lonnie, what were you *thinking* of by showing shit like this to Jack?"

Redoing his charts was, as I recall, an hour or two of work—at most. We looked at the old ones, and I would simply ask, "What do you want Jack to walk out of the room with from this?" He would answer, and I would then press him to clarify it and simplify it even more; and we would then make a chart with a key bullet or two, upon which Lonnie could look Welch in the eye and elaborate. We cleaned up Lonnie's presentation. He pitched Jack again, and was effusively praised to make up for the spanking he had suffered. Jack had kicked a golden retriever who had eaten his sock, and he felt bad.

Lonnie went back to Schenectady a relatively happy man, and didn't leave the company for another year or two.

You could not succeed at GE, or last in an executive role, without an IQ of 130 or higher. Welch's evaluation of people in the organization usually boiled down to an opinion of their intelligence. You could fail and be fired, as hundreds were, even if you had the requisite IQ, as decided by Jack; but I can only recall one senior guy who was awarded the label "not that bright," or "dumb" who still went on to remarkable success.

But I could not understand, after Jack's impassioned plea for clarity and simplicity in charts and presentations, why talented young GE managers had to continue to cry on my shoulder at Crotonville over the abortions the Six

Sigma presentations had become; with the business leaders tolerating the visual idiocies—and, in some cases, *ordering* them.

You can change the way your people communicate nearly overnight, by insisting on—demanding—simplicity and clarity in business presentations, and an end to the PowerPoint nightmares that bore and demoralize your people.

On Being a Leader Rather
Than a Projector Operator

Welch loves a captivating, simple, dramatic "depiction chart," and for years would rip a paper copy from a presenter's hands, and run around the company showing it to people, almost with the enthusiasm with which he shared his dirty, tattered Greg Norman score card.

He would often noodle an idea for a speech or a pitch in chart form, doodling and drawing, and crossing out and crumpling pad paper and running around the room until he had it right. And then, as often as not, the chart never saw the light of day.

The charts were vehicles for generating thoughts, and eventually, words.

This technique doesn't work for me, or I suspect, for most people; but it did for him. And, to be sure, while I saw him run around the company showing people "a great chart," never once did I see him express anything but disgust for a *word chart*.

I waged a 20-year war against the visual circus while I ran GE's meetings, largely with Welch's support. And—outside of corporate meetings—we lost.

Welch used visuals very moderately when presenting, typically throwing up one or two—maybe three—and then shutting the machine off and moving so the audience could focus entirely on him. I seldom saw him deliver a completely visualized pitch in 20 years—maybe sometimes to analysts, but *never* to employees.

He made a number of direct stabs at limiting the GE visual circus—not all of them successful.

Aircraft engines was addicted to using elaborate and obviously expensive videos as part of their Boca presentation—showing up the leaner, less cash-flush businesses like lighting and industrial systems.

The videos were admittedly interesting and well-done, and I, as a pilot, could watch them over and over in rehearsal, but what point did they make? What did they teach? What did the audience walk out with that they could use? That's the acid test, and *all* the videos failed it.

I asked Jack if I could ban *all* videos at the meeting, and he agreed, adding that we could allow the businesses—mainly Aircraft Engines—to show anything they wanted on video monitors *in the lobby during the coffee breaks.*

So I banned them all; politely of course, and couched the measure as a way to keep things focused on learning, and save money rather than "showing off," or showing "family movies." I had to listen to impassioned pleas from the jet engines' "communicator" to allow his boss to show a treasured clip. No. Medical systems wanted to show one, and I said No.

And Jack backed me up.

Both of the leaders of these businesses were crusty, old-school, customer-beloved GE leaders whom Jack valued and respected, and he scratched their egos and paid them enormous sums of money. But both were headed into their sixties, and neither had any place to go.

And besides, we were trying to get beyond this old GE "blow and go," dog-and-pony, canned, gee-whiz crap, in order to start sharing some *useful* things, and help each other. So the ban on videos held for almost a decade.

But—once again—at great personal cost to me. Both the medical systems and engines CEOs, in their Boca presentations, made sarcastic and devastating comments about how "a decentralized, empowered, multi-business company would allow a corporate bureaucrat (guess who) to dictate whether they could show videos as part of their presentations."

I was in the back of the hall at my roped-off "command table" feigning being shot or stabbed, slumping over in my chair, and indulging in other histrionics. I would then loudly whisper to my colleagues, "He didn't say *that* in rehearsal!"

Jack thought this was hilarious, spirited, contentious, and fun; but in his closing remarks, he showed the loyalty that is at the core of his character. Laughing at the lectern, he said, "Bill Lane took a number of shots at this meeting for cutting down on the slides and videos and visuals; but here's what we're trying to do here..." And he went on to enunciate the emerging philosophy of Boca: teach, share, help, and consult. No more show-off stuff. No more "reports." No more "bands on stage." No more train whistles.

Do It All in Five Charts

One year, Welch came up with this idea for one of our big meetings: "Bill, *I've got it!* Here's what I want them (the business leaders) to do. Everyone does the same pitch and this is what they talk about:

1. Description of your world markets;
2. Moves by competitors over the past three years;
3. *Your* moves over the past three years;
4. Competitors' moves over the coming *two* years; and
5. Your plan to counter or leapfrog them over the coming two years."

"That's it, Bill! That's what they do. And they do it *all on five charts.* That's all they're allowed. Got it?" Five Charts!!"

I thought it was a great idea at the time, although today both he and I would eventually hate it, because of its "cookie cutter" approach. It worked, marginally, at the meeting.

The one exception was the horrible disaster which befell the head of one of our businesses, "Tom," who was a transplant from an acquisition, an engineer, and a fine executive.

Tom saluted "my" edict from Fairfield about the format of the presentation. But with communications skills similar to someone sitting on a cheap overstuffed suitcase to get it to close, he simply *crammed the content of 20 or 25 charts into five*, creating a series of charts that appeared as the "microdots" that spies give each other; or pages xeroxed out of the Manhattan phone book.

I reasoned with him; I implored, and I got nowhere.

He was going to do "what Jack wanted."

At the meeting, the poor guy—who had early Helen Keller communications skills—began his presentation; the huge crowed began laughing *out loud* as the first chart hit the screen, quietly at first, and then with increasing gusto, as the second, third, and fourth charts, a nightmare of boxes and bullets, followed.

Tom "talked to them," with his back to the huge crowd.

The masterpiece came last, as Tom "threw up" on the screen his plan to "counter or leapfrog" the competition. This chart had all the boxes and bullets, but they were seemingly random with a series of arrows and connectors, themselves each containing words, or rather acronyms, numbers, and dates.

The crowd erupted in hysterics as the chart went up. It was totally unreadable to anyone except the front few rows, and headache-inducing to even them in its complexity.

The crowd in the back of the room couldn't read a single acronym, and just sat back and had a great time at the man's expense.

He waited—not mortified—until the laughter that greeted the last chart died out; and then began "talking to it."

Then he said it, as he was making yet another of the 200 or so points of which his pitch consisted, "As you can see from the chart..."

They lost it. One of my sound guys back stage told me afterwards that the hysteria level caused the "VU meter" to bounce off the peg.

But Tom wasn't done. As soon as the laughter and shouted witty comments abated (keep in mind that this is a senior executive and head of a multibillion-dollar GE business) he then announced yet another "point," and extracted a *laser pointer* from his blue-blazer pocket and began running it up one of the connecting arrows on the screen and through the boxes. And *he himself got lost,* and allowed the red dot to wander all over the mess. I thought people were going to be taken out of the meeting room on stretchers as he flopped around the slide in search of some arcane "point." He finally pretty much gave up, mumbling, crestfallen, through a close, and sat down, to *thunderous* sarcastic applause.

Engineers are generally unbelievably bad presenters (which is one reason Dilbert is an engineer). If a young engineer can learn how to present, clearly and effectively, without jargon and clutter and stupidity, he or she can start the career marathon with a five-mile head start.

This poor guy's presentation may, ironically, have been the most valuable pitch on the program, as several hundred people left the room with faces tear-stained from laughing, but with a grim determination never, *ever* to let that happen to them.

I spoke to a woman from a company in California last year who wanted me to come out and speak to her people. She agreed with my assessment of PowerPoint as a communications killer. "We had a meeting six months ago at headquarters, and we decided there would be no PowerPoint, *no visuals at all.* The presenters had to stand up and talk to the group and *tell* them what they wanted to say."

Consider, just consider, shutting the machine off and simply talking to people, rather than talking to a screen. If you have a great chart that will just blow them away, a chart that just underlines and slams the lid down on everything you've been trying to convey, throw it up on the screen and shout something like, "For the past 10 minutes I've been trying to convince you to turn your way of looking at inventory management 180 degrees. Believe me, it works. Or don't believe me (bar chart thrown up dramatically), but believe the results. Look at the cash flow! Please give this a try, or at least a look. It's the most important thing we've stumbled across in this business in 10 years."

Big, clear, bold type if you insist on using word slides. No "bullet point" more than seven or eight words.

Simple, clear, "depictions" (Jack's word, and a good one, meaning things like bar or pie charts). No legends; no footnotes. Ask yourself, crudely, I admit, as you complete each chart: "Why should anyone give a shit about this?"

Actually talk to people without a screen full of crap behind you! Try it!

At the End of the Day

Welch would simply not use clichés, jargon, or buzzwords. In Jack's terrifying phrase, you need to "ridicule and remove" them from the business presentations of your organization and its external pronouncements. He might use an interesting or evocative phrase he would pick up from somewhere, and then abandon it forever when it entered the current buzzword lexicon. Then it became what he called "business-ese," or "terms," something he scorned and snarled at. He would make *his* points using *his* own words rather than use the language of "sluggos" and "hacks," which is what buzzwords are.

Someone years ago gave me a copy of a game called "Bullshit Bingo," which, according to legend, came from Oxford and was popular for a while—perhaps still is—at the Harvard Business School.

Bullshit Bingo consists of a bingo-style matrix comprised of the most popular current buzzwords, arranged differently for each "player"—each member of the presentation audience. As the bore at the front of the room—usually an unsuspecting visiting professor or CEO or CFO—rambled and droned through his poorly prepared pitch, the class members would tick off the buzzwords on their cards. Usually a low but excited rumble of satisfaction would roll through the class as "proactive," "bandwidth," "pushback," "drill down," "no-brainer," "headwind," or "tailwind" were released by the flatulent jargon-monkey in the front of the room.

Finally, a gasp of satisfaction as "low-hanging fruit" sent one lucky MBA candidate over the top; and he or she excitedly shouted "Bingo!" while holding up the card, to congratulations and applause.

God only knows what the visiting bloviator thought was going on.

MBA candidates can be tough. I spoke to the class at Wharton a few years ago. It was about two weeks after Jack had talked to them, which put me in the enviable role of the guy with the push broom following the circus elephant down Main Street.

I then told them they were "wasting their money—or their parents' money"—if they alight in the world of business without the ability to deliver a great business presentation.

I quoted the imprecations and ridicule Jack had heaped on failing presenters.

I promised, *despite the limited time I had with them*, to tell them everything they needed to know about how to make a great pitch. I railed and yelled about the things I truly believe, and that I've been trying to tell you; and I only lost three or four of them—to the bathroom or other commitments, I like to think—and got a sincere round of applause at the end.

I was so wired after it that I went and had a double martini and bought a rare pack of cigarettes before grabbing Amtrak back to Connecticut. No "bingos" were yelled out because I gave them no ammo. *Intensity*, *utility*, and *passion* carried the day for me with these kids.

And that will do it for you, as well.

Bite your tongue if you feel that projectile-vomit such as "apples and oranges," "24/7," "think outside the box," "robust," "benchmark," or "metrics" is about to spew forth.

Or "buckets." Does your outfit use "buckets" to denote areas where financial resources are parked? That might have been a colorful expression the first time it was used, but it became an idiotic, repetitive, and cacophonous part of many GE pitches—at least while I was there.

I got a call from a friend, Phil Ameen, a finance VP at GE who reported in mock-horror, "Bill, it's out of control. A guy pitched to me today and described how he was going to 'bucketize' the resources for the business."

In the '80s, at GE, I would have to cite "leverage"—used as a verb or noun—as a deserving candidate. We were forever "leveraging our resources" in this market or that; or "leveraging our market position" to do this or that. It still makes an occasional appearance as a golden oldie. "Synergy" could've also been a "contenda."

During the latter '90s, the information technology crowd rolled through, aping the absurd, ruinous, and doomed dot-com model, along with its jargon. The conference rooms rang with protestations of how these people were working "24/7," although I would see them exiting the building at 6 p.m., when I did—or even earlier.

They looked, for inspiration, to the "gold standard" of some other company's Web site. The details would soon become more "granular," they assured us. They would soon "drill down" until we could all "plug and play" into the world of "clicks and mortar."

Trial balloons were actually floated by them about "concierge" service—people picking up your dirty underwear at work and cleaning it; or taking your car to be washed because of your bullshit "24/7" schedule. This never got anywhere near Welch, who would have puked.

He didn't buy any of this kind of stuff, and he hated the phoniness of using "businessese and terms."

At a GE meeting, in one of the final years of my career, I counted the phrase "at the end of the day" uttered *22* times over two half-days of presentations.

Saying stuff like this is just cause to have a "lightweight" sign stamped on your forehead. You have nothing to say, so you borrow someone else's hackneyed, meaningless cliché to barf at your audience.

Sit down when your terrific, useful, well-prepared presentation is complete and eliminate every buzzword that will mark you as a phony and a hack.

Use your own words, your own emotion, your own passion for what you want to say. And say it simply, and briefly, from your soul.

Love Story

Larry Bossidy once told me as we prepared for a speech, that after he had been named "CEO of the Year" while at Allied Signal he had walked down the hall after the presentation ceremony and heard a voice say, "Larry, what's it all mean?"

The voice was Herb Kelleher's, of Southwest Airlines. Herb had a reputation for "celebratin'." Larry was amused and suspicious, and turned to Herb and said, "I don't know, Herb. What does it mean?"

"It means, Larry, that it's all downhill from here."

Welch had gotten similar, and much more effusive awards and honors and, like Larry, never took them too seriously. He could have settled back and savored them, and ran several victory laps as late middle age moved in and retirement loomed. But he never did, until he turned things over to Jeff.

Cocktail conversation at GE tables often touched upon the question of whether Jack had mellowed over the years from the days Dennis Dammerman had described as his "violent period." And the answer is yes; to a degree, in his demeanor and volcanics, but the passion never waned, and the power of his communications—particularly with his team and his friends—if anything, increased.

Most of us in Fairfield *resented* his leaving us. I confronted him one quiet afternoon over a speech we were working on, and asked, "What did you do this for? You could have done another three years and not left us. Don't you ever wake up at night and, you know, think you made a mistake?"

Soft and quiet. "Yeah, Bill. I do. But it was time to give someone else a chance."

Welch never went into the tailspin Herb Kelleher might have predicted. His intensity, particularly in his communications with his people and his constituencies, continued until he stepped down. And still does, I guess.

I have attempted to show another side of Jack Welch—not a *dark* side; just a different side. He may not like the language, the craziness, the volcanic eruptions, the egomania, the boyishness in this book, but I hope I have conveyed at least a hint of the deep streak of *love* that ran through most of what he did. Love for the Company, for his friends, and those who through merit and very hard work, survived his incumbency.

Those who were "sent home" or otherwise organizationally brutalized by him, will think my use of the word "love" in any way connected with Jack Welch and business is absurd. Laughable. Bullshit.

Some of this "love" was tough: the cuts and closings and firings.

I rode with him out the gate of our locomotive plant in Erie, Pa., once after a visit for some now-long-forgotten reason. A crane with a wrecking ball and a bulldozer were noisily knocking down manufacturing buildings within sight and hearing of thousands of workers during a time when the labor environment at GE was not the best.

Jack watched for a second or two and then said, only partly to me: "A time-tested management technique."

He was, and is, a Darwinian capitalist, to be sure, but with an intense love of General Electric and the people it needed to make it work.

Welch turned to me one day in his conference room, with a big soft smile, a day after we had returned from the Boca meeting (he via Augusta National). The meeting had been a spectacular embodiment of everything we had been aiming for in communications since his "no more reports" epiphany a year or two before. Men and women shared, cajoled, warned, and taught their colleagues in the big hall. There was a warmth in that room that I've never seen in any business environment of that size before. No bragging, no dissembling, no recitations or reports. Only great people showing a form of affection for each other by helping each other with what used to be an instrument of torture: business presentations.

Jack, with more love in his voice for the Company than I have ever heard, said, "Bill, we've got ourselves *a learning company*."

The love for GE was thrillingly evident in his "close" at Boca a few years later—one of his last.

Many other successful CEOs would have preened and paraded around the stage accepting tribute. Not Jack. The teaching, the cajoling, the "telling people what to do" continued until he walked off the stage. Here's how he finished:

In mid-presentation, with a head of steam, voice lowers, and then quietly, softly, solemnly: "There's a place I would like everyone in this room to see. It's on the way from the airport to the golf course (Augusta). There's an old ramshackle, rundown mess of a building on the side of the road.

Windows all busted out, trees growing up from inside the building and out through the windows.

"And you can just barely see, on the side of the building, the outline of a sign that once said, 'General Electric.' You know what happened in that old building? Forty years or so ago, some people who sat in this meeting decided it would be a great idea to make a big business out of servicing GE apparatus (high value products like engines, motors, turbines, etc.).

"And it was a great idea! But you know what they *didn't* do?

"*They didn't put the new product technology we had into the machines we were servicing—and upgrade their capabilities for our customers.*

"And you know what happened? We became a bunch of high-cost 'wrench-turners' and oil-can carriers. We were one of the pack. And we got run out of the game by the lower-cost, mom-and-pop outfits."

Begging, imploring, hands extended—not misty-eyed, but not far:

"*Promise me* you will not fail to pour the very best technology GE has into the servicing of our products.

"PROMISE ME!

"IT'S THE FUTURE OF OUR COMPANY!!"

It was all Jack. I had nothing to do with this pitch, and I sat there in awe as it unfolded. I watched the executive's faces around me as Welch wound up this part of his "close." Heads nodding eagerly, eyes wide. Body and eye language saying, "sure, I promise. I *promise*. Do you want me to kill anybody? Because I'll do that too, if you want."

Think a few PowerPoint word charts would have helped him make his point more forcefully?

Was that presentation about "vanity"? Not that day. About love for his company and its leaders? Yeah, I think so.

I know so.

If you have no use for your colleagues, your employees, your organization, or your company, you need to get out fast.

But if you do care for them, wish them well, and wish to see them, your company, *and yourself* move toward greatness, you will never bore them, "report" to them, waste their time, or send them from the room with empty hands.

Trust me. If you structure every presentation you make around one or two insights, practices, or teachings that you know will be of *use* to your colleagues, you will never do another lousy presentation again in your life.

Everything else I have hectored you about in this book can be learned as you change and get better.

But change this and you change everything.

And if you are not instinctively adept at "feeding an audience"—as Jack Welch was—you *must* change.

Break a leg.

I can't, in good conscience, let you go just yet ...

Stay with me for just another minute or two, and return to me and to what follows every time you are facing a presentation whose outcome will determine how your colleagues, subordinates, or superiors think of you. And that, in my view, is every single one of them.

Look yourself in the mirror and answer, honestly:

- *Did I do my homework on this audience of one or a hundred; put myself in their place, and ask what I know would be useful to them?*
- *Are* their *needs the focus of my presentation?*
- *Will there be any question in their minds after the first minute as to why they should be listening intently to what I say?*
- *Have I scrubbed every needless detail, obscure acronym, and piece of trendy jargon from the pitch?*
- *Are all these charts necessary? Have I considered shutting down the visuals periodically and speaking to the faces in the crowd or across the table?*
- *Will every word and number be visible to every single individual in every part of the room?*
- *Could this presentation be shorter without losing anything of major significance to the audience? (Hint: Yes, of course, it could.)*
- *Did I rehearse it? Try it out on someone I respect? Did I incorporate that person's views and make changes?*
- *Do I simply want to "get this thing over with"?*
- *Or despite being nervous and stressed from the preparation workload, do I, like Jack Welch before his Bechtel presentation, find I just can't wait to get up in front of these people because I know my pitch is going to blow them away?!*

A

Ad-libbing, avoiding, 78
Akers, John, 44, 269
Alcohol
    at lunch, 181–183
    Welch's use of, 203
Allen, Marcus, 145
Allied Signal, 265
Ameen, Phil, 11
Anecdotes, 278–279, 282–283,
    285–288
Annual general managers meetings,
    69, 70
    facilities for, 149–151
    Lane's first, 79–81
    in 1950s, 13–14
    Welch's first, 24
Annual report, 1–3
Annual report letters, 240–248
    writing for oneself, 165–167,
    243–248
Annual shareowner's meetings,
    131–132
Appearance of presenter, 277–279
Army Congressional office, 73–78
Asea Brown-Boveri, 69
Asian presenters, 290
Association Island, 13

Audience
    bias of, 289–292
    conveying interest in, 38
    importance of information to, 33
    keeping interest of, 237–238,
    261–262
    knowing all about, 78
    powerful, importance of presenting
    to, 53
    providing with useful information,
    249–250, 257–259
    for rehearsal, 235, 239
Authority, maintaining, 293–296

B

Baird, Zöe, 116
Baker, Jim, 28, 69
Bartiromo, Maria, 219, 220
Bechtel, 211
Bechtel, Steve, 211
Begley, Charlene, 217–218
Bennett, Steve, 40
Best practices
    Frasier's project on, 29–31
    GE's adoption of, 31
Bias of audience, 289–292
Black and Decker, 56, 57
Black Catte, 13

Black male presenters, 289–290
Boca, decision to keep, 149–150
Bonuses, 10
"Bore test," 261–262
Bossidy, Larry, 25, 28, 35, 36, 37, 49,
    85, 200, 249, 311
    announcement of departure from
        GE, 243
    departure of, 263–264
    Execution by, 112
    intolerance for useless presentations,
        115, 138
    involvement of, 103
    on managers meetings, 70
    Midwest Massacre and, 183–184, 185
    move to Allied Signal, 112
    preparing for meetings and, 96
    Rabinowitz's promotion and, 31–32
    revision of presentations and, 205
    work ethic of, 224
Buffett, Warren, 214–215, 278
Bullshit, avoiding, 55–59, 61–64
Bullshit Bingo, 307
Bunch, Bruce, 5
Bunt, Jim, 18–21, 254
Burlingame, John, 23
Bush, Barbara, 201
Bush, George H. W., 201
Buzzwords, avoiding, 307–309

C

Calhoun, Dave, 217
    as candidate for CEO, 272–273
Candor, 55–59, 61–64, 127, 141–142
Charon, Ron, 35
Checklist for presentations, 315
Clichés, avoiding, 307–309
CNBC, 30
Compensation
    executive, 252–253
    incentive, 10
    perks for retired CEOs and, 178–179
Conaty, Bill, 49, 230
Connelly, John, 241

Corporate lawyers as poor presenters,
    116
Corporate officers meetings
    atmosphere of, 151–153
    facilities for, 151
    Lane's first, 88–93
    in 1986, 251–255
Country Club of Fairfield, 269
Credibility, enhancing, 155–157
Crotonville Management School
    effectiveness of, 126
    Lane's first time at, 35–42
    Lane's presentations at, 43
    party for Welch thrown at, 14
    regimen at, 39
    socializing at, 41–42
Culture of excellence, 129
Cynicism, public, intolerance of, 100

D

Dammerman, Dennis, 28, 59, 224,
    253, 297
    intensity of, 177
    intolerance for useless presenta-
        tions, 138, 139
    involvement of, 103
Defense industries, GE's presence in,
    131, 133–134
Demeanor, 278–279
Dietel, Bo, 294–295
Dingell, John, 170
Dingell Committee hearing, 169–171
Dishonesty, 63
    intolerance for, 139
Divorce
    of Welch, 178, 193, 203, 204
    of Wendt, 193–194
Doyle, Frank, 7, 11, 58, 81, 87, 115, 171
Drafts, unacceptable, handling, 97–98

E

Edelheit, Lonnie, 298–299
Excellence
    culture of, 129

importance of, 176
Execution (Bossidy), 112
Executive compensation, 252–253

F

Firings
    by Lane, 185–189
    Midwest Massacre and, 183–184,
        185
    during 1990s, 199
    of Wendt, 191–198
Fraiser, Mike, 29–31, 252
Fraud, 63–64
Fresco, Paolo, 125, 173, 174
    annual report letter and, 165, 240–242

G

Garry, Fred, 123
Gates, Bill, 215
GE Capital, 25, 149
GE Consumer Finance, 258
GE Corporate headquarters, 27
General managers meetings, 69, 70
    facilities for, 149–151
    Lane's first, 79–81
    in 1950s, 13–14
    Welch's first, 24
General Motors, 111, 258
Genworth Financial, 31
Glasses, 277
"Golden handcuffs," 265
Grossman, Ken, 229
Grossman, Larry, 147

H

Haines, Mark, 30
Heineman, Ben, 28, 277
Hergenhan, Joyce, 35, 37, 119, 147,
        151, 161, 204
    fear that Lane would leave GE, 264
    hiring of, 87, 185
    Lane's consultation about firing, 187
    retirement party at home of, 6, 11
Hilton, Jack, 51, 147

Hiner, Glen, 103
Honesty, 55–59, 61–64, 127, 141–142
    lying and, 63, 139
Hood, Ed, 23, 70, 103
Humor, using in presentations,
        278–279

I

IBM, 44
"Icarus syndrome," 52–53
Immelt, Jeff, 12, 71, 230
    on lying, 63
    pitch affecting stock, 164
    plant to eliminate speechwriter
        position, 15
    presentation following 9/11, 51
    selection as CEO, 14–15, 272
Importance of information to
    audience, 33
Imus, Don, 239, 294
Incentive compensation, 10

J

Jargon, avoiding, 307–309
Jensen, Warren, 47
Jett, Joe, 141
Jones, Reginald, 27, 269
    corporate offices moved by, 178
    demise of, 17, 18
    speechwriter for, 79
    successful performance of, 25
    successor chosen by, 24
    at White House reception, 67

K

Kelleher, Herb, 213, 311
Kidder Peabody, 141
Kissinger, Henry, 176
Knowledge
    about audience, 78
    of leader, 101–105

L

Lane, Beth, 229–231

Lane, Bill
   at Army Congressional office, 73–78
   first encounter with Welch, 23
   parents of, 65–67
   presentations at Crotonville, 43
   recruitment by General Electric, 8,
      179–180
   refusal to take credit for Welch's
      talks, 18
   Welch's auditioning of, 87
Lane, Billy, 180
Lang, Chet, 13–14
Lawyers, corporate, as poor presenters,
   116
Leadership, 87–93
   knowledge and, 101–105
   preparing one's own material and,
      151–152, 165–167
   required skills for, 273
   self-confidence and, 107–109
Lockheed Martin, 133
Long-range vision planning, Welch's
   rejection of, 25
Lying, 63
   intolerance for, 139

M

Magaziner, Ira, 35
Management awards, 152
Managers meetings, 69, 70
   facilities for, 149–151
   Lane's first, 79–81
   in 1950s, 13–14
   Welch's first, 24
Marsh, Lou, 7–8
McIntyre, Robert, 75
McLaughlin, John, 119
McLaughlin Group, 119–120
McNerney, Jim, 71
   as candidate for CEO, 271–272
Media coverage, 70–71
Meetings
   emphasizing points in, 97
   leadership of, 87–93

micromanaging, 100
in 1970s, 9
preparing for, 95–96
   (*See also* General managers
      meetings; Officers meetings)
"Meteors," 52, 53
Micromanaging, 100, 111–112
Midwest Massacre, 183–184
Mistakes
   admitting, 258
   pointing out, 97
The Monogram, 226–227
Motivational speakers, lack of use of,
   100
Murphy, Gene, 281, 282–283

N

Nardelli, Bob, 125
   as candidate for CEO, 71, 271, 272
   Welch's complimenting of, 217
NBC, 129, 138–139, 141, 147
Negative information, importance of
   presenting, 127
Nelson, Bob, 11, 46, 51, 199–200
Nissen, Dave, 258–259
Noonan, Peggy, 188
Nunn, Sam, 194

O

Officers meetings
   atmosphere of, 151–153
   facilities for, 151
   Lane's first, 88–93
   in 1986, 251–255
Outside speakers, avoiding, 100

P

Penske, Roger, 194
Perks for retired CEOs, 178–179
Philips, 69
Planning, Welch's lack of respect for,
   83–84
PowerPoint, shortcomings of,
   297–300

Preparation
   importance of, 122
   inadequate, 118
   for life-changing conversations,
     230–231, 264–267
   time spent on by Welch, 209–212
   (*See also* Rehearsal)
Presentation quality, importance of,
   49–50
Presentation skills, importance of,
   45–47

R

Rabinowitz, Steve, 31–32
RCA, 141
Reagan, Nancy, 12
Recommendations, useful, 127
Rehearsal, importance of, 230–236,
   239–242
Reiner, Gary, 192, 261, 291
Repeated pitches, 119–120
Retirement ceremonies
   for Lane, 5–12, 21
   for Welch, 14
Revising presentations, 205–206
Rogers, Jim, 143
Russell, Ed, 103

S

Salaries, 10
Sara Lee, 204, 206
Sarcasm, public, intolerance of, 100
Schlemmer, Carl, 111
Schwab, Charles, 211
Seinfeld, Jerry, 138
Self-confidence, 107–109
Shareowner's meetings, 131–132
Sherin, Keith, 253
Shultz, George, 211
Siemens, 69
Skilling, Jeff, 111
Speechwriters, 79–80
   hiring of, 187–188
   Welch's auditioning of, 87, 175

Starr, Ringo, 236, 239
Stephanopoulos, George, 129
Stock options, 161
Stock price
   increase during 1980s, 161
   as key to achieving wealth, 9–10
   Lane's retirement package and, 20
   raising of, 163–164
Strategic planning, Welch's lack of
   respect for, 83–84
Strawman technique, 169–171
Stuttering, of Welch, 117
Successes, discussing in presentations,
   258–259
Support, building, 275–276

T

Tape recorders, for revising presenta-
   tions, 205–206
Teel, Betti, 145
Thomson, 56
"Time messages," 293
Tinker, Grant, 147, 148, 158
Topic, speaker's caring about,
   173–174, 199–202
Toshiba, 69
Tower, John, 77
Trane, 56
Trotter, Lloyd, 257
Trotter Matrix, 257
Turner, Ted, 201

U

Unethical behavior, 63–64, 169–171
   (*See also* Lying)
Union leaders, Welch's discussion
   with, 104–105
Useless presentations, intolerance for,
   113–116, 138–139, 143–146
Utah International Coal, 161

V

Vachon, Mark, 45, 46, 114, 230
Van Fleet, "Van," 7

Vanity of communications, 1–3
Vickers, Len, 101
Visions, Welch's lack of respect for,
    83–84
Visuals
    judicious use of, 297–305
    overuse of, 85–86, 87–88
Voice, of Welch, 27–28

W

Warner, Sandy, 269
Welch, Carolyn, 176
Welch, Chuck, 144
Welch, Jane, 194, 201, 240–241, 269
Welch, Suzy, 218
Wendt, Gary, 25
    divorce of, 193–194

firing of, 191–198
Wendt, Lorna, 193, 196
Westinghouse Electric, 159–160
White male presenters, 289
"White Trash Day," 225–226
Williams, Brian, 138
Winning (Welch), 218
Women
    audience bias and, 290–292
    successful at GE, 217–220
Woodburn, Bill, 59
Work ethic, 217–227, 229–231
"Work Out" initiative, 31
Work-life balance, 217–220
Wright, Bob, 6, 129, 138–139,
    147–148, 192

I'd like to thank myself for sitting at the dining room table for the better part of a year cranking this out. Actually, it was fun, and I recommend it. I don't know if it's any good or not, although I think it's a fair, honest, and useful view on institutional communications, on Jack Welch, and on life.

Leah Spiro, my editor at McGraw-Hill, liked the book. Leah edited Jack and Suzy Welch's book, *Winning.* I assume—I *know*—I was easier to deal with than he was, and Leah and I became friends.

Terry Deal at McGraw-Hill read and reread her way through this thing, an experience that had to be one of root-canal proportions. A delightful intern named Tania Loghmani helped me through several hours of editorial changes one long afternoon, and thrilled me by saying she "had never worked with an author before." And Lydia Rinaldi and Keith Pfeffer helped get the word out.

Barbara Ray, my former secretary, put this mess into a coherent format, and we remain friends.

Vicky Wilchinsky, a gifted artist, did a great cover design, and one of the truest Jack caricatures I've ever seen. We didn't use it.

My 91-year-old mother, semi-computer literate and sharp as a tack, who asked me, after being warned, "Why would you put bad words in your book?" Sorry, Mom. That's the way everyone talked. GE is a combative, competitive company, an emotional company, and we spoke like combatants. That's not an excuse, maybe, but if I put a prettified, false face on conversations that actually occurred, I would be laughed off the earth by anyone who knew the cast of characters—particularly the lead character.

To my brothers Richie and Bobby, who always enjoyed my minor successes as much as they enjoyed their own—you're the best.

To Billy, Regan, and Tommy—who, fortunately, take after their mother in looks and brains—thanks for being happy and excited for your old man.

To my late father and sister, who were smarter and more talented than I ever was, but never had the breaks that I had. We'll get together again someday.

To the late Lou Marsh, who plucked me from the Washington I loved, and brought me to the world's greatest company, thanks.

To Jeff Immelt, walking on stage after the hardest act to follow in world business history: good job, so far.

To Walter Shaw, a friend and golf-enemy from my club, who, upon hearing an anecdote from my proposed book, said, "Oh, yeah, I'd pay $26.95 to read that bullshit." Walter, who is getting neither a free book, nor a signed *paid-for* book, will not even be allowed in any store where this thing is sold. But Walter *did*, in his desultory, random, crapulous fashion, hit the core idea: If it's not *useful*, it's not worth listening to, or, I guess, buying.

To the dozens of friends who had the identical, sophmoric, and obscene suggestion for a title to a sequel to *Jacked Up*. Not gonna happen.

And finally, to Jack, thanks for everything, and for the memories. I didn't let you mess with the manuscript because you are, as you once pondered with Larry Bossidy, "a meddler." But you are the greatest meddler I've ever met—or have even heard of.

Why did I write this? Jack, you have to understand vanity.